Student Guide with Map Exercises
to Accompany

THE ENDURING VISION

A History of the American People
Third Edition

by

**Paul S. Boyer • Clifford E. Clark, Jr. • Joseph F. Kett
Neal Salisbury • Harvard Sitkoff • Nancy Woloch**

Volume Two: From 1865

Barbara Blumberg
Pace University

D0162614

D. C. Heath and Company
Lexington, Massachusetts   Toronto

Address editorial correspondence to:

D. C. Heath and Company
125 Spring Street
Lexington, MA 02173

Copyright © 1996 by D. C. Heath and Company.

Previous editions copyright © 1990, 1993 by D. C. Heath and Company.

All rights reserved. No part of this publication may be reproduced or transmitted in any form or by any means, electronic or mechanical, including photocopy, recording, or any information storage or retrieval system, without permission in writing from the publisher.

Published simultaneously in Canada.

Printed in the United States of America.

International Standard Book Number: 0-669-39888-8

10 9 8 7 6 5 4 3 2

Preface

The *Student Guide with Map Exercises to Accompany The Enduring Vision,* Third Edition, is intended to help you master the history presented in *The Enduring Vision: A History of the American People.* It is *not* a substitute for reading the textbook. However, used properly as a *supplement* to the text, it should assist you in focusing on the important events, issues, and concepts in American history, as well as on the well-known figures and ordinary people alike whose ideas and actions help us to understand the past. It is also designed to build your vocabulary, improve your knowledge of geography, and enhance your understanding of how the historian learns about the past.

Each chapter in the *Student Guide* corresponds to a chapter in *The Enduring Vision* and is divided into the following sections:

- *Outline and Summary.* This follows the outline of the textbook chapter and summarizes the material discussed under each text heading. You should read it quickly before reading the textbook chapter to give yourself an overview of the contents. Then carefully read the text chapter. After completing the text chapter, reread the outline and summary as a review.

- *Vocabulary.* In this section social-science terms and other words used in the text chapter that may be new to you are defined. Look over the list before you read the textbook chapter. Familiarize yourself with any words that you do not already know.

- *Identifications.* Here you will find the important persons, laws, terms, groups, and events covered in *The Enduring Vision.* After reading the text chapter, test yourself by identifying who or what each item was and how this person or thing fits into the overall story. That is, what is its historical significance?

- *Skill Building.* In most of the chapters of the *Student Guide,* you will find either (a) a section designed to help you interpret charts and tables in the textbook or (b) a map exercise, asking you to locate places mentioned in the text chapter and to explain the historical significance of those geographical places. Some chapters contain both.

- *Historical Sources.* Too often we simply accept what we see in print as true and memorize it without stopping to ask how the author obtained the information and whether we should believe it. The purpose of the Historical Sources section found in most chapters is to explain where the historian gets his or her facts, and to assist you in evaluating the reliability of those sources and the conclusions based on them.

- *Multiple-Choice Questions, Short-Answer Questions, Essay Questions, and Answers to Multiple-Choice Questions.* After reading the corresponding chapter in *The Enduring Vision,* you should try to answer these questions. They are designed to help you review the significant material in the chapter; they will probably be similar to the kinds of questions and essays that your professor will give you to write on in papers, quizzes, and exams. Answers to the multiple-choice questions appear at the end of the *Student Guide*.

The last *Student Guide* chapter is intended to aid you in preparing for the final examination in your history course. It contains hints on studying, as well as multiple-choice and essay questions that ask you to consider and pull together the material presented in *all* of the chapters of *The Enduring Vision*.

For help in preparing the *Student Guide*, I would first like to thank the authors of *The Enduring Vision* for writing a lucid, informative political, social, and cultural history of the United States that is a pleasure to read and to write about. Second, I appreciate the help of the editors at D. C. Heath who made valuable suggestions. I am grateful to my husband, Alan Krumholz, and to my son, Mark, for their patience and support while I worked on this project.

Barbara Blumberg

Contents

Prologue
Visions of the Land   *1*

Chapter 16
The Crises of Reconstruction, 1865–1877   *5*

Chapter 17
The Trans-Mississippi West   *17*

Chapter 18
The Rise of Industrial America   *29*

Chapter 19
The Transformation of Urban America   *41*

Chapter 20
Daily Life, Popular Culture, and the Arts, 1860–1900   *51*

Chapter 21
Politics and Expansion in an Industrializing Age   *61*

Chapter 22
The Progressive Era   *77*

Chapter 23
World War I   *91*

Chapter 24
The 1920s   *107*

Chapter 25
Crash, Depression, and New Deal   *119*

Chapter 26
American Life in a Decade of Crisis at Home and Abroad   *133*

Chapter 27
Waging Global War, 1939–1945   *147*

Chapter 28
Cold War America, 1945–1952   *163*

Chapter 29
America at Midcentury   *179*

Chapter 30
The Turbulent Sixties   *193*

Chapter 31
A Troubled Journey: From Port Huron to Watergate   *207*

Chapter 32
Turning Inward: Society and Politics from Ford to Reagan   *221*

Chapter 33
Beyond the Cold War   *233*

Epilogue
Looking Ahead—Looking Back   *247*

Preparing for the Final Examination   *251*

Answers to Multiple-Choice Questions   *257*

PROLOGUE

Visions of the Land

OUTLINE AND SUMMARY

I. Introduction

Successive generations of North Americans have viewed their natural environment in different ways. They have also repeatedly reshaped the landscape to serve their physical and spiritual needs. Sometimes the modifications were intentional and benign; at other times, human use and abuse of the land caused unforeseen despoliation.

II. A "Howling Wilderness"

Before the arrival of Europeans, Native Americans in the Northeast killed trees selectively, opening up the forest floor. This practice enabled them to plant vegetable gardens and hunt game more easily. Native Americans saw themselves as living in harmony with nature.

Seventeenth-century European colonists, on the other hand, looked upon America as a frightening, "howling wilderness." It had to be subdued and made useful as quickly as possible by surveying the countryside, draining marshes, clearing pastures, and fencing, plowing, and planting crops they had known in Europe, such as wheat.

III. A Wondrous World

Mid-eighteenth century Americans no longer feared the wilderness. Rather, influenced by the Enlightenment view that, with the faculty of reason, human beings could understand and control the natural world, men such as William Bartram and Thomas Jefferson displayed great interest in the land. They studied, classified, and tried to find new uses for the flora and fauna of North America. By the time of the American Revolution most eastern forests were depleted and wildlife driven off. The hope of finding new and better resources further west, as well as curiosity, motivated explorations such as that of Lewis and Clark (1804).

IV. The Pastoral Ideal

In the nineteenth century, as America rapidly urbanized, people's earlier fear and then wonder about the land gave way to a romanticized vision, the pastoral ideal. In this view, shared at various times by landscape painters (Thomas Cole, Asher Durand, Albert Bierstadt), writers (Henry David Thoreau), park designers (Frederick Law Olmstead), and a majority of Americans, contact with the land ennobled and restored the human spirit.

1

V. The Legacy

By 1900 most of the nation was settled; little untamed, unexploited nature remained. Only then did some Americans begin to worry about conservation of resources and preservation of whatever wilderness was left. In our own day, we face the challenge of rediscovering the legacy of the Native Americans who understood "that the land—its life-sustaining bounty and its soul-sustaining beauty—is itself of inestimable value, and not merely a means to the end of material gain.

VOCABULARY

The following terms are used in the Prologue. To understand it fully, it is important that you know what each of them means.

bucolic   rural, countrified, rustic

ecologist   a scientist who studies the interaction of organisms and their environment

precursors   forerunners, ancestors

IDENTIFICATIONS

After reading the Prologue, you should be able to identify and explain the historical significance of each of the following:

Thomas Cole

Frederick Law Olmsted

Currier and Ives, "American Country Life"

Albert Bierstadt

Henry David Thoreau, *Walden*

Aldo Leopold

MULTIPLE-CHOICE QUESTIONS

Circle the letter of the item that best completes each statement or answers the question.

1. Native Americans living in the Northeast at the time of the arrival of Europeans
    a. did not practice agriculture and thus left the land unchanged.
    b. hunted so intensively that they had killed off most of the animals and game in the region before whites had much chance to hunt.
    c. killed trees selectively to make room for gardens of corn, squash, beans, and melons.
    d. concentrated on growing tobacco, which they smoked with great relish.

2. The Puritans of seventeeth-century New England looked on the American landscape as
   a. a frightening wilderness to be tamed and cultivated as rapidly as possible.
   b. the work of God to be treated with awe and thanksgiving, and to be carefully preserved.
   c. so similar to England's that they felt certain God had guided them to this land.
   d. barren and rocky, and therefore not capable of being farmed.

3. New England's forests had been mostly cut down by
   a. 1700.
   b. 1900.
   c. 1850.
   d. 1800.

4. A deepening conservation consciousness first appeared among Americans of European ancestry by
   a. 1900.
   b. the era of the Civil War.
   c. the end of the American Revolution.
   d. the post-World War II period.

5. The assumption that nature is nurturing and restorative is a part of the
   a. Puritan world view.
   b. Marxist theory of scientific socialism.
   c. romantic pastoral ideal.
   d. thinking of the "Age of Reason."

ESSAY QUESTION

---

1. Discuss the changing views of nature and the land that North Americans have held since the 1500s.

16

The Crises of Reconstruction, 1865–1877

OUTLINE AND SUMMARY

I. Reconstruction Politics

A. *Lincoln's Plan*

Differences between President Lincoln and Congress on reconstruction of the Confederate states began as early as 1863. In December Lincoln issued a plan that would allow the formation of a new state government when as few as 10 percent of the state's voters took an oath of loyalty to the Union and recognized the end of slavery. This plan said nothing about votes for the freedmen. Lincoln hoped with this plan to win over southern Unionists and draw them into the Republican party. Republicans in Congress thought the plan inadequate and passed the Wade-Davis bill instead. This bill required that at least 50 percent of the voters take an oath of allegiance, and it excluded from participation in government all those who had cooperated with the Confederacy. Lincoln pocket-vetoed the bill, and at the time of his death he and Congress were at an impasse.

B. *Presidential Reconstruction Under Johnson*

President Andrew Johnson, who was unconcerned about the blacks but wished to promote the interests of the poorer whites in the South, announced his Reconstruction plan in May 1865. Johnson required whites to take an oath of allegiance to the Union, after which they could set up new state governments. These had to proclaim secession illegal, repudiate Confederate debts, and ratify the Thirteenth Amendment (abolishing slavery). Whites who had held high office under the Confederacy and all those with taxable property of $20,000 or more could not vote or hold office until they applied for and received a special pardon from the president. During the summer, Johnson undermined his own policy of excluding planters from leadership by handing out pardons to them wholesale. The new governments created under Johnson's plan were soon dominated by former Confederate leaders and large landowners. Some of the Johnson governments refused to ratify the Thirteenth Amendment, and all showed their intention of making black freedom only nominal by enacting "black codes." Horrified by such evidence of continued southern defiance, the Republican-dominated Congress, in December 1865, refused to recognize these governments or to seat the men they sent to the House and Senate.

C. Congress Versus Johnson

The Radical Republicans, who wished to give black men the vote and transform the South into a biracial democracy, were in a minority in 1866. The majority Moderate Republicans wanted only to get rid of the black codes and protect the basic civil rights of blacks. The Moderates attempted to accomplish these limited goals by continuing the Freedmen's Bureau and passing the Civil Rights Act of 1866. When Johnson vetoed both of these measures, he drove the Moderates into alliance with the Radicals, and together they overrode his vetoes. The now radicalized Republicans also moved to protect the provisions of the Civil Rights Act by embodying them in a constitutional amendment.

D. The Fourteenth Amendment

With the Fourteenth Amendment, the federal government for the first time defined citizenship and intervened to protect persons from state governments. The amendment stated that all persons born in the United States or naturalized were citizens. No state could deny any person's rights without due process of law or deny equal protection of the law. States that refused black men the vote could have their representation in Congress reduced. Former Confederate officials were excluded from voting and officeholding until pardoned by a two-thirds vote of Congress. The southern states, except for Tennessee, refused to ratify the amendment and Johnson denounced it, but in the congressional elections of 1866 the Republicans won huge majorities, giving them a mandate to force ratification of the Fourteenth Amendment and proceed with congressional Reconstruction of the South.

E. Congressional Reconstruction

In 1867 and 1868 Congress enacted its Reconstruction program over Johnson's vetoes. The earlier Johnson governments, black codes, and all other laws they had passed were invalidated. All the former Confederate states except Tennessee, which had been readmitted, were divided into districts under the temporary rule of the military. Each state was required to write a new constitution enfranchising black men and to ratify the Fourteenth Amendment. When these things had been done, Congress could readmit the state to the Union. Congressional Reconstruction was more radical than Lincoln's or Johnson's, since it enfranchised blacks and temporarily disfranchised many whites. It did not, however, go as far as the Radicals wanted, since it failed to confiscate southern land and redistribute it to blacks and poor whites. Johnson, as commander in chief of the army, dragged his feet in enforcing congressional Reconstruction, thus convincing Republicans that he had to be dealt with.

F. The Impeachment Crisis

In March 1867 Congress passed laws aimed at reducing the president's power. Johnson violated one of them by firing Secretary of War Stanton, at which point the Republicans in Congress began impeachment proceedings. Some Republicans wavered, however, fearing that removal of Johnson would upset the constitutional balance of power. As a result, the vote to convict and remove the president fell one short of the necessary two-thirds of the Senate.

G. The Fifteenth Amendment

Congress passed a final amendment to complete its Reconstruction program. The Fifteenth Amendment stated that the right to vote could not be denied because of race, color, or previous condition of servitude. The Republicans hoped with this amendment to protect southern blacks, extend suffrage to northern blacks, and gain many new voters for their party. When Congress refused to include women's suffrage, some feminists denounced the amendment and its Republican sponsors. By 1870 the three new amendments—ending slavery, guaranteeing the rights of citizens, and enfranchising black men—were a part of the Constitution and Congress had readmitted all the former Confederate states. Thereafter congressional efforts at Reconstruction weakened.

II. Reconstruction Governments

A. A New Electorate

The Reconstruction laws of 1867–1868 created a new electorate in the South by enfranchising blacks and temporarily disfranchising 10 percent to 15 percent of the whites. This new electorate put in power Republican governments that were made up of a coalition of carpetbaggers (northerners who had come south for a variety of reasons), scalawags (cooperating southern whites), and blacks.

B. Republican Rule

The Republican Reconstruction governments democratized southern politics by abolishing property and racial qualifications for voting and officeholding, redistricting state legislatures, and making formerly appointive offices elective. They undertook extensive public works, offered increased public services, and established the South's first public schools. All of this cost money, and therefore taxes rose. Southern landowners bitterly resented the increased taxes and accused the state governments of corruption and waste. Some of their charges were true, but many were exaggerated.

C. Counterattacks

White southern Democrats refused to accept black voting and officeholding and launched a counterattack to drive the Republican Reconstruction governments from power. White vigilante groups began a campaign of violence and intimidation against blacks, Freedmen's Bureau officials, and white Republicans. Congress investigated this reign of terror and attempted to suppress it with the Enforcement Acts, but only a "large military presence in the South could have protected black rights" and preserved the black electorate. By the 1870s Congress and President Grant were no longer willing to use military force to remake the South.

III. The Impact of Emancipation

A. Confronting Freedom

Freedmen, usually lacking property, tools, capital, and literacy, left the plantations where they had been enslaved and searched for family members from whom they had been separated. Once reunited many took the first opportunity to legalize their marriages so that they could raise their children and live an independent family life.

B. Black Institutions

The desire to be free of white control also led blacks to establish their own institutions. Most important were the black churches, which played major religious, social, and political roles. Many black schools were started with the help of the Freedmen's Bureau and northern philanthropists, including the earliest black universities: Howard, Atlanta, and Fisk. Segregation of all facilities in the South became a way of life despite Charles Sumner's Civil Rights Act of 1875, which was unenforced and later invalidated by the Supreme Court.

C. Land, Labor, and Sharecropping

Above all freedmen wanted to become landowning, independent farmers, but few did because the Republicans believed that property rights were too sacred to violate by confiscation and redistribution of white planters' land. Besides, blacks did not have the capital to buy land and agricultural tools. With the end of slavery, the planters continued to own the land but had no work force. Therefore, landless laborers and landholding planters developed the form of tenantry known as sharecropping. Many white small farmers also lost their land and became sharecropping tenants. By 1880, 80 percent of the land in the cotton states was worked by landless tenants.

D. Toward a Crop-Lien Economy

Rural merchants (often themselves landlords) sold supplies to sharecroppers on credit—with a lien on the tenants' share of the crop as collateral. Because interest rates were exorbitant, cotton prices low, and merchants often dishonest, sharecroppers fell deeper and deeper into debt. Southern law prohibited their leaving the land until they had fully repaid their debts. Thus sharecroppers were locked into poverty and "debt peonage."

IV. New Concerns in the North

A. Grantism

The popular Civil War hero Ulysses S. Grant won the presidency in 1868 on the Republican ticket. His administration was marred by rampant corruption, as were many state and local governments of the time. In 1872 Republicans disgusted by the scandals broke with Grant and formed the Liberal Republican party.

B. The Liberals' Revolt

The Liberal Republicans nominated Horace Greeley for president, and the Democrats endorsed him as well. The regular Republicans renominated Grant, who won the 1872 election, but the split in Republican ranks seriously weakened Republican efforts to remake the South.

C. The Panic of 1873

During Grant's second term the nation suffered a financial panic and a severe economic depression. These produced business failures, mass unemployment, heightened labor-management conflict, and disputes over the country's currency system, all of which further diverted Republican attention from Reconstruction.

D. Reconstruction and the Constitution

The Supreme Court in the last quarter of the nineteenth century also undermined Republican Reconstruction. In a series of decisions, the Court interpreted the Fourteenth and Fifteenth amendments in a way that made them all but useless for protecting black citizens. It declared the Civil Rights and Enforcement acts unconstitutional and upheld state segregation laws.

E. Republicans in Retreat

By the 1870s the Republicans were abandoning their Reconstruction policy. Most of them were more interested in economic growth than in protecting black rights. The Radicals who were committed to biracial democracy in the South were dead or had been defeated in elections. Many northerners wanted to normalize relations with the white South. They shared the racist belief that blacks were inferior to whites, and the federal government could not force equality.

V. Reconstruction Abandoned

A. Redeeming the South

After 1872 congressional pardons restored voting and officeholding rights to all ex-Confederates. These men and the South's rising class of businessmen led the Democratic party in a drive to redeem the South from Republican rule. Using economic pressure, intimidation, and violence, the Democrats had regained control of all the southern states but South Carolina, Florida, and Louisiana by 1876. Once in power the Democrats cut taxes and public works and services, and they passed laws favoring landlords over tenants. Some blacks responded to the deteriorating situation by migrating from the South, but most were trapped where they were by debt and poverty.

B. The Election of 1876

The Republicans nominated Rutherford Hayes; the Democrats, Samuel Tilden. Tilden won in the popular vote, but because of fraud and intimidation at the polls, the electoral votes in four states were disputed. A special electoral commission stacked in favor of the Republicans awarded all the disputed votes to Hayes. The Democrats refused to accept the finding until a compromise deal was worked out by southern Democrats and Republican supporters of Hayes. In exchange for southern acceptance of Hayes as president, the Republicans promised (1) to let Democrats take over the last Republican Reconstruction governments in Louisiana, South Carolina, and Florida; (2) to remove the remaining troops from the South; (3) to give more federal patronage to southern Democrats; and (4) to provide federal aid for building railroads and for other internal improvements in the South.

VI. Conclusion

By the end of the Reconstruction era the Republicans had firm support in the Northeast and Midwest; the Democrats were solidly entrenched in the South and would remain so for nearly a century. Many historians today look back on Reconstruction as a democratic experiment that failed partly because Congress did not redistribute land to the freedmen, and without any property they were too economically vulnerable to hold on to their political rights. The Republicans also were unwilling to continue using military force to protect blacks and remake southern society. Reconstruction did, however, leave as a lasting legacy the Fourteenth and Fifteenth amendments. During that brief era, southern blacks reconstituted their families, created their own institutions, and for the first time participated in government.

VOCABULARY

The following terms are used in Chapter 16. To understand the chapter fully, it is important that you know what each of them means.

suffrage   the vote; the right to vote

enfranchisement   the giving of the rights of citizenship and voting (the taking away of these rights is called disfranchisement)

allegiance   faithfulness and obligation to a person, idea, country, or government

amnesty   a general pardon for offenses against a government

partisan   a supporter of a political party or cause; having to do with actions motivated by support of a political party or cause

yeomen   nonslaveholding, small landowning farmers

status quo antebellum   the way things were before the war

referendum   the procedure of submitting legislative measures to the voters for approval or rejection

mandate   instruction about policy given or supposed to be given by the voters to a legislative body or government

confiscate   to seize private property by government authority

impeachment   the charging of a public official, such as a judge or president, with misconduct in office

vigilantes   members of extralegal citizens' groups organized to maintain order and punish offenses

electorate   the body of persons entitled to vote in an election

stereotype   a characteristic or set of characteristics, usually negative, attributed to all members of a group

coalition   a combination or alliance between different groups, parties, or states in support of a particular cause, individual, or purpose

mulatto   the offspring of one white and one black parent; a person of mixed black and white ancestry

mobilization   putting forces or resources into active service for a cause

writ of habeas corpus   a formal order requiring that an arrested person be brought before a judge or court and be charged with a specific crime or released; the right to such a writ is guaranteed in the U. S. Constitution

capital   wealth (especially money) that can be used to produce more wealth

segregation   the act of separating or setting apart from others, especially on the basis of race (the undoing of such separation is called desegregation or integration)

collateral   security or property pledged for the payment of a loan

debt peonage   the practice of holding someone in servitude or partial slavery until that person's debt is paid off

speculator   one who trades in commodities, securities, or land in the hope of making a profit from changes in their market value; a person who engages in business transactions that involve considerable risk but offer the chance of large gains

filibuster   to use delaying tactics, such as long speeches, to prevent a vote or action by a legislative body

IDENTIFICATIONS

After reading Chapter 16, you should be able to identify and explain the historical significance of each of the following:

Charles Sumner, Thaddeus Stevens, and the Radical Republicans

Lincoln's 10 percent plan versus Wade-Davis bill

Thirteenth Amendment

black codes

Freedmen's Bureau

Civil Rights Act of 1866

Fourteenth Amendment

Reconstruction Act of 1867

Tenure of Office Act

Fifteenth Amendment

Elizabeth Cady Stanton and Susan B. Anthony

carpetbaggers and scalawags

Ku Klux Klan, Enforcement Acts (Ku Klux Klan Act)

Civil Rights Act of 1875

Jay Gould and Jim Fisk

Crédit Mobilier

William M. Tweed

"Seward's Ice Box"

Liberal Republicans and Horace Greeley

greenbacks and the Greenback party

Slaughterhouse cases

Mississippi Plan and redemption

"Exodus" movement

Rutherford B. Hayes, Samuel J. Tilden, and the Compromise of 1877

SKILL BUILDING: CHARTS

1. Look at the table titled "The Duration of Republican Rule in the Ex-Confederate States" on page 527 in the textbook.
   a. For how many years on average did Republicans control the governments of the ex-Confederate states?
   b. Can you explain why Republican rule lasted less than a decade in every one of them?
   c. Which state was readmitted to the Union before the start of congressional Reconstruction? After reading the chapter, can you explain why?
   d. In what three states did Republicans hold power the longest? Can you explain what brought about the return of the Democrats to power in those three states?
2. Look at the table titled "Percentage of Persons Unable to Write by Age Group, 1870–1890, in South Carolina, Georgia, Alabama, Mississippi, and Louisiana" on page 518 of the textbook.
   a. What percentage of whites in each age group were unable to write in 1870? After reading the textbook, can you explain why these figures are so high?
   b. Did the educational levels of whites improve by 1890? Can you explain why it did or did not?
   c. Was the educational level of blacks higher or lower than that of whites in 1870? What about 1890? How might a critic of Republican Reconstruction of the South use these figures?
   d. After reading the text, can you explain the reasons for the differences between whites and blacks?

HISTORICAL SOURCES

Among the many historical sources used in Chapter 16 are three that are often useful to historians writing political history: (1) law codes, statutes, and constitutional amendments passed by the states and the federal government; (2) records of congressional speeches, remarks, and votes, as found in the *Congressional Globe,* later named the *Congressional Record;* (3) records of congressional hearings and investigations that are printed and made public by the federal government.

Page 503 of the text refers to laws known as black codes passed by the ex-Confederate states. By studying these laws, what does the historian learn about the intentions and attitudes toward blacks among the governing whites? What other conclusions does the textbook come to on the basis of this source?

Find at least three places in Chapter 16 where remarks of congressmen or important votes in the House or Senate are discussed. In each example, analyze what the author is illustrating or proving with this evidence.

Page 515 of the text cites testimony about vigilante violence in the South that was given before a joint congressional committee. Why are records of hearings and investigations by congressional committees a rich source for historians? Could a historian get a distorted or biased view of a past situation by relying solely on such a source? Why or why not?

Intensive studies of local or regional areas also provide useful historical insights. Look at "A Place in Time: A Georgia Plantation, 1865–1880." What light does this account of the Barrow plantation shed on the questions of why and how the sharecropping system developed? In what ways would the article written in 1881 by David Barrow for *Scribner's* magazine be a good historical source for learning about blacks and sharecropping? Why should the historian using it also be skeptical about its claims and observations?

MULTIPLE-CHOICE QUESTIONS

Circle the letter of the item that best completes each statement or answers the question.

1. Lincoln's plan of reconstruction
   a. required southern states to enfranchise blacks.
   b. required that 50 percent or more of white voters in an ex-Confederate state take an oath of allegiance to the Union before a new state government could be established.
   c. was intended to gain the support of southern Unionists and attract them to a southern Republican party.
   d. was eventually accepted by Congress.

2. Which of the following statements about Andrew Johnson is *incorrect*?
   a. He wanted to exclude the planters from political leadership in the South, but then he undermined his intention by granting many pardons to this group.
   b. He cared deeply about obtaining just treatment for the freedmen.
   c. He was a lifelong Democrat with no interest in building the strength of the Republican party.
   d. He vetoed all of the congressional Reconstruction acts, only to have Congress override his vetoes.

3. The black codes
   a. were imposed by Congress on the ex-Confederate states.
   b. guaranteed such basic liberties as freedom of movement and employment, the right to testify in court, and the use of all public facilities.
   c. were seen by Thaddeus Stevens and other Radical Republicans as a necessary legal step to help blacks make the transition from slavery to freedom.
   d. were laws passed by the Johnson governments in the South to keep blacks as a semifree, cheap labor force.

4. Which of their plans did Radical Republicans persuade Congress to embody in the Reconstruction acts and in the Fourteenth and Fifteenth amendments?
   a. black suffrage, a period of military occupation of the South, temporary exclusion of ex-Confederates from voting and officeholding
   b. confiscation and redistribution of land in the South, imprisonment of ex-Confederate leaders
   c. forty acres and a mule for each freedman, temporary disfranchisement of whites, enfranchisement of blacks
   d. exile of Jefferson Davis and other ex-Confederate leaders, upholding of all Civil War debts, extending the right to vote to all citizens over age twenty-one

5. Andrew Johnson was impeached but not convicted because
   a. he proved that he had not violated the Tenure of Office Act.
   b. he resigned before the Senate voted on his guilt.
   c. seven Republicans, fearing that removal of the president would upset the balance of power among the three branches of government, voted ''not guilty'' with the Democrats.
   d. the Supreme Court ruled that he had not engaged in misconduct in office.

6. The Fifteenth Amendment
   a. defines citizenship and requires states to extend to all persons equal protection of the laws.
   b. states that no one shall be denied the right to vote because of race, color, or previous condition of servitude.
   c. extends suffrage to all citizens over twenty-one years of age.
   d. gives Congress the power to deny seats in the House to states that do not allow black men to vote.

7. In the Republican Reconstruction governments of the South, the group that held the most political offices consisted of
   a. carpetbaggers.
   b. scalawags.
   c. blacks.
   d. the planter elite.

8. The Republican Reconstruction governments of the South
    a. gave the region the most honest, efficient governments it had ever had.
    b. excluded almost all whites from officeholding and were run almost exclusively by blacks.
    c. created public-school systems, built and repaired roads and bridges, and opened institutions to care for orphans and the disabled.
    d. cut taxes and passed laws favoring the interests of landlords over those of tenants and sharecroppers.

9. The sharecropping and crop-lien systems that developed in the post–Civil War South
    a. contributed to soil depletion, agricultural backwardness, and southern poverty.
    b. reduced the portion of southern land owned and controlled by the planter elite.
    c. forced most black people out of agriculture and into southern cities.
    d. tied white planters and black tenants together economically but had no effect on white small farmers.

10. Most historians today view Radical Reconstruction as a democratic experiment that failed because
    a. it left blacks without property and thus economically unable to defend their political rights.
    b. it relied on excessive military force instead of political persuasion.
    c. it was unrealistic in its expectation that illiterate blacks could be turned into responsible citizens overnight.
    d. it was overly vindictive and harsh toward all white southerners.

SHORT-ANSWER QUESTIONS

1. What actions of President Johnson drove Moderate Republicans in Congress into cooperation with Radical Republicans?

2. Why did Elizabeth Cady Stanton, Susan B. Anthony, and some other feminists oppose the Fifteenth Amendment?

3. Why did the Liberal Republicans break with President Grant? What impact did the split have on Republican Reconstruction?

4. Explain how Supreme Court decisions in the 1870s and 1880s undermined Republican Reconstruction.

5. What were the terms of the Compromise of 1877? Which of the terms were actually carried out after the inauguration of Rutherford B. Hayes?

ESSAY QUESTIONS

1. Compare and contrast Lincoln's, Johnson's, and Congress' plans of reconstruction (as represented by the Reconstruction Acts of 1867–1868 and the Fourteenth and Fifteenth amendments). What were the objectives of each plan? Why did each fail to achieve its goals?

2. Discuss the transformation of southern agriculture during the Reconstruction period. Why did the sharecropping and crop-lien systems evolve? What were the consequences of those systems for the economy of the South and for white and black farmers?

3. Discuss the achievements and failures of the Republican Reconstruction governments in the South. Who supported and who opposed them? Why? Why and how were they driven from power?

4. Imagine that you are a Freedmen's Bureau agent in the South during the Reconstruction period. Using the information in Chapter 16, write an account of what you have seen black people doing and experiencing. As such an agent, how have you been involved with the blacks in your district?

5. Write an essay discussing the Grant administration. What were its policies on Reconstruction and the freedmen? What was meant by "Grantism" and Grant's "Great Barbecue"? What successes and failures did the administration have in foreign policy? Why did the Liberal Republicans break with Grant?

17

The Trans-Mississippi West

OUTLINE AND SUMMARY

I. Native Americans and the Trans-Mississippi West

A. *The Plains Indians*

In the mid-nineteenth century, the Sioux, Blackfoot, Cheyenne, Arapaho, Crow, and other Indian tribes roamed the northern Great Plains. In the central and southern Plains lived the Five Civilized Tribes and the Comanches, Kiowas, Pawnees, and others. Such diverse peoples as the Hopis, Zunis, Navajos, Apaches, southern Arapahos, and southern Cheyennes inhabited the Southwest. Many of the Plains Indians, among them the Dakota Sioux, Blackfeet, Crows, and Cheyennes, hunted the migrating buffalo herds. They ate the meat and used the hides for tepees and clothing, the sinews and bones for tools and weapons, and skulls and other parts for religious rituals. In the 1870s the demand for buffalo hides in the eastern markets grew so great that white hunters, aided by the expanding railroads, became professional buffalo killers. By the 1880s hunting had reduced the once great herds to only a few thousand animals and doomed the nomadic, buffalo-centered way of life of the Plains tribes.

B. *The Transformation of Indian Life*

Not only did white hunters destroy most of the game on the Great Plains, but settlers began to invade the area as well. In the 1850s and 1860s the U.S. government forced the Dakota Sioux to cede 24 million acres of land in the Minnesota Territory in exchange for promises of payments, agricultural help, and two reservations. When the government failed to deliver promised supplies and farming help, the angry Sioux attacked white settlers in Minnesota, only to be defeated and pushed out of the territory almost entirely. By the time of the Civil War, the government was pressuring other Plains tribes to surrender their vast hunting grounds and settle as farmers on restricted reservations. Some tribes, such as the Pueblos and Crows, accepted the change peacefully, but in the 1860s and 1870s some 100,000 Indians of the Sioux, Cheyenne, Arapaho, Kiowa, Comanche, and other tribes engaged in almost constant warfare with the army over possession of the Great Plains and the Southwest. In this struggle both whites and Indians committed atrocities, such as the Chivington and Fetterman massacres. In 1868 the government signed peace treaties with many of these tribes that assigned most of them to two large reservations, one in present-day Oklahoma (then known as the Indian Territory) and the other the Great Sioux Reserve in present-day Montana and South Dakota. The government failed to keep its promises of supplies and help with learning to farm, and much of the land was unsuitable for cultivation. The Indians, therefore, left the reservations and harried white pioneers. The army retaliated by attacking any bands off their reservations, even if those groups did not happen to be the ones that had committed hostile acts.

C. Custer's Last Stand

When the Sioux refused to report to the government-run agencies on their reservation and to sell the Black Hills part of their reserve, on which gold had been discovered, the army made war against them. The most famous casualties in that campaign were Colonel George A. Custer and his Seventh Cavalry, whom the Sioux annihilated at the Battle of the Little Bighorn in 1876. Despite their brief triumph, the Sioux were subsequently forced to settle near the government agencies and to surrender the Black Hills. In the late 1870s the army crushed brief resistance by Chief Joseph's Nez Percés and Chief Dull Knife's northern Cheyennes.

D. "Saving" the Indians

Humanitarian reformers in the East began to cry out against government mistreatment of the Indians. In 1881 Helen Hunt Jackson's *A Century of Dishonor* called attention to the sorry record. These reformers thought the best way to end the injustice was to assimilate Indians quickly into mainstream white society. Therefore, well-intentioned reformers, as well as whites who were interested only in seizing more Indian land, supported the 1887 Dawes Severalty Act. The law ended collective tribal ownership of land and split the reservations into 160-acre farms that were assigned to the head of each Indian family. Any remaining reservation land was sold to whites. At the end of twenty-five years, the Indians were to receive full title to their farms and U.S. citizenship. The government also attempted to suppress tribal languages and culture. The new policies proved disastrous for most Indians. By 1934 the total acreage owned by Indians had fallen by 65 percent. What was left in Indian hands was often too dry or infertile to be farmed.

E. The Ghost Dance and the End of Indian Resistance on the Great Plains

Desperate because of their plight, the Sioux and other tribes turned to the Ghost Dance movement. The army's decision to stop the movement led to the last battles between whites and Indians and the 1890 Wounded Knee massacre of three hundred Sioux.

II. Settling the West

A. The First Transcontinental Railroad

With the meeting of the Union Pacific and Central Pacific tracks at Promontory Point, Utah, in 1869, the United States completed its first transcontinental railroad. Construction had been authorized by the Pacific Railroad Act of 1862, and much of the labor was performed by Chinese and Irish immigrants. Because the government granted land to the companies for every mile of track laid, the railroads emerged as the biggest landlords in the West. By the end of the 1800s, nine major railroads linked the country, making westward travel and shipping much faster and easier.

B. Settlers and the Railroad

The railroad attracted settlers to the Great Plains. To encourage railroad companies to lay track across the country, state and federal governments granted them millions of acres of land. Eager both to sell these lands and to create future customers for rail service, the companies made all-out efforts to attract settlers. They opened land bureaus, sent agents to the East Coast and Europe, offered easy credit and free transportation out west to potential purchasers, and promised land buyers that the railroads would transport their future crops to market inexpensively. The railroads wielded great economic and social influence over western development. Their pressure for quick payment from land buyers pushed western farmers into concentrating on producing a single cash crop, such as wheat or corn, which made them very vulnerable to price fluctuations on the world market.

C. Homesteaders on the Great Plains

Settlers also were attracted to the Great Plains by the Homestead Act, which provided a free 160-acre farm to anyone who would live on and improve it over a five-year period. This offer was especially attractive to immigrants from western and northern Europe, where land was extremely expensive. Some 400,000 families registered claims under the Homestead Act between 1862 and 1900, although there were flaws in the provisions and implementation of the law that allowed the most valuable western land to end up in the hands of the railroads, land speculators, lumber companies, and big ranchers.

D. New Farms, New Markets

Railroads, improved farm machinery, soaring eastern demand for food, and improved milling techniques all led to the development of 2.5 million new farms and the doubling of American agricultural production between 1870 and 1900. Starting a new farm on the Great Plains was a risky business. Most settlers had to go heavily into debt to acquire horses, machinery, and seed even if they obtained free land. To meet debt payments to railroads and banks, farmers specialized in growing cash crops, which made them vulnerable to world market conditions and dependent on the railroads to reach the markets. Uncertain rainfall and severe weather conditions added to the farmers' problems.

E. Building a Society and Achieving Statehood

The difficulties of living in crude frontier conditions—sod houses, backbreaking labor, isolated surroundings, storms, and extremes of heat and cold—drove out many early settlers. Within a decade, however, most of those who stuck it out had built decent wood houses. "Civilized" communities with churches, schools, lyceums, libraries, and social clubs began to emerge. Residents drew up state constitutions, and one after another Kansas, Nevada, Nebraska, and Colorado entered the Union in the 1860s and 1870s. Most of the northern portions of the Great Plains achieved statehood in the late 1880s and 1890s. With the entrance to the Union of Oklahoma, Arizona, and New Mexico early in the twentieth century, the trans-Mississippi West completed its transition from frontier territories to statehood. Although most western governments were conservative, they did lead the eastern states in granting women's suffrage. By 1910 Idaho, Wyoming, Utah, and Colorado women had full voting rights.

F. The Grange

When prices of wheat and other agricultural products dropped in the 1870s, debt-burdened farmers fell on hard times. They responded by forming the first nationwide agricultural organization, the Patrons of Husbandry, or Grange, led by Oliver H. Kelley. The Grange tried to help farmers economically by organizing cooperatives to market their crops and buy supplies. It also lobbied state legislatures to regulate the railroads, which were overcharging farmers, giving discounts to large shippers, and bribing state officials. A number of states did pass "Granger Laws," but they were bitterly attacked by the railroads as unconstitutional. At first federal courts upheld state regulation, but in the *Wabash* case (1886) the Supreme Court ruled that states could not regulate interstate railroads. Congress stepped into the void by passing the Interstate Commerce Act (ICA) (1887), which created the Interstate Commerce Commission (ICC) to investigate and oversee railroad practices. The ICA did little to curb railroad abuses, but the law and the ICC set a precedent for future federal regulation of interstate commerce. The failure of the Granger Laws and the Grange's other efforts to help farmers economically led to the organization's decline after 1878.

G. The Southwestern Frontier

After the Mexican War, American ranchers and settlers in the Southwest took over the territorial governments and forced most of the Spanish-speaking population off the land. The Mexican minority tended to become low-paid day laborers who faced discrimination and periodic violent attacks. The large numbers of Mexicans in the region nonetheless gave the Southwest a strongly Spanish cultural and linguistic coloration.

III. Exploiting the West

A. The Mining Frontier

Starting with the California gold rush in 1849, a series of mining booms swept the West. In the 1850s gold rushes took place in the Sierra Nevada and in British Columbia. New gold and silver strikes followed in Nevada, Colorado, Idaho, Montana, Wyoming, South Dakota, and the Alaskan Klondike. Each new discovery brought a rush of eager prospectors who believed in the get-rich-quick myth of the West. Infamous boomtowns such as Virginia City, Nevada, sprang up and then declined into ghost towns when the mines were depleted. Although a few individual prospectors with picks, shovels, and strainers did make their fortunes, most barely earned a living. The real profits from the mining frontier went to large mining companies backed by European and eastern capital. They had the expensive equipment necessary to mine the gold and silver deposits deep underground.

B. Cowboys and the Cattle Frontier

Confinement of the Plains Indians on reservations, extension of the railroad into Kansas, and the construction of new stockyards at railheads such as Abilene made possible the open-range cattle industry. Railroad promoters enticed thousands of people to enter the business by predicting great profits. For a time open-range ranchers did make fortunes, although this was not true for the ordinary cowboys who tended the cattle on the long drives to the railheads. Most cowboys were poorly paid young men, about one-fifth of them black or Mexican. The open-range cattle bonanza reached its peak in the years 1880–1885. Thereafter the industry declined rapidly because of overgrazing, fencing of the open range by farmers, and freezing winters in 1885 and 1886 that killed 90 percent of the steers in some regions. The open range and great cattle drives disappeared, to be replaced by smaller, fenced-in ranches that were close to one of the many rail lines serving the West by the 1890s.

C. Bonanza Farms on the Plains

Believing that enormous profits could be made in large-scale wheat growing, speculators in the late 1870s and 1880s established ten-thousand-acre farms and invested heavily in the latest equipment. For a while these bonanza farms did reap handsome profits, but overproduction, poor weather conditions, and falling wheat prices sent most of the enterprises into bankruptcy by 1890.

D. The Oklahoma Land Rush

The federal government initially set aside Oklahoma as a reservation for various Indian tribes, but as pressure from land-hungry farmers mounted, the government reconsidered. In 1889 Congress opened some 2 million acres in the heart of the Indian Territory to white settlers. Within weeks Oklahoma pioneers filed six thousand homestead claims, and in the following years, under the provisions of the Dawes Act, more and more Oklahoma land passed into the hands of whites.

IV. The West of Life and Legend

A. The American Adam and the Dime-Novel Hero

In the 1860s and 1870s eastern dime-novel writers created the western novel, with its frontiersman hero who fought Indians and "bad guys" and rescued maidens. One of the novelists, Ned Buntline, made Buffalo Bill so famous that his real-life model, William F. "Buffalo Bill" Cody, cashed in on the fame by founding a Wild West touring show that became extremely popular.

B. Revitalizing the Frontier Legend

The dime novels and Wild West shows caught the fancy of three young members of the eastern elite: Theodore Roosevelt, Frederic Remington, and Owen Wister. The three visited the West and made it the subject of their histories, art, and novels. In doing so they fostered the frontier legend of the West as a testing ground in which the fittest and best survived and as the home of the cowboy, who embodied the essence of manly virtue.

C. Beginning a Conservation Movement

The frontier legend aroused limited public interest in protecting some of the West's natural beauty and wonders. Also, in response to the work of John Wesley Powell, Henry D. Washburn, George Perkins Marsh, and John Muir, the nation created its first national parks (Yellowstone and Yosemite), and Muir founded the first organization dedicated to conservation, the Sierra Club.

V. Conclusion

In the 1890s, as the untamed West vanished, historian Frederick Jackson Turner advanced his thesis that American self-reliance, inventiveness, individualism, and freedom had been nurtured by the frontier experience. While most modern historians reject Turner's "frontier thesis," they do acknowledge the important role of the West and its resources in "influencing our thinking about society, government, and ourselves."

VOCABULARY

The following terms are used in Chapter 17. To understand the chapter fully, it is important that you know what each of them means.

entrepreneur one who owns, launches, manages, and assumes the risks of a business venture

cede to hand over land or valuable rights, usually by treaty

severalty the legal situation in which property, such as land, is held or owned by separate or individual right, as opposed to collective ownership

polygamy the practice of having several spouses at one time

lobby to seek to influence legislators' votes for or against a bill; many groups hire persons called lobbyists to do this for them

indigenous native to a region or to the original population of an area

bonanza a rich mass of ore, as in mining; a sudden find of wealth

subsidize to give governmental aid to a private business to encourage its development

cavalier disdainful, dismissive, showing superiority toward others

IDENTIFICATIONS

After reading Chapter 17, you should be able to identify and explain the historical significance of each of the following:

John M. Chivington and the Sand Creek Massacre

Fetterman Massacre

Great Sioux Reserve

Sitting Bull

George Armstrong Custer

Chief Joseph

Chief Dull Knife

Carlisle Indian School

Helen Hunt Jackson, *A Century of Dishonor*

Dawes Severalty Act, 1887

Wovoka, the Ghost Dance, and Wounded Knee

Pacific Railroad Act, 1862

Homestead Act, 1862

Timber Culture, Desert Land, and Timber and Stone acts, 1870s

the Grange and the Granger Laws

Wabash v. *Illinois*, 1886

Interstate Commerce Act, 1887

Henry Comstock and the Comstock Lode

Joseph G. McCoy and the cattle frontier

Oklahoma "sooners"

Frederick Jackson Turner's "frontier thesis"

Ned Buntline and William F. "Buffalo Bill" Cody

John Wesley Powell, Henry D. Washburn, George Perkins Marsh, John Muir, and the birth of the conservation movement

---

SKILL BUILDING: MAPS

1. On the outline map of the Great Plains and the Far West, identify each state and indicate the decade in which it entered the Union.

2. Each of the following places was significant in the history of the frontier West. Locate each and explain its importance.

   100th meridian

   Sierra Nevada

   Rocky Mountains

   Virginia City, Nevada

   Denver, Colorado

   Missouri River and Great Sioux Reserve

   Indian Territory (Oklahoma)

   Black Hills, South Dakota

   Little Big Horn, Montana

   Wounded Knee, South Dakota

   Abilene, Kansas

   Chisholm Trail

   Promontory Point (near Ogden, Utah)

   Colorado River

   Yellowstone National Park

   Yosemite National Park

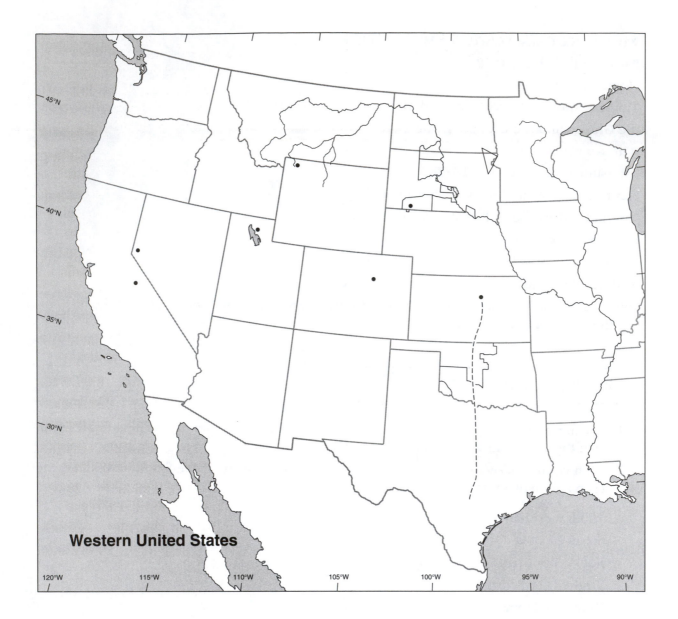

Western United States

HISTORICAL SOURCES

Historians try to discover not only what life was like for different groups of people living in the past but also what those people believed, valued, and perceived. Unless we know these things, it is difficult to understand motivation, to answer the question, Why did people do what they did?

In Chapter 17 the author uses popular novels published in the last forty years of the nineteenth century to shed some light on beliefs, values, and perceptions. Some examples are Edward L. Wheeler, *Deadwood Dick* (1877), cited on pages 559–560; and Ned Buntline, *Buffalo Bill, King of the Border Men* (1869), cited on pages 562–563. What do each of these popular novels try to convey to the reader? Why are popular novels good historical sources? How can we know whether their readers shared the values and perceptions of their authors?

While these novels may be historical sources, they have little lasting literary merit. In Chapter 17 the author also uses the works of more gifted writers and artists as historical sources. Hamlin Garland wrote vivid stories about farm life on the Great Plains. On page 554 the author refers to two of Garland's books. What do *Son of the Middle Border* and *Main-Travelled Roads* illustrate? Page 557 refers to a book by Mark Twain, one of the best nineteenth-century writers, and page 563 discusses the paintings and sculptures of Frederic Remington, the fine western artist. How does the author use the work of Twain and Remington? What is illustrated in each case? Look at some reproductions of Remington paintings and sculptures of cowboys and Indians. Do you see the same message in them as the author does in Chapter 17?

Look at "A Place in Time: Like-a-Fishhook." How does this capsule history of the Hidatsas illustrate the generalizations made in Chapter 17 about Plains Indian culture and the adjustments forced on Indians?

MULTIPLE-CHOICE QUESTIONS

Circle the letter of the item that best completes each statement or answers the question.

1. Most Great Plains Indians in the mid-nineteenth century
   a. lived in semipermanent villages and did some farming.
   b. lived in nuclear family units and seldom saw others beyond their immediate relatives.
   c. hunted the migratory buffalo herds and utilized the animals' meat, hides, and bones.
   d. adjusted quickly to reservation life because they were used to living in tribal communities.

2. Custer's Last Stand occurred during an army campaign aimed at
   a. suppressing the Ghost Dance.
   b. forcing the Sioux to settle at government agencies and give up the Black Hills.
   c. forcing Dull Knife and his northern Cheyennes to return to their reservation in Wyoming.
   d. capturing Chief Joseph and his fleeing band of Nez Percés.

3. The Dawes Severalty Act
   a. was opposed by Helen Hunt Jackson and other eastern friends of the Indians.
   b. gave each tribe legal title to its reservation land.
   c. attempted to preserve Indian culture once the Indians were no longer a military threat.
   d. benefited land-hungry whites much more than it did Indians.

4. Which of the following statements about the Homestead Act is *incorrect?*
   a. It attracted many immigrants from Northern and Western Europe to the Great Plains.
   b. Because of this law, the great majority of federal government land on the Great Plains went to pioneering family farmers.
   c. The law provided 160-acre farms to anyone who would live on the land for five years and improve it.
   d. Because of flaws in the law and its enforcement, much of the best land went to speculators and railroads.

5. In the latter half of the nineteenth century, the federal government attempted to confine all Plains Indian tribes on two big reservations located in
   a. Texas and Arizona.
   b. California and Oregon.
   c. Nebraska and Kansas.
   d. Oklahoma and South Dakota.

6. In the case of *Wabash* v. *Illinois*, the Supreme Court ruled that
   a. states could regulate railroads and other businesses serving the public so as to protect public safety.
   b. the federal government could not interfere in businesses operating wholly or partly in a particular state.
   c. states could not regulate interstate railroad rates.
   d. the Interstate Commerce Act was unconstitutional.

7. Although the new state governments in the West were generally conservative, the one area in which they were ahead of the eastern states was in
   a. granting women suffrage.
   b. ending all discrimination on the basis of race.
   c. enacting legislation against prostitution.
   d. desegregating public education.

8. Whose campaign to protect the wilderness led to establishing Yosemite National Park and the founding of the Sierra Club?
   a. Joseph G. McCoy
   b. Hamlin Garland
   c. Owen Wister
   d. John Muir

9. The days of the open range and great cattle drives came to an end after 1886 for all of the following reasons *except*
   a. overgrazing and crowding of the range.
   b. severe winters and dry summers in 1885 and 1886.
   c. a decline in the demand for beef.
   d. expansion of the railroads throughout the West.

10. He was the Indian leader who helped defeat Custer at the Little Big Horn, traveled with Buffalo Bill's Wild West show, and was killed in 1890 by reservation agents trying to suppress the Ghost Dance.
    a. Chief Joseph
    b. Chief Dull Knife
    c. Goodbird
    d. Sitting Bull

SHORT-ANSWER QUESTIONS

1. What was the Grange? What did it attempt to do for farmers? Did it succeed? Why or why not?

2. Discuss early state and federal efforts to regulate railroads. Why were they ineffective?

3. What happened to the Hispanic population of the Southwest after 1848?

4. What was Frederick Jackson Turner's "frontier thesis"? How do today's historians regard it?

5. Discuss the beginnings of the conservation movement. Who were some of its early advocates? What were their motives?

ESSAY QUESTIONS

1. One historian has written a book about the Plains Indians in the period 1840–1900 titled *The Long Death*. Drawing on the material in Chapter 17, explain why this is an appropriate title. Include in your discussion the impact of the slaughter of the buffalo, the reservation policy, the Dawes Act, and the attempts of government and reformers to "civilize" and assimilate the Indians.

2. The railroads, more than any other agency, stimulated settlement of the Great Plains and shaped the pattern of development there. Discuss this statement, explaining why and how railroads helped shape the West.

3. The myth of the frontier celebrated the economic opportunities that the West offered to everyone. Judging from the material in Chapter 17, how much truth was there in that myth? (Cite as much specific evidence as possible.)

4. Compare and contrast the picture of cowboys and their lives in the West as presented in Chapter 17, Owen Wister's novel *The Virginian,* and the dime novels of writers such as Ned Buntline.

5. "Unlike earlier westward expansion, almost every aspect of the settlement of the final frontier was influenced by the transformation occurring within American industry and the American economy." Explain and illustrate this statement with material about the development of farming, mining, and cattle raising found in Chapter 17.

18

The Rise of Industrial America

OUTLINE AND SUMMARY

I. The Character of Industrial Change

A. *Railroad Innovations*

By 1900 the United States had more rail miles tying the country together than did all of Europe. Building this extensive railroad system opened a vast internal market to American industry. The railroad companies also led the way in developing financial and managerial practices that made large-scale corporate enterprise possible, such as the sale of stock to raise needed capital. Railroad management innovations became the model for other businesses trying to sell products in a national market.

B. *Creativity, Cooperation, and Competition*

A group of innovative and unscrupulous railroad entrepreneurs, including Collis P. Huntington, Jay Gould, and James J. Hill, bought out their smaller competitors one by one. By the 1890s they had established great trunk lines that controlled most of the track. These integrated lines, with their standardized equipment and track gauge, carried goods all over the country much more efficiently than had been done formerly. The railroad companies also abused their powers. They cheated investors by watering their stock, bribed politicians with free passes and other favors, and gave rebates and kickbacks to big shippers while over-charging small businesses and farmers.

Suffering from these railroad abuses, small shippers demanded legislation to curb the unfair practices. In the 1870s many midwestern states outlawed rate discrimination, and in 1887 Congress passed the Interstate Commerce Act, which established the Interstate Commerce Commission (ICC) to investigate complaints and unreasonable rates. The legislation proved ineffective for several reasons, among them federal court decisions, which nearly always sided with the railroads.

In the early twentieth century, under the guidance of investment bankers, railroad consolidation proceeded still further. By 1906 seven giant corporations controlled two-thirds of all the track. These companies had become the largest business enterprises in the world, pioneering new accounting and organizational methods and stimulating iron, steel, and other industries with their need for rails and engines.

C. Applying the Lessons of the Railroads to Steel

Andrew Carnegie's career illustrates the close connection between railroad expansion and the growth of heavy industry. Carnegie's best customers were the railroad companies. From his early experiences working in the railroad industry, he learned the organizational, accounting, and managerial innovations that he later applied to his steel business. He also copied the railroad practice of consolidating smaller enterprises into fewer and fewer huge companies. Carnegie integrated his business both vertically and horizontally. When J. P. Morgan's Federal Steel and Carnegie Steel combined in 1901 to form U.S. Steel, it was the world's first corporation capitalized at over $1 billion.

D. Consolidating the Industrial Order

By 1900 the consolidation process that had placed the railroad and steel businesses in the hands of a few corporate giants had also taken place in the oil, sugar, meat-packing, and many other industries. In the oil-refining business, John D. Rockefeller led the way toward consolidation. His Standard Oil Company, like Carnegie Steel, was quick to adopt the latest technology. He advertised heavily, made deals with the railroads to get special shipping discounts, engaged in deception and aggression to ruin competitors, and created the first trust to extinguish all competition in oil refining.

The growth of trusts and monopolies in one industry after another led to public pressure for government intervention. In 1890 Congress passed the Sherman Anti-Trust Act, which outlawed all contracts and consolidations that were in restraint of trade in interstate commerce. The law proved ineffective in stopping the growth of trusts because it was vaguely worded, presidents rarely brought suits against companies under it, and the Supreme Court in the *E. C. Knight* case interpreted the meaning of interstate commerce so narrowly as to prevent the law's use against manufacturing corporations. In fact, between 1897 and 1903, large-scale consolidations in industry accelerated.

E. The Triumph of Technology

The invention and patenting of new machines in the period 1860–1900 also brought about the growth of huge corporations. For example, Alexander Graham Bell's invention of the telephone in 1876 gave rise to Bell Telephone, which by 1900 had installed some 800,000 phones in the United States. Thomas A. Edison, with the founding of his Menlo Park laboratory, perfected the light bulb and invented the phonograph, microphone, motion-picture camera, and over a thousand other items. These men proved that new inventions could be the foundation of profitable big business.

F. Mass Production, Mass Marketing

Aggressive marketing and advertising were effective in expanding sales and beating out competitors in the late nineteenth century. Procter and Gamble, American Tobacco, and Pillsbury Flour all built huge demand for their products this way.

G. Industrialization: Costs and Benefits

By 1900 the chaos of thousands of small companies competing for the national market had been replaced by an economy dominated by a small number of enormous corporations offering a dazzling array of new products. The price of these accomplishments was the crushing of thousands of small- and medium-sized businesses, the exploitation of millions of workers, and the fouling of the environment.

II. The New South

A. Obstacles to Southern Economic Development

The South industrialized more slowly than the North and until 1900 lagged far behind it. The reasons for this included the destruction of the South's credit system by the Civil War and its subsequent shortage of capital. Other factors were federal government policies that hurt the South economically, such as high protective tariffs, and the South's poor educational facilities and high rate of illiteracy.

B. The New South Creed and Southern Industrialization

In the 1870s southern newspaper editors, planters, and businessmen began to preach the "New South Creed"—the region must industrialize. Eager to attract northern capital, southern states offered tax exemptions for new businesses that would locate there. They also held industrial fairs, leased convicts from state prisons as cheap labor, and practically gave away land, forests, and mineral rights to northern corporations. Northern lumber syndicates cut down the forests of Alabama, Louisiana, and other southern states, making lumber production soar. Iron and steel production expanded dramatically around Birmingham, Alabama.

C. The Southern Mill Economy

Southern industry developed in its own distinctive pattern. Unlike the North, where factories were usually in or near urban areas, southern textile mills opened in the countryside, and towns and villages were created around them. Most of the textile mills were located in the Piedmont region of Virginia, the Carolinas, Georgia, and Alabama. The southern mills combined northern technical expertise with southern rural paternalism. They recruited workers from the poor white farm population of the Piedmont, hiring whole families, including many women and children. The owners, despite substantial profits, paid the laborers 30 percent to 50 percent less than New England mills did. The textile companies dominated life in the mill towns they started. They provided their employees with housing, stores, schools, and churches. Because the mills underpaid their workers and overcharged for rent and supplies, the employees often fell into debt to the companies, just as sharecroppers were indebted to their landlords and credit-merchants.

D. The Southern Industrial Lag

Despite impressive advances, southern industrialization occurred on a smaller scale and at a slower pace than in the North. Furthermore, the southern economy remained essentially in a colonial status, owned largely by northern firms. U.S. Steel, for example, controlled the foundries in Birmingham.

III. Industrial Work and the Work Force

A. From Workshop to Factory

As the number of industrial workers in the United States climbed from 885,000 to 3.2 million by 1900 and the trend toward large-scale, increasingly mechanized production speeded up, the nature of work changed markedly. There were fewer artisans, and the remaining skilled workers had less control over their work and derived less satisfaction from it. Factories hired more low-skilled, low-paid women and children to do jobs that had become simple, machine-paced, repetitive, and boring.

B. The Hardships of Industrial Labor

Already by the 1880s almost one-third of the labor force in the steel and railroad industries were unskilled workers. Common laborers drifted from city to city and from industry to industry, working for wages that were one-third of those paid to skilled artisans. In the expanding factories and on railroads, workers were exposed to a variety of industrially induced diseases, such as black and brown lung. They also had appallingly frequent accidents resulting in permanent disability or death. The excessive hours of work and the presence of many child laborers contributed to the high rate of industrial accidents. Employers rarely paid compensation to injured workers and opposed passage of state health and safety codes.

C. Immigrant Labor

More and more, immigrants filled the least skilled, lowest-paid, dirtiest, and most dangerous jobs in the expanding mines, factories, and railroads. Impoverished French Canadians crossed the border to work in the New England textile mills; the Chinese constructed railroads and mined ore in the West. If immigrant workers stayed healthy, they often lived better than they had in their homelands. They even saved small amounts of money. Although most of the immigrants worked very hard, they did not adjust easily to the fast pace and monotony of factory work. As much as possible, they resisted management's attempts to tighten factory discipline and increase production quotas. When worker resentment boiled over in response to wage cuts and speed-ups, they struck and often became violent.

D. Women and Work in Industrializing America

Since women could be paid even less than men and could do unskilled industrial jobs just as well, management hired more and more women. Married, working-class women and their children often spent hours finishing garments, rolling cigars, and performing other labor for manufacturers in their tenement apartments. Young, single women readily took jobs in factories because they preferred them to domestic service, almost the only alternative for uneducated females. Immigrant parents regularly sent their daughters into the mills and factories to supplement inadequate family incomes. By 1900 women made up 17 percent of the labor force. In the late nineteenth and early twentieth centuries, women also began to enter clerical positions. Office work paid better and offered more prestige than factory jobs, but women clerical workers had almost no chance of moving up to managerial positions.

Despite the increase in female wage earners, women's work outside the home was viewed as temporary. A woman's career was that of housewife and mother.

E. Hard Work and the Gospel of Success

Newspapers and magazines preached the gospel that, for male workers, America was the land of opportunity and hard work led to success. The papers were filled with rags-to-riches stories of poor immigrant boys such as Andrew Carnegie who rose to become heads of major corporations. In fact, Carnegie was the exception. Ninety-five percent of executives of big corporations came from middle- and upper-class families. There was some opportunity, however, for skilled workers to move into ownership and management of small businesses. For unskilled immigrant laborers, there was less mobility. At best they moved from unskilled to semiskilled or skilled industrial jobs, and they remained in the working class. A huge gulf existed between the rich and poor. By 1890 America's richest families, the top 10 percent, owned 73 percent of the country's wealth. At the other extreme, better than 50 percent of all industrial laborers earned incomes that placed them below the poverty line.

IV. Labor Unions and Industrial Conflict

A. Organizing the Workers

In response to the unfavorable changes that rapid industrialization was forcing upon them, workers turned to labor unions. In 1866 William H. Sylvis recruited workers from several trades into the National Labor Union. As it declined in membership in the 1870s, it was overshadowed by the Knights of Labor, led by Terence V. Powderly. The Knights called for advanced social and economic reforms, including equal pay for men and women; abolition of child labor; inclusion of black workers in unions; a graduated income tax; and cooperative ownership of factories, mines, and other businesses. Despite its egalitarian ideals, the Knights and other labor groups favored immigration restriction. Labor opposition to the Chinese, whom they accused of working so cheaply that they undercut native-born workers, was especially strong. The federal government responded to anti-Chinese sentiment by passing the Chinese Exclusion Act in 1882. When the Knights won a series of strikes in the 1880s, workers rushed to join, swelling its membership to 700,000. In the late 1880s, however, the Knights suffered setbacks: it lost several big strikes, its craft unions broke away to form a separate American Federation of Labor, and its membership declined to 100,000.

The AFL, led by Samuel Gompers, did not attempt to organize unskilled workers, and it dropped the far-reaching social-reform goals of the National Labor Union and the Knights. Instead, the AFL concentrated on winning short-term improvements in wages and hours for its skilled members. The AFL grew, but by 1900 less than 5 percent of America's workers belonged to it or any other union. The development of unions was seriously impeded by splits in the labor force between skilled artisans and common laborers, religious and ethnic divisions, and differences among labor leaders concerning goals and tactics.

B. Strikes and Labor Violence

Between 1881 and 1905 almost thirty-seven thousand strikes took place, involving nearly seven million workers. In many of these, violence erupted as strikers attacked employers' property and the scab laborers hired to replace them. Some of the biggest and most violent confrontations were the railroad strikes of 1877, the eight-hour strikes of 1886, the Haymarket Square bombing (for which four anarchists were unjustly convicted and executed), the Homestead steel strike, and the Pullman strike.

   To combat labor unrest, employers forced workers to sign yellow-dog contracts and hired their own private police forces. Because of the violence, the public regarded strikers as dangerous radicals. The federal government intervened repeatedly on the side of management, using the army to quell disturbances and injunctions to order union members back to work. When injunctions were disobeyed, union officers like Eugene Debs, leader of the Pullman strike, were thrown in jail. As a result of employer, public, and government hostility, strikes almost always failed and unions languished.

C. Social Thinkers Probe for Alternatives

The growing extremes of poverty and wealth and the violent clashes between labor and management troubled middle-class Americans. A number of social commentators tried to explain these developments and put forward their own solutions. Conservative Social Darwinists, like Andrew Carnegie and William Graham Sumner, believed that labor's misery was an inevitable product of the constant struggle for survival that weeded out all but the fittest. They opposed any government interference with the workings of these natural laws. On the other hand, Lester F. Ward, Henry George, and Edward Bellamy attributed the social problems to a man-made economic system that placed private property and unrestrained profit seeking above all else. They called, respectively, for government regulation, tax reform, and a cooperative commonwealth. Tiny socialist and anarchist groups preached that only the overthrow of the capitalists and the government that protected them would make possible a just and humane society.

V. Conclusion

Industrialization had brought great benefits to America: international power status, lower-cost goods, more jobs, and a tremendous array of new consumer products. But the price had been high. Shoddy business practices and polluted factory sites abounded. Much of the industrial work force lived in urban slums and grinding poverty. Exploited laborers periodically vented their rage and frustrations in violent outbursts and strikes. Middle-class Americans were ambivalent about the new industrial order. They wanted to keep the benefits but somehow alleviate the accompanying social evils.

VOCABULARY

The following terms are used in Chapter 18. To understand the chapter fully, it is important that you know what each of them means.

"watering" stock   issuing stock certificates far in excess of the value of a corporation's assets; stock in a company that has overissued in this manner is called "watered stock"

rebate   a return of part of an original amount paid for some service or merchandise

pool   an agreement among formerly competing companies to set uniform prices and divide the business among themselves according to a predetermined formula; the purpose is to maximize profits by ending competition

vertical integration   organization of a single corporation to control all stages of manufacturing, from obtaining raw materials to marketing the finished product

horizontal integration   organization of a single corporation, through consolidation measures, to gain broad control over all manufacturing of a particular product

postbellum   after the war; usually meaning after the Civil War

"bread-and-butter" unionism   (also trade unionism "pure and simple") the union practice of concentrating on issues of immediate concern to its members, such as reducing hours and raising wages, rather than promoting broad social reforms

yellow-dog contract   an agreement that employers forced employees to sign swearing that they would not join unions or strike

anarchist   a person who advocates the overthrow of all established governments and of capitalist economic institutions

injunction   a court order requiring a person to do or not do a particular thing

laissez faire   the doctrine that government should intervene as little as possible in economic affairs, such as regulating business

---

IDENTIFICATIONS

After reading Chapter 18, you should be able to identify and explain the historical significance of each of the following:

Jay Gould

Interstate Commerce Act and Interstate Commerce Commission, 1887

J. Pierpont Morgan

Andrew Carnegie

John D. Rockefeller and Standard Oil

Sherman Anti-Trust Act, 1890

United States v. *E. C. Knight Co.*

Thomas A. Edison

Henry W. Grady and the "New South Creed"

William H. Sylvis and the National Labor Union

Terence V. Powderly and the Knights of Labor

Mother Jones

Chinese Exclusion Act, 1882

Samuel Gompers and the American Federation of Labor

railroad strikes of 1877

Haymarket Square bombing, 1886

Homestead strike, 1892

Pullman strike, 1894

Eugene Debs

William Graham Sumner and conservative Social Darwinism

Lester Frank Ward

Henry George, *Progress and Poverty*

Edward Bellamy, *Looking Backward*

Marxist socialists

SKILL BUILDING: MAPS

Locate each of the following sites and explain why each was important in the rise of industrial America from 1860 to 1900:

Pittsburgh, Pennsylvania

Homestead, Pennsylvania

Mesabi range, Minnesota

Titusville, Pennsylvania

Birmingham, Alabama

Piedmont region of Virginia, the Carolinas, Georgia, and Alabama

Cincinnati, Ohio

Chicago, Illinois

Pullman, Illinois

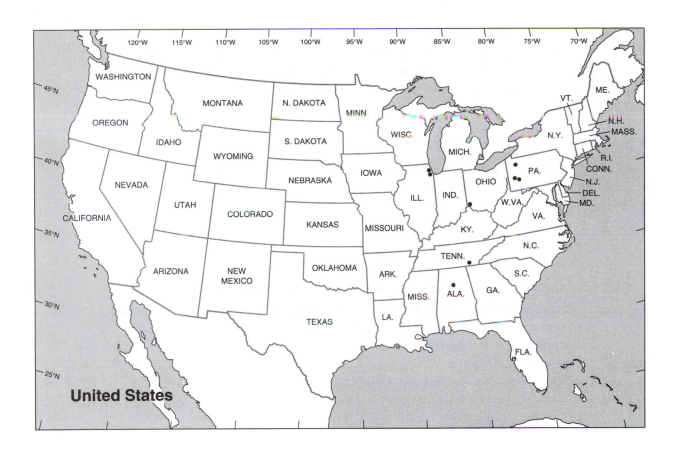

MULTIPLE-CHOICE QUESTIONS

Circle the letter of the item that best completes each statement or answers the question.

1. Rapid industrial development in the United States between 1860 and 1900
   a. increased the demand for and importance of skilled artisans.
   b. produced by 1900 an economy dominated by enormous corporations.
   c. increased the opportunities by 1900 for small- and medium-sized companies to succeed.
   d. reduced by 1900 the use of women and child laborers in mines and mills.

2. Why did the South's industrialization lag behind the North's?
   a. The post-Civil War South lacked capital and technically trained personnel.
   b. Southern industry paid higher wages than northern factories and therefore could not compete effectively with northern plants.
   c. The South had almost no natural resources and not enough people to supply the necessary industrial labor force.
   d. The South clung to its agrarian tradition and rejected the building of factories and mills.

3. The Interstate Commerce Act
    a. outlawed trusts and monopolies in manufacturing in interstate commerce.
    b. was effective in stopping railroad abuses of small shippers.
    c. stopped the trend toward a few giant companies' controlling most of the economy.
    d. created the Interstate Commerce Commission but left enforcement of the law to the federal courts, which seldom upheld ICC rulings.

4. The first U.S. corporation capitalized at over $1 billion and created by merging more than two hundred companies was
    a. Standard Oil.
    b. Union Pacific.
    c. U.S. Steel.
    d. American Telephone and Telegraph.

5. The Supreme Court in *United States* v. *E. C. Knight Company*
    a. diminished the effectiveness of the Sherman Anti-Trust Act by ruling that manufacturing was not interstate commerce.
    b. declared the Granger Laws unconstitutional because states could not regulate interstate commerce.
    c. ruled that all trusts and monopolies in interstate commerce are illegal and can be broken up by the federal government.
    d. held that employers could force employees to sign and abide by yellow-dog contracts.

6. The New South Creed preached the need for the South to
    a. industrialize.
    b. combat racial prejudice.
    c. promote the interests of agriculture ahead of those of industry.
    d. bring its wage scale up to that prevailing in the North.

7. Studies of top managers in large corporations in the late nineteenth century show that
    a. the majority of them rose from the ranks of skilled workers.
    b. the majority of them started out as poor but ambitious immigrant boys like Andrew Carnegie.
    c. the great majority of them came from middle- and upper-class families.
    d. women were beginning to make their way into executive positions.

8. Which of the following explains why unions did not have much success in the nineteenth century?
    a. Workers had little interest in joining unions because their real wages were rising and their conditions improving.
    b. Most workers did not remain in the working class permanently but quickly went on to become self-employed farmers or small businessmen.
    c. Labor and management saw eye-to-eye on most issues, and as a result there was little need for unions.
    d. Public, employer, and government hostility toward unions as well as divisions within the labor force impeded union growth.

9. Which of the following people argued that poverty was *not* the result of unchangeable natural laws and could be eliminated by government intervention and social planning?
    a. William Graham Sumner
    b. Lester Frank Ward
    c. Andrew Carnegie
    d. John D. Rockefeller

10. In the Pullman strike
    a. the federal government used an injunction and troops against workers and threw the union leaders in jail.
    b. the state of Illinois tried eight anarchists for throwing a bomb, found them guilty, and executed four of them.
    c. workers walked out to protest conditions at Carnegie's steel mills but eventually returned to work without gaining any improvements.
    d. the Knights of Labor led railroad workers in demands for an eight-hour day and finally won this concession from the railroads.

SHORT-ANSWER QUESTIONS

1. Explain how the building of the nation's railroad network stimulated American industrialization and the growth of large corporations.

2. Discuss government attempts to stop the growth of trusts and monopolies in the late nineteenth century. Why were these efforts ineffective?

3. Explain the actions Andrew Carnegie and Henry Clay Frick took at Homestead to crush unionism in the steel industry.

4. How were the objectives of the American Federation of Labor different from those of the earlier National Labor Union and Knights of Labor?

5. What was the theme of Horatio Alger's novels? How realistic were these books in terms of late-nineteenth-century American experience?

6. Explain what a conservative Social Darwinist would believe that government should do about poverty and exploitation of labor. How would the Social Darwinist justify such recommendations?

ESSAY QUESTIONS

1. Discuss the reasons for rapid industrial expansion and the growth of huge corporations between 1860 and 1900. What were some of the benefits the American people reaped from these developments? What were some of the social and economic costs or problems produced by industrialization and the growth of big business?

2. Discuss the impact on labor of industrial development in the post–Civil War period. In your answer include the effects on skilled, unskilled, southern, immigrant, and women workers.

3. Discuss the contemporary intellectual response to late-nineteenth-century industrialism and the social problems that accompanied it. Be sure to include in your answer the ideas of the conservative Social Darwinists, such as William G. Sumner, and their opponents, including Lester F. Ward, Henry George, and Edward Bellamy.

4. Discuss the industrialization of the South in the post–Civil War period. Why did the South lag behind the North? How much had the South's industry grown by 1900? In what ways was southern industrial development different from that in the North? Why?

5. Between 1881 and 1905, there were almost thirty-seven thousand strikes, and workers made numerous attempts to unionize. Yet by 1900 less than 5 percent of the labor force belonged to any union, and workers lost most strikes. What obstacles stood in the way of unionization and successful strikes?

19

The Transformation of Urban America

OUTLINE AND SUMMARY

I. Introduction

In the post–Civil War years, the United States experienced rapid urbanization. By 1900 New York, Chicago, and Philadelphia each had more than 1 million inhabitants, and 40 percent of all Americans lived in cities. Because they offered work and other opportunities, cities attracted thousands from the surrounding rural districts and most of the 11 million immigrants who arrived in this nation between 1870 and 1900. The runaway population growth swamped municipal services and facilities, and terrible housing and sanitary conditions developed. The physical deterioration, ethnic diversity, and social instability alarmed native-born reformers who tried to clean up cities and quickly "Americanize" the often resistant immigrants.

II. Urban Expansion

A. The New Urban World

Urbanization changed people's way of life. Small-town residents knew each other and usually shared a common heritage and similar traditions and values. The city bristled with activity, anonymity, and heterogeneity. City industry or industries also polluted the urban environment and surrounding lands and waterways.

B. A Revolution in Transportation

Advances in transportation—first horse-drawn streetcars, later regional steam railroads and electric trolleys—transformed cities. The "walking" city of the early 1800s was compact, with the wealthy living near the commercial center and the poor occupying basements scattered around town. As new transportation facilities made it possible to commute to work, upper- and middle-class residents moved outward along the streetcar lines to more desirable neighborhoods, while the poor remained behind in subdivided homes abandoned by the affluent. The commercial centers became busy shopping areas easily accessible to all.

C. A Mobile Population

In search of better homes and jobs, the working, middle, and upper classes moved frequently from place to place within the same city and from one metropolis to another.

D. Migrants and Immigrants

In the post–Civil War years thousands of young people, especially women, moved from farms to cities to find employment. Also between 1860 and 1890 some 10 million Northern European immigrants, mostly German, English, and Irish, settled in East Coast and midwestern cities. In the late nineteenth century, these "old immigrants" were joined by the "new immigrants" from Southern and Eastern Europe—Italians, Slavs, Greeks, and Jews–as well as Armenians from the Middle East. Faster and cheaper steamship travel facilitated the immigrants' arrival. By 1890 the foreign-born and their children accounted for four-fifths of the population of Greater New York. Most who disembarked on the East Coast came through the immigration reception centers at Castle Garden (1855–1891) or Ellis Island (1892 on) in New York. German and Scandinavian newcomers, bringing a little capital with them, tended to migrate to midwestern cities and to farms on the prairies beyond. Italians and Irish, usually without cash, took the first jobs they found in eastern cities.

E. Adjusting to an Urban Society

To ease their adjustment, immigrants clustered together in ethnic neighborhoods where they could speak their native language, buy their traditional foods, and celebrate traditional holidays with compatriots and even persons from the same village or district. Though rich in cultural, social, and institutional life, these ethnic enclaves were horribly overcrowded and provided miserable slum housing. The various immigrant groups improved their social and economic status at different rates. The Irish came in such great numbers that they were able to dominate the Democratic party and Catholic church leadership in New York and Boston, where they accounted for 16 percent and 17 percent of the population, respectively. Nationality groups that had high rates of remigration, such as Italians and Chinese, experienced slower upward mobility and assimilation. By the end of the nineteenth century, resentment of the newcomers, from whatever country, was growing.

F. Slums and Ghettos

Neighborhoods deteriorated into slums as landlords packed more and more people into their buildings. The poorer the residents, the greater the crowding and the faster the area's decline. Ethnic slum neighborhoods became ghettos when discrimination and law kept members of the minority group, whether racial or immigrant, from obtaining housing elsewhere, even if they had the money to do so. For example, black ghettos grew in Chicago and Philadelphia, Mexican in Los Angeles, and Chinese in San Francisco. In slums and ghettos, disease, death, and crime rates soared. Middle-class Americans, even reformers who wanted to clean up the slums, tended to blame the deplorable conditions on the residents rather than the socioeconomic forces that oppressed minorities.

G. Fashionable Avenues and Suburbs

In contrast to the slums, grand millionaires' mansions lined Fifth Avenue in New York, Commonwealth Avenue in Boston, Lake Shore Drive in Chicago, and fashionable boulevards in other cities. The wealthy and the middle class also moved to newer, more desirable suburbs on the edges of the old, compact cities. Thus, American cities became increasingly segregated along class as well as ethnic and racial lines.

III. The Urban Challenge

A. Policing the City

Urbanization inevitably brought increased crime. Many cities established professional police forces in the 1830s and 1840s and authorized them to carry clubs and revolvers in the 1850s. The police sometimes fought with immigrant gangs but generally did not enforce state laws curbing gambling, saloons, prostitution, and Sunday business operations in ethnic neighborhoods where the social customs ran counter to such moralistic legislation. The 1894 Lexow investigation in New York discovered that, in exchange for regular payoffs, officers winked at these activities. At least a portion of the bribes ended up in the hands of political bosses who hired and fired the police. Reformers demanded that appointment and supervision of law-enforcement officers be turned over to nonpartisan police commissioners, which was starting to happen by the 1890s.

B. Governing the City

Urban political machines, headed by powerful political bosses, emerged to govern the unwieldy cities with their many competing interests. The machines awarded contracts and franchises to favored businessmen in return for payoffs and gathered the votes of poor immigrants by providing them with relief, legal help, and city jobs. Some bosses, such as Cincinnati's George B. Cox, were relatively honest, whereas others, such as New York's William Marcy Tweed, were grossly corrupt and greedy. By the late nineteenth century middle- and upper-class good-government reformers ("goo-goos") had begun their drives against the bosses.

C. Battling Poverty

Middle-class reformers also set out to relieve poverty. They often tended to blame the problem on character flaws of the poor and "self-destructive" cultural practices of the immigrants. Therefore, reformers concentrated on moral uplift and Americanization campaigns among the needy. Typical were Robert M. Hartley's New York Association for Improving the Condition of the Poor (AICP) and Charles Loring Brace's New York Children's Aid Society. Hartley's organization sent visitors to slum dwellers' homes to urge sobriety, hard work, and responsibility on them. The AICP also called for pure milk laws, public baths, and improved housing. Brace founded dormitories, reading rooms, and workshops for indigent boys and sent thousands of them to live with and work for families in the Midwest. In addition, the Young Men's and Young Women's Christian associations offered rural young people arriving in the cities temporary housing, recreation, and moral strictures against alcohol and other vices.

D. New Approaches to Social Work

By the 1880s the Salvation Army and Josephine Shaw Lowell's Charity Organization Society (COS) had joined the fight against poverty. Lowell's group preached a tough-minded approach to charity, insisting that the needy must meet the standards of responsibility and morality set by the COS's "friendly visitors" to receive aid. Critics charged, with some justification, that the COS was more interested in "controlling the poor than in alleviating their suffering."

E. The Moral-Purity Campaign

Middle- and upper-class reformers attacked what they considered urban vice. Crusaders such as Anthony Comstock and Charles Parkhurst demanded that city officials close down gambling dens, saloons, and brothels and censor obscene publications. In 1894 the nonpartisan Committee of Seventy elected a New York City mayor committed to moral purification, but within three years the effort failed, and the more tolerant political machine was back in power.

F. The Social Gospel

The Social Gospel movement developed in the 1870s and 1880s among a small group of Protestant clergymen. Founded by Washington Gladden, a Congregational minister, the movement preached that urban poverty was caused in part by actions of the rich and well-born and "that true Christianity commits men and women to fight social injustice head on, wherever it exists." Walter Rauschenbusch, a Baptist pastor in New York's "Hell's Kitchen" slums, made the clearest statement of the movement's philosophy in his 1907 book *Christianity and the Social Crisis*.

G. The Settlement-House Movement

Like the Social Gospel ministers, the settlement-house founders blamed poverty not on the poor but on social and environmental causes. Settlement-house leaders, such as Jane Addams and Ellen Gates Starr, believed that middle-class relief workers must reside among the immigrant masses and learn what services they needed by firsthand experience. At Hull House, for example, Addams and Starr ran a day-care nursery, gave legal and health aid, helped find employment, and offered classes in English and other subjects for their immigrant Chicago neighbors. Settlement-house workers also published studies of the terrible housing and sanitation they encountered, and they lobbied legislators for improved services and corrective laws. By 1895 more than fifty settlement houses in various cities were training a generation of young college students, many of whom would become state and local government officials applying the lessons they had learned.

IV. Reshaping the Urban Environment

A. Parks and Public Spaces

Whereas Social Gospelers and settlement-house workers tried to solve the problems of the urban poor, landscape artists such as Frederick Law Olmsted and architects such as Calvert

Vaux attempted to improve the quality of city life by designing and constructing spacious parks as "tranquil country refuge[s] within the city."

B. Boston's Back Bay

The kind of urban planning and design advocated by Olmsted and many other architects was carried out in Boston's Back Bay development between 1857 and 1900.

C. Rebuilding Chicago

The 1871 Chicago fire that destroyed the city's commercial center gave architects, engineers, and businessmen the chance to pioneer in new urban design as they rebuilt. The greatest innovation developed by Louis Sullivan and others was the skyscraper. It was soon imitated in other cities. The changes in Boston and Chicago and the exhibits at the 1893 Chicago Columbian Exposition stimulated the growth of the city-beautiful movement. Municipal art societies, park associations, and civic-improvement leagues strove to grace their cities with imposing civic buildings; sparkling fountains; outdoor sculptures; and landscaped parks, squares, and roadways. Like the followers of architect Richard Morris Hunt, they believed that attractive urban areas would produce better citizens and reduce social disorder. In the early twentieth century the city-beautiful movement evolved into the new field of city planning.

D. Toward a Metropolitan America

Cities slowly began to develop the centralized administrative structures and managerial tools that their large, diverse populations and great size required. Armed with centralized administrative powers, municipal officials in the late nineteenth century built adequate city-wide sewer and water systems that finally brought an end to the cholera, typhoid, and other epidemics that had plagued urban America. In the course of centralization, many cities incorporated surrounding lands or annexed adjacent municipalities. The joining of Brooklyn, Queens, Staten Island, the Bronx, and Manhattan into Greater New York in 1898 represents the biggest of these consolidations.

V. Conclusion

The unprecedented growth of cities between the time of the Civil War and 1900 forced millions of Americans—old, urban upper and middle classes; newly arrived rural migrants; and old and new immigrants—to make tremendous adjustments. The cities often became arenas for class and ethnic conflict over issues such as temperance, moral uplift, the role of the political machine and boss, and the causes and cures for urban poverty. By 1900, however, new conceptions of the services and responsibilities that municipal government had to undertake to make the metropolis livable were beginning to crystalize. In the coming progressive era, this enlarged vision of government would slowly make its way into national politics.

VOCABULARY

The following terms are used in Chapter 19. To understand the chapter fully, it is important that you know what each of them means.

demographer   one who studies vital and social statistics and trends concerning births, deaths, marriages, diseases, and population

exodus   a going out; a departure or emigration, usually of a large group of people

compatriots   fellow countrymen and countrywomen; persons from the same country

remigration   the return of immigrants to their country of origin

ghetto   any neighborhood or quarter in which a minority group is required to live by law or discrimination (originally, Jews in Venice, Italy)

patina   a film or coloring on a surface—for example, the greenish coloring on old bronze produced by oxidation

tacitly   not openly expressed or permitted but understood

symbiosis   the living together of two organisms, with each dependent on the other—for example, the fungus and alga that together make up lichen

bombastic   high-sounding; inflated (style of speech)

tycoon   a businessman who has great wealth and power

IDENTIFICATIONS

After reading Chapter 19, you should be able to identify and explain the historical significance of each of the following:

Jacob Riis, *How the Other Half Lives*

"walking" cities

trolleys

"old immigrants"; and "new immigrants"

Castle Garden and Ellis Island

"dumbbell tenements"

Horatio Alger

political boss, machine, and ward captain

Tammany Hall

"Big Jim" Pendergast

William Marcy Tweed

Thomas Nast

"goo-goos"

Robert M. Hartley and the New York Association for Improving the Condition of the Poor

Charles Loring Brace and the Children's Aid Society

Josiah Strong, *Our Country*

Josephine Shaw Lowell and the Charity Organization Society

Anthony Comstock

Charles Parkhurst

Washington Gladden, Walter Rauschenbusch, and the Social Gospel

Jane Addams and Hull House

Florence Kelley

Frederick Law Olmsted and Calvert Vaux

Boston's Back Bay

city-beautiful movement

SKILL BUILDING: GRAPHS

After looking carefully at the line graph titled "The Changing Face of U.S. Immigration, 1865–1920" on page 608 of the textbook, you should be able to answer the following questions:

1. In which years did overall immigration to the United States exceed 1 million?

2. In which periods did overall immigration to the United States drop significantly? From your knowledge of American history, can you account for this? Were things happening in this country during those periods that might have discouraged immigrants from coming?

3. Where did the so-called old immigrants come from? During which years did this old immigration peak?

4. Where did the new immigrants come from? During which years did the new immigration peak? Did the numbers of new immigrants arriving during their peak years exceed the numbers of old immigrants arriving during their peak period?

5. During which years did Asian immigration to the United States hover close to zero? Can you account for this from your knowledge of American history?

Now look at the line graph "Immigration of Skilled and Unskilled Workers, 1860–1900" on page 611 of your text. Based on this graph, answer the following questions:

1. During the period 1860–1900, did the percentage of unskilled laborers arriving in the United States exceed the percentage of skilled workers? How do you account for this?

2. During the years 1860–1900, what was the overall trend for the proportion of unskilled laborers among immigrants? Based on your knowledge of American history during these years, explain why this trend may have occurred.

3. In the same period, did the proportion of skilled workers entering the United States show an overall trend or merely periodic dips and peaks?

4. Do the dips in percentage of unskilled laborers entering the United States seem to correspond to periods of economic depression in the U.S. economy?

HISTORICAL SOURCES

One historical source the author of this chapter used is letters that persons who immigrated to the United States wrote to friends and family. On pages 608–609 one such letter is quoted. What does the author wish to illustrate with these letters? Thousands of letters and transcripts of oral interviews of immigrants have been collected in archives of immigrant and ethnic history. The newest of these collections is being developed at Ellis Island, where the main building has been restored as an immigration museum.

Look at "A Place in Time: Immigrant Milwaukee in the 1890s." What does this capsule history demonstrate about the causes of conflict between immigrants and native-born city authorities?

The author of Chapter 19 also uses as historical evidence architects' and landscape artists' plans and buildings that were constructed in the late nineteenth century and are still standing. For example, on pages 623–624 the author cites Olmsted's and Vaux's original plan for Central Park; on pages 624–625 the author refers to the layout and major buildings found in Boston's Back Bay section; and on page 626 the Reliance Building, Masonic Temple, and other Chicago skyscrapers are used as evidence. In each case what conclusions does the historian draw about ideas, values, and technology prevalent in nineteenth-century America?

MULTIPLE-CHOICE QUESTIONS

Circle the letter of the item that best completes each statement or answers the question.

1. In the "walking" city of the early nineteenth century,
   a. the rich and poor lived in distinctly different neighborhoods.
   b. the wealthy lived near the commercial center.
   c. the poor lived near downtown, the wealthy at the outer edges of the city.
   d. few people owned their own homes.

2. An electric streetcar system was first developed in
   a. Richmond, Virginia.
   b. Chicago, Illinois.
   c. Denver, Colorado.
   d. New York, New York.

3. Which of the following statements about American cities between 1860 and 1900 is *incorrect?*
   a. Runaway growth of urban population swamped municipal services and facilities.
   b. Terrible housing and sanitary conditions developed in them.
   c. By 1900 the majority of the American people lived in them.
   d. Their neighborhoods became increasingly segregated along class, ethnic, and racial lines.

4. By 1890 the foreign-born and their children made up what portion of New York City's population?
    a. one-half
    b. one-third
    c. two-thirds
    d. four-fifths

5. Which of the following immigrant groups was made up mostly of poor peasants who settled heavily in northeastern cities and had a high rate of remigration?
    a. Germans
    b. Eastern European Jews
    c. Italians
    d. Armenians

6. The urban political machines and their political bosses
    a. were always Democrats, rather than Republicans, in the late nineteenth century.
    b. angered building contractors by having municipal construction done by city employees on a not-for-profit basis.
    c. dispensed city jobs, legal help, and relief to poor immigrants in exchange for their votes.
    d. were often controlled by the native-born, wealthy elite groups who secretly ran them.

7. Which of the following would be most likely to challenge the statement that moral deficiencies of the immigrant poor caused their poverty?
    a. Josephine Shaw Lowell and the Charity Organization Society
    b. William S. Rainsford and the Social Gospel ministers
    c. Josiah Strong in his book *Our Country*
    d. Robert M. Hartley and the Association for Improving the Condition of the Poor

8. Jane Addams and her coworkers at Hull House did all of the following *except*
    a. establish a day-care nursery for the children of working mothers.
    b. pressure Congress to restrict the flow of poor immigrants to the United States.
    c. pressure legislators to enforce sanitation regulations and pass laws protecting the urban poor.
    d. run classes, a laundry, an employment bureau, and recreation programs.

9. Which of the following people were most closely associated with designing parks as tranquil country refuges within the city?
    a. Frederick Law Olmsted and Calvert Vaux
    b. Richard Morris Hunt and John Wellborn Root
    c. Louis Sullivan and Richard Morris Hunt
    d. Thomas Nast and "Big Jim" Pendergast

10. The Lexow investigation found
    a. that the police permitted gamblers, prostitutes, and saloonkeepers to operate unmolested in poor immigrant neighborhoods in exchange for payoffs.
    b. that landlords permitted their dumbbell tenement buildings to become unsanitary, overcrowded firetraps.
    c. that blacks, Italians, Chinese, and other minorities were kept out of middle-class neighborhoods by restrictive real-estate covenants.
    d. that New York's inadequate sewage system contributed to recurrent outbreaks of typhoid and cholera.

SHORT-ANSWER QUESTIONS

1. Explain the reasons for conflict between immigrants and native-born reformers in the late nineteenth century.

2. What did Social Gospel ministers preach?

3. Explain how the approach to and attitudes toward the poor of Jane Addams and Hull House differed from those of Josephine Shaw Lowell and the Charity Organization Society.

4. In what ways did the settlement house movement prepare the way for progressive reform in the early twentieth century?

ESSAY QUESTIONS

1. Discuss the impact of transportation improvements in the nineteenth century on American cities. How did transportation changes affect who came to cities, where people lived in cities and suburbs, and where they worked and shopped?

2. Between 1870 and 1900 nearly 11 million immigrants entered the United States. Discuss who came, why they came, where they settled, how they fared, and the impact they had on urban America.

3. Discuss the rise of the urban political machines and bosses. Why did they emerge? What roles did they play? Who supported them and why? Who fought them and why?

4. Discuss the city-beautiful movement of the late nineteenth century. What was it? Who was behind it? What assumptions about the city and its peoples did it make? What precedents for the future did it create?

5. Discuss the varied responses of nineteenth-century middle-class reformers to urban ethnic diversity, poverty, and crime.

20

Daily Life, Popular Culture, and the Arts, 1860–1900

OUTLINE AND SUMMARY

I. Everyday Life in Flux

A. *Rising Standards of Living*

The rapid industrialization in the second half of the nineteenth century brought a rising standard of living to millions of Americans. Clothing mass-produced by factory sewing machines allowed great expansion in the wardrobes of the middle and working classes. Kellogg's and Post's breakfast cereals and a host of other commercially prepared foods transformed the national diet. By 1900 urban upper- and middle-class families enjoyed centrally heated homes that had electric lights, telephones, indoor plumbing, mechanical washing machines, and many other conveniences.

B. *Bringing New Commodities to Rural and Small-Town America*

In the 1870s and 1880s, Aaron Montgomery Ward and Richard Warren Sears published catalogs and established mail-order companies that acquainted rural Americans with urban middle-class fashions and sold, at modest prices, an array of consumer goods. Chain stores, such as F. W. Woolworth's and the A&P, also brought a variety of products to buyers at relatively low prices. While all these goods made life more comfortable for the upper and middle classes and raised their social status, many farm and working-class families could not afford to purchase the same quantity and quality of items, and thus the sense of difference between the haves and the have-nots widened.

C. *A Shifting Class Structure*

Industrialization and the growth of big business sharpened class distinctions. The number of unskilled workers increased, and a large gap in wages and self-identification opened between them and the skilled craftsmen. The middle class also expanded as national corporations required armies of trained white-collar, professional, and sales personnel. The middle class, with higher incomes and more job security than industrial laborers, achieved a lifestyle that allowed more socializing, planning ahead, buying of expensive possessions, and educating of their children. The rich industrialists and financiers flaunted their worth by building mansions in town and at summer resorts; purchasing racehorses, yachts, and art collections; traveling abroad; and endowing museums. By 1900 the class disparities were striking. Workers (about 44 percent of the population) possessed only 1.5 percent of the national wealth; the middle class (also about 44 percent) possessed 12.5 percent of the wealth; and the upper crust (about 12 percent) owned a whopping 86 percent of the national assets and income.

D. The Changing Family

The level of family income affected family size, life expectancy, infant mortality, and the relationship between parents and children. Overall between 1860 and 1900 Americans lived in nuclear families that had a decreasing birthrate and increasing life expectancy. But the class differences in these matters were substantial. For example, working-class families, needing their children's earnings to survive, had a higher birthrate than upper- and middle-class families. In Buffalo in 1900, laborers averaged 5.7 offspring; business owners and managers, 3.5. The smaller families of the upper and middle classes afforded women some free time and children more attention and education.

E. Working-Class Family Life

Because of their low incomes, working-class black and immigrant families had to rely on the help of children, women, and relatives to make ends meet. Thus the extended kinship network often replaced the nuclear family household. To supplement the breadwinner's earnings, families took in boarders, women took in laundry, and children went to work at ten to twelve years of age. The pooling of many family members' incomes sometimes made it possible for working-class families to buy homes and acquire possessions commonly owned by the middle class.

II. Middle-Class Society and Culture

A. Manners and Morals

The manners and morals of the middle class during much of the nineteenth century were influenced by the Victorian worldview. This outlook held that human society was on an upward course from barbarism to civilization and that progress could be ensured only by strenuous moral effort of the sort exercised by the upper and middle classes. Important virtues, in this view, included sobriety, industriousness, and self-restraint. Workers were told that if they emulated their betters, they would rise to more privileged positions. Victorian morality also stressed the civilizing importance of "culture": fine manners, uplifting literature and art, and classical music. In keeping with this, the wealthy founded and the middle ranks visited a network of cultural institutions, such as the New York Metropolitan Museum of Art and the Boston Museum of Fine Arts, in the 1870s. Displaying proper etiquette, appreciating culture, and exercising moral restraint became badges of status and heightened the visible distinctions between the middle and lower classes.

B. *The Cult of Domesticity*

Victorian morality assigned a special place to women. Whereas men tended to business and public affairs, women used the domestic sphere to provide the genteel, sensitive, and spiritual influences that moved society toward higher civilization. They decorated their homes as richly and artistically as their means permitted and fostered the family's sense of cultural appreciation. At no time, however, were all middle-class women satisfied with devoting their whole life to this cult of domesticity.

C. *Department Stores and Hotels*

Innovative entrepreneurs, such as Rowland H. Macy, John Wanamaker, and Marshall Field, developed urban department stores that appealed particularly to the Victorian outlook of the upper and middle echelons. These giant emporiums advertised high-quality goods at low cost and encouraged buyers to believe that owning the right material possessions contributed to civilized living. The department stores were designed to look like palaces, with marble staircases, sparkling chandeliers, and thick carpets, and the deferential sales staff made the upper- and middle-class shoppers feel that their status was being rightfully acknowledged. Grand hotels built in the late nineteenth century, such as New York's Waldorf Astoria and Chicago's Palmer House, also attracted affluent Victorians with "luxury, convenience, and service."

D. *The Transformation of Higher Education*

Higher education was still restricted to the upper and upper-middle classes. As late as 1900 only 4 percent of youths between eighteen and twenty-one years of age were enrolled in colleges or universities. Indeed, these institutions were seen as the training schools for the future business and professional elites. Wealthy capitalists, such as John D. Rockefeller and Leland Stanford, made large donations to already existing universities or started new ones. With private contributions and state support, more than 150 additional colleges and universities were founded between 1880 and 1900. In this period, the research university was developed and major reforms were instituted in medical and other professional training.

III. Working-Class Leisure in the Immigrant City

A. *Streets, Saloons, and Boxing Matches*

The neighborhood streets, especially in summer, served as the arena of social life and free entertainment for shop girls, laborers, and poor immigrant families. For workingmen the saloons offered male companionship, reinforcement of group identity, and centers for immigrant politics. One of the favorite spectator sports among workingmen was bare-knuckle prizefighting. In the 1880s and 1890s boxing began to attract a following among upper-class males as well.

B. *The Rise of Professional Sports*

Americans were the first to turn what had been a children's game into the professional sport of baseball. The earliest teams were the New York Knickerbockers and the Cincinnati Red Stockings. Team owners organized the National League in 1876, and by the 1890s baseball had become big business. It appealed to members of all social groups, particularly workers. Horse racing and boxing contests also drew spectators from all social levels. The most popular sports hero of the nineteenth century was heavyweight boxing champion John L. Sullivan.

C. Vaudeville, Amusement Parks, and Dance Halls

Vaudeville shows, amusement parks like New York's Coney Island, and dance halls were popular with working-class women as well as men.

D. Ragtime

Although the middle class preferred hymns or songs that carried a moral lesson, the masses became fans of ragtime, which originated with black musicians in the saloons and brothels of the South and Midwest. Ragtime's most famous composer, Scott Joplin, introduced this music at the 1893 Chicago Columbia Exposition, and Tin Pan Alley music publishers spread it to a national audience.

IV. Cultures in Conflict

A. The Genteel Tradition and Its Critics

In the 1870s and 1880s a group of upper-class writers and magazine editors, among them Charles Eliot Norton and E. L. Godkin, attempted to set standards for fine writing and art. They insisted that literature must avoid sexual allusions, vulgar slang, disrespect for Christianity, and depressing endings. High-toned journals like *The Century* and the *North American Review* upheld this genteel standard by banishing from their pages authors who violated these rules. Many emerging writers refused to fit into the mold. The works of regionalists like Sarah Orne Jewett, realists like William Dean Howells, and naturalists like Stephen Crane all violated the canons of the genteel tradition in one way or another. Mark Twain's *Adventures of Huckleberry Finn* (1884) and Theodore Dreiser's *Sister Carrie* (1900), among the best novels of the period, were both condemned by proponents of Victorian ideals.

Social scientists such as Thorstein Veblen and W. E. B. Du Bois criticized the business elite and challenged middle-class notions about the link between moral worth and economic standing. The depression and labor unrest of the 1890s further undermined the smug Victorian outlook and its genteel culture.

B. Modernism in Architecture and Painting

Some architects and artists began questioning Victorian ideals of beauty. Modernist architects William Holabird, John Wellborn Root, and Frank Lloyd Wright refused to copy European design. Rather, they looked to their vision of the future for inspiration and argued that a building's form should follow its function. Winslow Homer and Thomas Eakins rejected sentimentality in favor of tough realism in their paintings.

C. From Victorian Lady to New Woman

Although Frances Willard and her Woman's Christian Temperance Union (WCTU) did not openly challenge the cult of domesticity, they broadened the scope of women's social responsibilities. The WCTU, with a membership of 150,000 by 1890, became America's first mass organization of women. Through its crusade against liquor, women gained experience as lobbyists, organizers, and lecturers. Middle- and upper-class club women founded the General Federation of Women's Clubs in 1892 and were getting involved in social welfare projects and tenement reform by the end of the century. As more women pursued higher education—they accounted for more than one-third of all college students in 1900—they developed the self-confidence to break with the Victorian belief in women's separate sphere and went out to compete with men in the public arena. The so-called new woman broke Victorian restraints about dress and exercise, and the most advanced thinkers, such as Charlotte Perkins Gilman, advocated women's economic independence from men through work outside the home. Following Gilman's advice, a growing number of female college graduates entered journalism, social work, education, and other professional careers. However, the new-woman emphasis on economic and social independence and equality had little impact on the lives of working-class women.

D. Public Education as an Arena of Class Conflict

Starting in the 1870s middle-class reformers, such as federal commissioner of education William Torrey Harris, campaigned to expand public schools, bring them under central control, and make attendance mandatory. Harris viewed the public schools as instruments for indoctrinating the masses with middle-class values and outlook. By 1900, as a result of the work of education advocates, thirty-one states had passed laws requiring school attendance for all children from eight to fourteen years of age, the illiteracy rate had dropped significantly, and more than half a million students were attending some five thousand high schools. Centralized urban public-school systems, however, aroused opposition from various quarters. Poor immigrant parents, who needed the wages of their children to survive, objected to laws that kept youngsters in school beyond the elementary level. Catholics disliked the Protestant orientation of the public schools and organized their own parochial systems, and upper-class parents preferred to send their offspring to exclusive, private academies.

V. Conclusion

In the latter part of the nineteenth century, the upper and middle classes, with their genteel Victorian morality and ideals, were dismayed by the raucous, vibrant culture of the working masses. "Respectable" people periodically attempted to suppress "indecent" lower-class enjoyments such as gambling; gathering in dance halls, saloons, and amusement parks; and attending Sunday baseball games and bare-knuckle prizefights. However, Victorian standards of decency were weakening by the 1890s as they came under attack from younger middle-class writers, artists, social scientists, and "new women," as well as the working and immigrant masses. By 1900 the two cultural traditions were reaching an accommodation that blended elements of both. National pastimes became highly commercialized, and the working-class amusements of the nineteenth century evolved into the mass culture of sports spectaculars, movies, and theme parks of modern America.

VOCABULARY

The following terms are used in Chapter 20. To understand the chapter fully, it is important that you know what each of them means.

armoire   a large movable cupboard with doors and shelves used to hold clothing

puddler   a skilled worker who converted pig iron into wrought iron by heating and stirring the molten metal and an oxidizing agent in a reverberatory furnace

nuclear family   a family made up of parents and their minor children (as opposed to *an extended family* or *a kinship network,* which includes grandparents, grown children and their spouses, aunts, uncles, cousins, and so on)

fertility rate   the average number of children born to females between fourteen and forty-five years of age

surrogate   one appointed to act for another; a substitute for another

certitudes   certainties; things you are sure of

effeteness   the condition of having lost vigor or energy; being worn-out or unable to produce

patrician   an aristocrat; aristocratic, noble; befitting an aristocrat or noble

hyperbole   obvious exaggeration for effect

prototype   the original or model from which other things are formed

mores   customs of central importance accepted without question and embodying the fundamental moral views of a group, people, or social class

ethos   dominant assumptions of a people or period; the fundamental spiritual characteristics of a culture

caustic   sarcastic, sharp, biting

platitudes   flat, dull, or trite remarks, especially uttered as if they were fresh and profound

IDENTIFICATIONS

After reading Chapter 20, you should be able to identify and explain the historical significance of each of the following:

John Harvey Kellogg and Charles W. Post

Aaron Montgomery Ward and Richard Warren Sears

F. W. Woolworth

Victorian morality

Henry Ward Beecher

Catharine Beecher, *The American Woman's Home*

cult of domesticity and "the woman's sphere"

Rowland H. Macy, John Wanamaker, and Marshall Field

Charles W. Eliot

Andrew D. White

New York Knickerbockers and Cincinnati Red Stockings

John L. Sullivan

Scott Joplin and ragtime

the new woman

Charles Eliot Norton, Richard Watson Gilder, E. L. Godkin, and genteel culture

Henry James

Mark Twain (Samuel Langhorne Clemens)

Sarah Orne Jewett and the regionalists

Stephen Crane and the naturalists

Theodore Dreiser, *Sister Carrie*

Thorstein Veblen, *The Theory of the Leisure Class*

Frank Lloyd Wright

Winslow Homer, Thomas Eakins, and Albert Pinkham Ryder

Frances Willard and the Woman's Christian Temperance Union

Charlotte Perkins Gilman, *Women and Economics*

"Gibson girls"

Kate Chopin, *The Awakening*

William Torrey Harris

Creoles, Cajuns, Storyville, and Dixieland jazz

HISTORICAL SOURCES

In Chapter 20 the author has used the records of business corporations, among other sources, as historical evidence. For instance, on page 635 a Campbell's soup jingle of the late nineteenth century is quoted. On pages 635–636 Montgomery Ward's and Sears catalogs from the 1890s are described, and a customer's letter to Montgomery Ward's is quoted. How does the historian use this evidence?

In the section on "The Changing Family," the historian turns to data from the federal census. A census has been taken every ten years since the adoption of the Constitution. Originally the census takers simply counted people to facilitate reapportioning of seats in the House of Representatives as population grew and shifted. Recently the census takers have asked many more questions and have gathered much valuable demographic information. Using those data, however, can prove tricky. Why does the author say on page 638 that "historians are cautious in their use of aggregate federal census statistics" from the late nineteenth century? What does the author use the data to illustrate?

Look at "A Place in Time: New Orleans in the 1890s." How does this description of the city's musical culture fit the theme of this chapter about conflicts between middle- and upper-class white genteel culture and working-class and black popular culture? In what ways was New Orleans unique among American cities? In what respects did it mirror the racial and class tensions of the period 1860–1900? In what ways did New Orleans's culture anticipate twentieth-century American trends?

MULTIPLE-CHOICE QUESTIONS

Circle the letter of the item that best completes each statement or answers the question.

1. The overall impact of industrialization on American life in the late nineteenth century was
   a. to reduce the gulf between the standard of living of the rich and the poor.
   b. to make class distinctions less apparent.
   c. to improve the standard of living for many families.
   d. to drive fine-quality goods off the market in favor of mass-produced, shoddy products.

2. Which of the following correctly states income distribution in late-nineteenth-century America?
   a. The middle class was the largest one, controlling more than 50 percent of national wealth.
   b. The working class made up more than 40 percent of the nation but controlled only 1.5 percent of its wealth.
   c. The upper-class elite controlled about 20 percent of the country's wealth.
   d. The wealth was almost evenly divided among classes, with the upper, middle, and working classes each controlling roughly one-third of the national income.

3. Which of the following statements about American families between 1860 and 1900 is correct?
   a. Working-class families generally had fewer children than upper- and middle-class families.
   b. Blacks and immigrants were more likely to live in nuclear families; the upper and middle classes formed extended kinship networks.
   c. Immigrant working-class families expected children to go to work by age ten or twelve, and all members of the family contributed to its support.
   d. Birth control was unknown, and all families continued to have seven or eight children on average.

4. In the late nineteenth century, middle- and upper-class Americans generally frowned on
   a. flaunting their wealth by wearing expensive clothes and lavishly decorating their homes.
   b. women from good families going outside their homes to shop in downtown department stores.
   c. people of good reputation frequenting the grand hotels in cities such as New York, Chicago, and San Francisco.
   d. saloons, vaudeville, and ragtime as immoral, low class, and vulgar.

5. Between 1860 and 1900 all of the following advances in education occurred *except*
    a. the public schools banned physical punishment of children and deemphasized discipline.
    b. the research university developed, and improved training was given to medical and other professional students.
    c. the number of high schools and students attending them rose.
    d. the illiteracy rate fell for persons older than ten years of age.

6. "Prairie-school" houses featuring low silhouettes and rejecting the bulk and clutter of the typical Victorian home were the creation of
    a. John L. Sullivan.
    b. Thomas Eakins.
    c. Andrew D. White.
    d. Frank Lloyd Wright.

7. A member of the working class in the late nineteenth century would have been most likely to read
    a. *The Nation.*
    b. *The Century.*
    c. *Atlantic Monthly.*
    d. *The National Police Gazette.*

8. Who coined the term *conspicuous consumption* to describe the excessive materialism and flaunting of wealth of America's captains of industry?
    a. Mark Twain
    b. Annie MacLean
    c. Thorstein Veblen
    d. W. E. B. Du Bois

9. A good example of naturalism in American fiction is found in
    a. Stephen Crane's *Maggie: A Girl of the Streets.*
    b. Henry James's *The Bostonians.*
    c. Catharine Beecher's *The American Woman's Home.*
    d. Charlotte Perkins Gilman's *Women and Economics.*

10. Compulsory attendance at urban public schools of the late nineteenth century was fought by
    a. Catholic immigrants because of the Protestant orientation of the public schools.
    b. poor working-class families who needed to send youngsters over age ten to work.
    c. upper-class parents who did not want their children mingling with the immigrant masses.
    d. all of the above.

SHORT-ANSWER QUESTIONS

1. Explain the roles of Aaron Montgomery Ward and Richard Warren Sears in marketing products and shaping tastes in rural and small-town America.

2. How did department stores in the period 1860 to 1900 try to appeal to consumers, especially women?

3. Why did Theodore Dreiser's *Sister Carrie* shock guardians of genteel culture in the Victorian age?

4. Describe the changes that took place in American higher education between 1860 and 1900.

5. How did the middle and upper classes in the Victorian period explain why they were more economically successful than the working class?

ESSAY QUESTIONS

1. Discuss the effects of industrialization and the growth of big corporations on the American standard of living and class structure and distinctions in the period 1860–1900.

2. Compare and contrast the patterns and attitudes of immigrant and black working-class families with those of white middle- and upper-class families in the period 1860–1900.

3. Explain the Victorian genteel tradition in the arts. Discuss the writers, painters, architects, and social scientists who broke with it in the late nineteenth century.

4. Discuss the Victorian view of the role of women. How did the so-called new woman of the late nineteenth century challenge the Victorian ideal? Which women were the most affected by the new-woman patterns? Which were least affected by the changes?

5. In the conclusion to Chapter 20, the author writes that in the 1890s, "middle- and upper-class Americans battled against what they deemed 'indecent' lower-class behavior," yet "the . . . frequently denounced working-class culture of the late-nineteenth-century immigrant city can be seen, in retrospect, as nothing less than the fertile seedbed of twentieth-century mass culture." Explain what the author means by this statement, and illustrate your answer with as many specific examples as possible.

21

Politics and Expansion in an Industrializing Age

OUTLINE AND SUMMARY

I. Introduction

From 1877 to 1896 national politics largely ignored the social problems arising from industrialization. This happened in part because the business leaders influential in both political parties preached the doctrine of laissez-faire as far as government regulation was concerned, although they were happy to receive federal subsidies and tariff protection. Rather than tackling substantive issues, politicians spent most of their time fighting over the spoils of office. Meanwhile, agrarian discontent grew and reached a climax in the 1890s with the Populist party and the election of 1896, which was the first election in years to see opposing candidates who truly differed on political-economic policies. In the late 1890s, with domestic problems still unresolved, the nation turned much of its attention to imperialist expansion.

II. Party Politics in an Era of Social and Economic Upheaval

A. *Patterns of Party Strength*

Politics in the period 1870–1900 was a male world, with women neither voting nor holding office. Male voter turnouts were high, and the two political parties—Democratic and Republican—were closely matched in strength. The main Democratic support came from the solid South, states that bordered the South, and recent immigrants in the big cities. The Republicans generally won the votes of rural and small-town New England, Pennsylvania, and the upper Midwest and of native-born businessmen, professionals, and white-collar workers.

B. *The Stakes of Politics*

Tariffs, the currency supply, and benefits for Civil War veterans were the main issues addressed in late-nineteenth-century national politics.

C. The Hayes White House: Virtue Restored

Rutherford B. Hayes's main accomplishments were to restore reasonable honesty to the presidency and to win respect for it after the Grant scandals.

D. Regulating the Money Supply

The nation split on the questions of how much money the government should issue and what should back it. Bankers, creditors, most businessmen, economists, and politicians all believed that, to maintain economic stability and avoid inflation, the money supply must be limited to that which the government could back with its holdings of gold. Debt-ridden southern and western farmers and some manufacturers wanted a larger money supply, including retention of the unbacked Civil War currency (greenbacks), issue of notes backed by silver and gold, and the minting of silver coins. They believed this larger money supply would raise falling farm prices and make it easier to pay off debts. In the 1870s the Greenback party tried to further this program. Even after the party's demise, debtor groups continued to demand a larger money supply and got a little help from the 1890 Sherman Silver Purchase Act.

E. The Spoils System

The spoils system had operated since the days of Andrew Jackson. A group of reformers, including Carl Schurz, E. L. Godkin, and Josephine Shaw Lowell, saw its defects and in 1881 founded the National Civil Service Reform League.

F. Civil-Service Reform

After a crazed job seeker assassinated President James A. Garfield, the civil-service reformers were finally able to convince Congress in 1883 to pass the Pendleton Act. It created a civil-service commission to prepare competitive examinations for federal jobs, and it prohibited politicians from asking government employees for campaign contributions. Gradually it began to raise the honesty and competence of the federal bureaucracy.

III. Politics of Privilege, Politics of Exclusion

A. 1884: Cleveland Victorious

In 1884 the Republicans nominated James G. Blaine, who was tainted by the corruption of the Grant era and was identified with the spoils system. When the Democrats chose Grover Cleveland, who had a reputation for fighting the spoilsmen, a number of Republican civil-service reformers bolted their party to support him. This Mugwump switch helped Cleveland win the presidency.

B. Tariffs and Pensions

Cleveland, a believer in laissez-faire, had little understanding of the social problems caused by industrialization. He did, however, attempt to lower the tariff, arguing that reduced rates would remove a potentially corrupting government surplus of funds, reduce prices for consumers, and slow the growth of trusts. Lower tariffs appealed to farmers and many

Democrats from the West and South but alarmed manufacturers and those Republican politicians who looked out for their interests. Cleveland also angered Civil War veterans when he halted wholesale granting of disability pensions to them.

C. 1888: Big Business and the GAR Strike Back

The tariff became a major issue in the election of 1888. The Democrats renominated Cleveland; the Republicans chose Benjamin Harrison and stood behind high protective tariffs. Industrialists contributed heavily to the Republicans. Although Cleveland received more popular votes than Harrison, he lost in the electoral college. In 1890 the victorious Republicans passed the McKinley Tariff, raising rates to an all-time high. They also rewarded Civil War veterans with generous pensions.

D. Southern and Western Farmers Organize

Farmers believed that the federal government was unresponsive to their needs. Western and southern farmers suffered from falling agricultural prices, a tight money supply, and high interest rates. They were heavily in debt and were overcharged by industrial trusts, grain elevator operators, and railroads. Earlier, farmers had turned to the Grange and the Greenback party to redress their grievances. When these failed, farmers joined the Southern, National Colored Farmers', and Northwestern alliances. The alliances called for tariff reduction, a graduated income tax, public ownership of railroads, and "free silver," among other things. In 1892 the alliances founded the People's or Populist party and wrote a platform based on their program. They also endorsed direct election of senators and other electoral reforms and nominated James B. Weaver for president.

E. African-Americans After Reconstruction

After Reconstruction white Democrats in the South increasingly deprived black southerners of the right to vote. At first the whites used intimidation and terror, but after 1890 they found even more effective means in poll taxes, literacy tests, and grandfather clauses. Southern blacks also were victimized by segregation laws, the convict-lease system, and lynching. Some southern Populists attempted to combat prejudice and encourage white and black farmers to unite against their exploiters, but the southern Democratic elite purposely inflamed racial antagonism to keep poor farmers divided.

The federal government did nothing to protect black rights. The Supreme Court gave its stamp of approval to segregated but equal facilities in *Plessy* v. *Ferguson* (1896). It also upheld poll taxes and literacy tests (1898).

Blacks responded to these abuses in several ways. Some fled the South only to find de facto discrimination in the North. Booker T. Washington advised fellow blacks to accept their second-class status for a time and concentrate on getting ahead economically and educationally. The old abolitionist Frederick Douglass still called on blacks to demand full equality. With the disfranchisement of blacks and the defeat of southern populism, the South became a one-party region, always controlled by the Democrats.

IV. The 1890s: Politics in a Depression Decade

A. 1892: Populists Challenge the Status Quo

In 1892 the Democratic candidate, Grover Cleveland, regained the presidency from the incumbent Republican, Benjamin Harrison. Populist James B. Weaver received more than a million votes, but few of them came from the urban Northeast. The Populists also gained less than one-quarter of the votes of the agricultural South, largely because of the race issue.

B. The Panic of 1893: Capitalism in Crisis

Soon after Cleveland was inaugurated, the nation suffered a financial panic that ushered in a severe depression.

C. The Depression of 1893–1897

During the depression thousands of banks and businesses failed; between 20 percent and 25 percent of the labor force was unemployed; and agricultural prices fell more than 20 percent, completing the ruin of many farmers already in economic difficulty. Hard times increased the appeal of the Populists and spawned strikes and protests. In 1894 Jacob Coxey led a march of the unemployed on Washington to demand a public-works program to create jobs. He was arrested, and the demonstration was broken up. The heightened unrest frightened the middle class.

D. Conservatives Hunker Down

Cleveland, in keeping with laissez-faire doctrine, opposed government help for victims of the depression. His use of force against the Pullman strikers and Coxey's marchers appeared heartless. He angered farmers when, in defense of the gold standard, he induced Congress to repeal the Sherman Silver Purchase Act. Cleveland's actions split his party, as Democrats from agricultural states began to favor free silver. Hard times also led many Americans to question the laissez-faire doctrine.

V. The Watershed Election of 1896

A. 1894: Protest Grows Louder

The voters repudiated Cleveland in the 1894 midterm elections. Congress went Republican, and the vote for Populist candidates climbed more than 40 percent above their 1892 tallies.

B. The Silver Issue

The issue of free silver came to symbolize the deep split between economic classes. Creditors feared that abandonment of a strictly gold standard would cause runaway inflation and ruin. Debt-ridden farmers saw silver as the panacea that would raise farm prices and return prosperity.

C. Silver Advocates Capture the Democratic Party

At the 1896 Democratic convention, western and southern delegates gained control, wrote a platform calling for free silver, and nominated silver advocate William Jennings Bryan. The Republicans nominated William McKinley, who promised to maintain the gold standard and raise the protective tariff. The Populists, though not completely satisfied with the Democratic platform, feared that if they ran their own candidate, they would split the farm vote, ensuring the election of McKinley. The Populists, therefore, endorsed Bryan but nominated one of their own, Tom Watson, for vice president.

D. 1896: Conservatism Triumphant

McKinley received huge campaign contributions from businessmen who feared Bryan. Besides having less money, Bryan was handicapped by the lack of appeal of free silver to factory workers and the urban middle class. They realized that it would probably bring about higher food prices. McKinley won the election, carrying the Northeast, Midwest, and most cities. His party also kept its majority in Congress. As promised, McKinley and the Republicans maintained the gold standard and raised the tariff to an all-time high. These policies aroused little opposition, however, because prosperity returned, more gold became available with new discoveries, and farm prices began to rise. McKinley easily beat Bryan for a second term in the election of 1900. Indeed, the elections of 1894 and 1896 ushered in a long period of Republican dominance in American politics that lasted almost unbroken until the 1930s. The Populist party disintegrated after 1896, but many of the reforms it had advocated were enacted by progressives after 1900.

VI. Expansionist Stirrings and War with Spain

A. Roots of Expansionist Sentiment

In the late nineteenth century the United States showed heightened interest in overseas empire. The example of European nations and Japan, which were seizing colonies in Asia and Africa, stimulated U.S. expansionism. During the depression of 1893–1897 American businessmen and politicians argued that the United States must capture overseas markets to maintain prosperity. Inspired by Alfred T. Mahan's *The Influence of Sea Power upon History*, Republican politicians—including Theodore Roosevelt, Henry Cabot Lodge, and John Hay—claimed that, to be a great power, the United States must build up its navy and obtain far-flung colonies in which to establish fueling stations and bases. Combining religion and racism, Josiah Strong's *Our Country* (1885) told Americans that, as members of the superior Anglo-Saxon race, they were destined to spread Christianity and civilization to "inferior" peoples.

B. Pacific Expansion

Expansionist enthusiasm led the United States to establish a joint protectorate with Germany and Great Britain over the Samoan Islands and to annex Hawaii in 1898.

C. Crisis over Cuba

The Cubans revolted against Spanish rule in 1895, and the Spanish authorities brutally attempted to suppress the rebellion. Public opinion in the United States turned against the Spanish as William Randolph Hearst's *Journal* and Joseph Pulitzer's *World,* using yellow-journalistic sensationalism, featured daily accounts of atrocities. President McKinley did not want to intervene, but he sent the battleship *Maine* to Havana to protect the lives and property of Americans on the island. On February 15, 1898, an explosion on the *Maine* killed 266 of its crewmen. The yellow press immediately accused the Spanish of blowing up the ship, and the public demanded revenge. Bending to popular pressure, McKinley asked Congress to declare war on Spain, which it did in April 1898. It also passed the Teller Amendment proclaiming that the United States had no designs on Cuba and would leave the island as soon as its independence was ensured.

D. The Spanish-American War

The fighting against Spain lasted less than four months. On orders from Assistant Secretary of the Navy Theodore Roosevelt, Admiral George Dewey attacked the Spanish fleet in the Philippines and American troops took Manila. By July 1898 the Spanish were driven from Cuba. The defeated Spanish recognized Cuba's independence and ceded to the United States the Philippines, Puerto Rico, and Guam.

VII. Deepening Imperialist Ventures: The Philippines, China, Panama

A. The Platt Amendment

Contrary to the Teller Amendment, the United States occupied Cuba from 1898 to 1902, then withdrew its forces only after Cuba agreed to the conditions set forth in the 1901 Platt Amendment. This amendment limited Cuba's sovereignty by, among other things, reserving to the United States the right to intervene in Cuba and to maintain a naval base there. Although the Platt Amendment was abrogated in 1934, the United States still retains the base at Guantanamo Bay in Cuba.

B. Guerrilla War in the Philippines

President McKinley was persuaded that the United States should keep the Philippines by the arguments of the expansionists and the desire of businessmen to use the islands as a way of penetrating nearby Chinese markets. That American decision led to a war against Filipino independence fighters. To crush the guerrilla resistance of the Filipinos, the United States used brutal tactics and lost ten times as many soldiers as it had in the Spanish-American War. The United States ruled the Philippines until July 4, 1946, when it finally granted the country its independence.

C. Critics of Empire

Some Americans were horrified by their nation's actions in the Philippines. Among these people were civil-service reformers Carl Schurz and E. L. Godkin, agricultural spokesmen such as William Jennings Bryan, settlement-house founder Jane Addams, and writers and intellectuals such as Mark Twain and William James. They founded the Anti-Imperialist

League, which pointed out that imposing American rule on other peoples by military force violated the principles of human equality and liberty championed in our own Declaration of Independence.

D. The "Open Door": Competing for the China Market

American businessmen, who dreamed of penetrating the Chinese market, became alarmed at developments there. European powers and Japan were forcing the weak Chinese government to lease that country's ports to them—and then they closed those ports to trade and investment by businessmen of any country but their own. U.S. secretary of state John Hay attempted to aid American business by sending his 1899 Open Door notes to the nations involved, asking them to keep their leased Chinese ports open to trade and investment from all countries on equal terms. He received noncommittal replies. Soon thereafter the United States joined those countries in putting down a Chinese uprising against foreign imperialists known as the Boxer Rebellion. Some nations wanted to use the rebellion as an excuse for carving China up into colonies for themselves. Hay announced U.S. opposition to this plan in his 1900 Open Door notes. He asked all countries to respect the territorial integrity of China and repeated the demand for equal trading and investment opportunities there. The Open Door notes became a cornerstone of U.S. policy in Asia and helped shape this country's response to the Japanese drive to conquer China in the 1930s.

E. The Panama Canal: Hardball U.S. Diplomacy

For commercial and strategic reasons, the United States wanted to build a canal across the Isthmus of Panama. In 1902 the United States negotiated a treaty leasing a canal zone from Colombia, the country that owned the isthmus at the time. However, the Colombian senate, hoping for more money, rejected the treaty. An infuriated President Roosevelt conspired with directors of a bankrupt French company that had been trying earlier to build a canal and hoped to profit from the United States' taking over its land lease. Philippe Bunau-Varilla, an official of the company, fomented revolution in Panama, and Roosevelt sent an American warship in 1903 to see to it that the uprising succeeded. The United States then recognized Panama's independence and negotiated a treaty leasing the land, with Bunau-Varilla appointed to speak for Panama. The canal, a great engineering feat by the U.S. Army, opened in 1914, but the imperialistic methods Roosevelt used to seize the area created lasting ill will toward the United States in Latin America.

VIII. Conclusion

The burst of expansionism in the late nineteenth and early twentieth centuries never fully diverted U.S. attention from domestic issues. The Populist party, though it went down to defeat in 1896, left behind the feeling that government must free itself from business domination and play a more active role in solving the economic and social problems arising from industrialization. After the turn of the century, the progressive movement would build on that new attitude.

VOCABULARY

The following terms are used in Chapter 21. To understand the chapter fully, it is important that you know what each of them means.

disfranchisement   depriving persons of the right to vote

myriad   a great number of persons or things

bureaucracy   the body of officials administering the agencies or bureaus of government or other large organizations; excessive governmental or institutional red tape and routine

pliable   easily influenced

spoils system   the practice whereby the victorious political party rewards its supporters with appointments to government jobs, regardless of their qualifications for the positions

patronage   the control of appointments to public office or of other political favors

agrarian   rural, agricultural

lynch   to kill a person by mob action for some alleged offense without due process of law

caveat   warning or caution

de facto   in fact; in reality (as opposed to de jure: according to law or required by law)

reactionary   extremely conservative; favoring a return to the social or political conditions of a past time

panacea   a remedy for all ills or difficulties; a cure-all

jingoism   an aggressive, bellicose spirit or foreign policy that advocates seizing new territories and/or securing national advantages by use of force

sovereignty   independence; self-government or authority of a nation or state

imperialism   the policy of extending the rule or authority of an empire or nation over foreign countries or of acquiring and holding colonies and dependencies

protectorate   the relationship of a strong state toward a weaker state or territory that it protects and partly controls

subjugate   to conquer; to bring under complete control

territorial integrity   condition of a country being whole, entire, and self-governing rather than broken up into the colonies of other countries

IDENTIFICATIONS

After reading Chapter 21, you should be able to identify and explain the historical significance of each of the following:

Rutherford B. Hayes

greenbacks and the Greenback party

Carl Schurz, E. L. Godkin, Josephine Shaw Lowell, and the Civil Service Reform League

James B. Weaver

Pendleton Civil Service Act

Grover Cleveland

Mugwumps

Southern, Northwestern, and National Colored Farmers' alliances

Tom Watson, Mary E. Lease, and the Populist party

poll tax, literacy test, and grandfather clause

Plessy v. *Ferguson*

Booker T. Washington

Jacob Coxey

free silver

William Jennings Bryan

William McKinley

Alfred T. Mahan, *The Influence of Sea Power upon History*

Josiah Strong, *Our Country*

Henry Cabot Lodge

Liliuokalani versus Sanford B. Dole

William Randolph Hearst, the *Journal*, and yellow journalism

Joseph Pulitzer and the *World*

Teller Amendment versus Platt Amendment

Emilio Aguinaldo

Anti-Imperialist League

John Hay and the Open Door policy

Boxer Rebellion

Philippe Bunau-Varilla and the Hay–Bunau-Varilla Treaty

SKILL BUILDING: MAPS

1. On the map of Asia and the Pacific, locate each of the following. Explain the significance of each on late-nineteenth-century and early-twentieth-century U.S. foreign policy.

   Samoa

   Hawaiian Islands, Honolulu, Pearl Harbor

   Philippines, Manila Bay, Manila, Luzon

   Guam

   China, Manchuria, Beijing (Peking)

   Japan

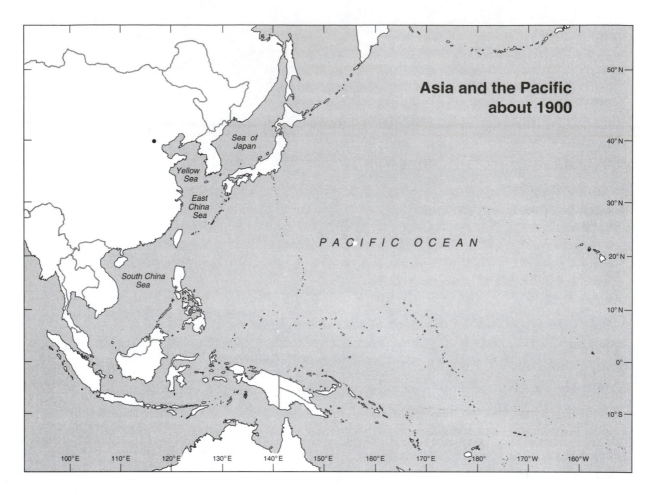

2. On the map on page 71 of the Caribbean and Central and South America, locate the following. Explain the significance of each on late-nineteenth-century and early-twentieth-century U.S. foreign policy.

Cuba, Havana, Santiago de Cuba, Guantanamo

Puerto Rico

Colombia

Panama Canal Zone

Panama

Nicaragua

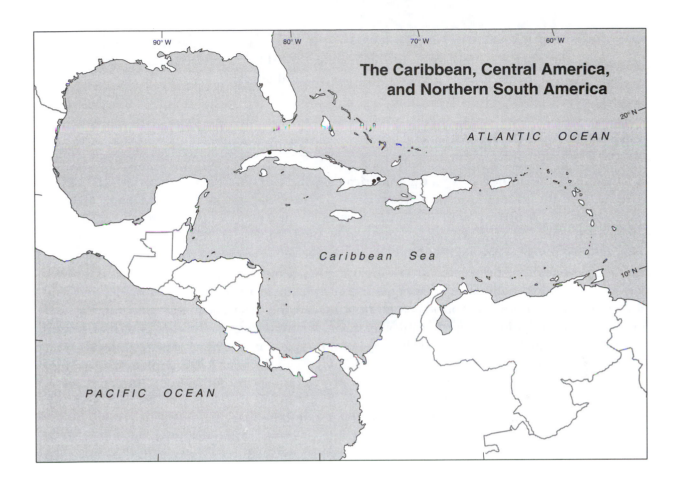

SKILL BUILDING: TABLES

Look at the election tables in Chapter 21. What can you conclude about the relative strength of the two major parties between 1880 and 1892? What had happened to the balance between them by 1900? After reading the chapter, can you explain the reasons for the change? In what election did the candidate with the greater popular vote lose the election? Can you explain how this is possible and could happen again?

Look at the line graph titled "Consumer Prices and Farm-Product Prices, 1865–1913" on page 675 of the text. After studying this graph you should be able to answer the following questions:

1. Was the period 1875–1897 one of overall economic inflation or deflation?
2. During that period, which generally dropped lower: total cost of living for consumers or prices of farm products?

3. During which years did farmers' incomes fall the farthest below their expenditures? Based on what you have read in this chapter, would you say that those years corresponded to the periods of greatest agrarian political unrest?

HISTORICAL SOURCES

In Chapter 21 the author tells us that Americans in the late nineteenth century were bitterly divided over the money question. How does the historian know that? On page 683 the author cites two sources that give historians clues about issues of concern to people at various times in the past. One is a book published in 1894, William H. Harvey's *Coin's Financial School*. Since it sold more than 400,000 copies in the next two years, we can assume that its topic, the money question, interested a great many people. By reading this book, the historian can find out the kinds of arguments the silver standard propagandists made, and one can see from the book's emotional tone how heated the discussion was. Second, the text reproduces a pro–gold standard political cartoon. What message did it convey to its viewers? The historian can find such political cartoons in copies of old newspapers, journals, and books. For example, a cartoon in *Harper's Weekly* from the year 1896 depicts William Jennings Bryan pressing down on the brow of a protesting laborer a fifty-cent "bunco dollar." The historian can certainly tell how this journal, published in the Northeast and read primarily by business and professional people, felt about free silver.

Now look at the sections in Chapter 21 titled "Roots of Expansionist Sentiment" and "Crisis over Cuba." Does the author cite similar historical sources to explain the desire for expansion and feelings of anger against Spain?

Finally, look at "A Place in Time: Chicago in the 1890s." How does this capsule history of Chicago and its Columbian Exposition illustrate the economic, social, and political impact of rapid industrialization on Americans at the time?

MULTIPLE-CHOICE QUESTIONS

Circle the letter of the item that best completes each statement or answers the question.

1. The Pendleton Act provided for
    a. civil-service reform.
    b. using silver as well as gold to back paper currency.
    c. separate but equal facilities for blacks and whites.
    d. higher protective tariff rates.

2. Which of the following was *not* a goal of the Populist party?
    a. having government take over and run the railroads
    b. increasing the money supply
    c. raising the protective tariff
    d. having the people elect U. S. senators instead of state legislatures choosing them

3. Which of the following results of the Spanish-American War aroused the greatest controversy in the United States?
    a. payment of $20 million to Spain
    b. acquisition of the Philippine Islands
    c. removing the Spanish from Cuba
    d. annexation of Puerto Rico

4. American imperialists argued that U.S. participation in the race for colonies would do all of the following *except*
    a. cause lower taxes in the United States.
    b. provide bases for the U.S. Navy.
    c. provide the United States with new markets.
    d. bring civilization to backward peoples.

5. The Populist party was launched chiefly by leaders of the
    a. farmers' alliances.
    b. Grange.
    c. American Federation of Labor.
    d. Progressive party.

6. The free-silver position of the Democrats and Populists in 1896 failed to win much support from urban labor because
    a. it would destroy labor unions.
    b. factory workers were relatively prosperous in the 1890s.
    c. workers liked Grover Cleveland and laissez-faire.
    d. workers feared it would result in higher food prices.

7. The Teller Amendment was later partially repudiated by
    a. the Platt Amendment.
    b. the Hay–Bunau-Varilla Treaty.
    c. *Plessy* v. *Ferguson*.
    d. the Sixteenth Amendment.

8. The yellow journalism of William R. Hearst's *Journal* and Joseph Pulitzer's *World* probably contributed to
    a. Bryan's defeat in 1896.
    b. Cleveland's election in 1884.
    c. the passage of poll taxes, literacy tests, and grandfather clauses.
    d. America's declaration of war on Spain.

9. Which nineteenth-century political figure championed civil-service reform, joined the Mugwump revolt against James G. Blaine, and criticized American imperialism?
    a. Alfred T. Mahan
    b. Benjamin Harrison
    c. Carl Schurz
    d. John Hay

10. In the case of *Plessy* v. *Ferguson,* the U.S. Supreme Court ruled that
    a. poll taxes, literacy tests, and grandfather clauses were unconstitutional devices for undermining the Fifteenth Amendment.
    b. segregated public facilities did not violate the Fourteenth Amendment as long as the separate accommodations were equal.
    c. a federal income tax was unconstitutional.
    d. the convict-lease system violated constitutional guarantees of fair trial and no cruel and unusual punishment.

SHORT-ANSWER QUESTIONS

1. Discuss the causes of agrarian discontent in the period 1870 to 1897.

2. Why did American farmers between the 1870s and 1897 generally favor issuing greenbacks and adopting "free silver"?

3. Discuss the effects of the depression of 1893–1897 on national politics.

4. Why did the Populists decide to endorse the 1896 Democratic presidential candidate, William Jennings Bryan, instead of nominating a member of their own party to run?

5. Explain the relationship the United States established with Cuba after the Spanish-American War.

6. Theodore Roosevelt said, "I took the Canal Zone." Explain how he took it. What were the consequences of his actions for the United States?

ESSAY QUESTIONS

1. Discuss what happened to African-Americans in the post-Reconstruction South. How did the federal government react to these developments? What impact did these developments have on national politics?

2. Write an essay on the rise of populism in the 1890s. How and why was the Populist party founded? What did it hope to accomplish? Why did it fail to become a major party and gain control of the federal government? Did it accomplish anything?

3. Discuss the election of 1896. Who were the candidates? What were the issues? What was the outcome? Why was it an important watershed election?

4. In 1898 the United States declared war on Spain, although there seemed to be little provocation. Why did the majority of Americans and most government leaders favor war?

5. With the annexation of the Philippines, the United States for the first time imposed its rule on a distant people by military force. How can you account for this change in U.S. foreign policy? What pressures and groups led the nation in this imperialistic direction? Were there countergroups trying to prevent this course? If so, why were they unsuccessful?

22

The Progressive Era

OUTLINE AND SUMMARY

I. A Changing American Society and Economy

A. *Immigrant Masses and a New Urban Middle Class*

Cities grew rapidly between 1900 and 1920 as rural Americans and some 17 million immigrants moved into them. Most of the immigrants were fleeing poverty in their native lands. Many of the newcomers huddled in burgeoning urban slums in terrible conditions. Overwhelmed and often corrupt municipal governments failed to provide them with adequate services and public facilities. Settlement-house workers, Social Gospel ministers, and reform journalists had been telling middle-class Americans about the plight of slum dwellers for years; the resulting consciousness of urban poverty helped set the stage for the progressive movement.

The urban middle class, mostly native-born, also was expanding and becoming increasingly self-aware and influential. Especially, college-educated, urban, middle-class women organized social-welfare efforts and revived the feminist movement.

B. *African-Americans in a Racist Age*

In 1900 two-thirds of the 10 million black Americans were still in the rural South, mostly living as sharecroppers. To escape from poverty, disfranchisement, Jim Crow laws, and violence, blacks began migrating to cities and to the North. In the North they encountered de facto segregation and discrimination. Under these difficult circumstances, blacks developed their own communities, culture, and music.

C. *Corporate Boardrooms, Factory Floors*

Domination of the economy by corporate giants accelerated in the first years of the twentieth century. The real wages of industrial laborers rose after 1900 but were still so inadequate that in many families the mothers and children had to go to work to make ends meet. In 1910 at least 1.6 million youngsters between ten and fifteen years of age worked full-time. Industrial laborers spent on average nine and a half hours a day in mills and shops that were often hazardous to their health and safety, as demonstrated by the Triangle Shirtwaist fire. Employers, inspired by efficiency experts such as Frederick W. Taylor, tried to get still more work out of their employees.

D. Workers Organize; Socialism Advances

To improve their lot, workers kept trying to unionize. However, their right to strike was frequently curtailed by conservative court decisions such as *Danbury Hatters*, and employers often hired recent immigrants as scabs when employees struck. Because of these obstacles, the AFL craft unions grew primarily in the skilled trades, leaving most factory workers unorganized. Two unions attempted to help semiskilled and unskilled workers: the International Ladies' Garment Workers' Union, which led successful strikes in the needle trades, and the Industrial Workers of the World (IWW). The IWW signed up western miners, lumberjacks, and migratory farm workers and won a major strike in 1912 in the textile mills of Lawrence, Massachusetts. Unlike the American Federation of Labor, the IWW preached revolution to overthrow capitalism.

The Socialist Party of America, which hoped to end capitalism through the ballot box rather than revolution, also was gaining followers. When party leader Eugene Debs ran for president in 1912, he received 900,000 votes. The same rising discontent that won support for the IWW and the Socialists also opened the way for the progressive movement.

II. The Progressive Movement Takes Shape

A. Progressivism: An Overview

The reform movement known as progressivism arose in response to the problems spawned by industrialization. Progressivism and the earlier populist movement shared the belief that government must become involved in ameliorating these problems, but populism was primarily a farmers' movement; progressivism's main strength lay in the urban middle class. The progressive movement also won important support from urban and immigrant workers, and even some backing from business leaders.

Most progressives accepted the capitalist system; they merely wanted to reform the worst abuses that had developed under it. There was never one unified movement, but many different groups of reformers. Some preached regulation of big business; others concentrated on passing laws to protect workers. Still others thought that the way to solve social ills was to outlaw liquor and prostitution or restrict immigration. Progressives generally attempted to be "scientific" in their approach, backing their demands for change with scholarly studies of deplorable conditions to be remedied.

B. Intellectuals Lay the Groundwork

Many intellectuals criticized laissez-faire and called for an activist government that would regulate business practices and protect the economically vulnerable. These intellectuals included economist Thorstein Veblen, historians Charles and Mary Beard, and journalist Herbert Croly. William James's pragmatic philosophy also undermined fixed dogma about laissez-faire.

C. New Ideas About Education and the Law

New educational and legal ideas paved the way for the progressive movement. John Dewey preached that schools must foster in students respect for the values of democracy and cooperation. Supreme Court justice Oliver Wendell Holmes, Jr., attacked conservative judges for being guided entirely by legal precedent. He insisted that the "law must evolve as society changes."

D. Novelists and Journalists Spread the Word

Muckraking journalists and novelists played an important role in stimulating the progressive movement by exposing to middle-class Americans political corruption and corporate wrongdoing. Muckraking journalists included Lincoln Steffens, who wrote about urban political machines and bosses, and Ida Tarbell, who revealed the cutthroat competitive practices of Standard Oil Company. Magazines such as *McClure's* and *Collier's* specialized in muckraking articles. Novelists Frank Norris in *The Octopus* and Theodore Dreiser in *The Financier* also told tales of business abuses and political corruption. Meanwhile, "Ashcan School" artists and photographers such as Lewis Hine, depicted the harsh world of the immigrants and factory workers.

E. Reforming the Political Process

The earliest signs of the progressive movement appeared in cities where municipal reformers battled corrupt political machines and elected activist mayors dedicated to change. Reform mayors such as Hazen Pingree of Detroit and Tom Johnson of Cleveland generally brought honesty to municipal government, provided city dwellers with improved municipal services and facilities, and forced transportation and utility companies to lower rates and pay their fair share of taxes. Other municipal reformers experimented with commission and city-manager forms of government.

The reform efforts soon moved up to state government. Progressives attempted to democratize politics by establishing secret balloting, the direct primary, the initiative, the referendum, and recall and by helping to enact the Seventeenth Amendment, which provided for popular election of U.S. senators. In practice these measures fell short of producing the democratic results that their progressive authors had hoped for.

F. Protecting Workers, Beautifying the City

Under progressive influence, state governments enacted important social measures: maximum number of hours per workday for female employees, such as Oregon's ten-hour law; factory safety codes, such as the one enacted in New York after the Triangle Shirtwaist fire; workers' compensation acts; bans on child labor; and housing codes. Progressive reformers also began to beautify cities with more parks and playgrounds, broad boulevards, and impressive municipal buildings.

G. Corporate Regulation

States moved to regulate big business, too. The pioneer was Wisconsin, under Governor Robert La Follette. Between 1901 and 1906 he convinced the legislature to introduce the direct primary, create a state railroad commission, increase corporate taxes, and limit business contributions to political campaigns, among other reforms. These progressive measures and La Follette's method of relying on the expertise of academics at the state university became known as the "Wisconsin Idea."

III. Progressivism and Social Control: The Movement's Coercive Dimension

A. Moral Control in the Cities

Some reformers tried to guard morality by inducing cities to censor movies and outlaw gambling and prostitution.

B. Battling Alcohol and Drugs

Prohibition became the biggest moral crusade of the Progressive Era. Due to the efforts of the Anti-Saloon League, the Woman's Christian Temperance Union, and various church groups Congress in 1918 passed the Eighteenth Amendment, which outlawed the manufacture, sale, and shipment of alcoholic beverages. Progressives also enacted the earliest laws regulating the then-widespread use of such addictive drugs as morphine, heroin, and cocaine.

C. Immigration Restriction

Some people believed that immigrants caused poverty and immorality. In 1894 Senator Henry Cabot Lodge and other prominent Bostonians founded the Immigration Restriction League. In 1917, over President Wilson's veto, Congress excluded illiterate immigrants.

D. Eugenics: Scientific Bigotry

Eugenicists claimed that humans and society could be improved by controlled breeding. Inspired by their ideas, a few states passed laws during the Progressive Era allowing forced sterilization of criminals and sex offenders. Pseudo-scientific racism was spewd by some so-called progressive writers, such as Madison Grant in *The Passing of the Great Race* (1916).

E. Racism and Progressivism

Racism in American society reached a peak during these years. Many progressives either ignored racial discrimination or were themselves racists. Southern progressives such as James K. Vardaman combined advocacy of economic and political reform with vicious attacks on blacks. Woodrow Wilson, during his presidency, condoned segregation and discrimination practiced by the federal government. On the other hand, white progressives such as Mary White Ovington helped found the National Association for the Advancement of Colored People (NAACP).

IV. Blacks and Women Organize

A. Controversy Among African-Americans

Booker T. Washington, America's best-known black leader between 1890 and 1915, advised blacks to concentrate on economic advancement through vocational education and, for the time being, accept the South's Jim Crow and disfranchisement laws. Northern black intellectuals and professionals—William Monroe Trotter, Ida Wells-Barnett, and W. E. B. Du Bois—urged blacks to fight for economic, political, and educational equality.

B. *The Founding of the NAACP*

In 1905 Du Bois and other black critics of Washington formed the Niagara Movement. In 1909 Du Bois and other members of the Niagara Movement joined with white progressives in organizing the NAACP, which rejected Washington's accommodationist advice and began the long fight for racial justice.

C. *Revival of the Woman-Suffrage Movement*

A new group of feminists emerged to revitalize the women's movement. Carrie Chapman Catt, who became president of the National American Woman Suffrage Association in 1900, led her members in lobbying, distributing literature, and demonstrating. They convinced a number of states to grant women the vote. Impatient with the pace of change, however, Alice Paul organized the Woman's party to bring direct pressure on the federal government. She and her followers picketed the White House and went on a hunger strike. Congress finally passed the Nineteenth Amendment in 1919, and by 1920 it was ratified.

D. *Breaking Out of the "Woman's Sphere"*

Feminists challenged the assumption that the only proper roles for women were those of wife, mother, and homemaker. Women like Florence Kelley, Margaret Sanger, and Alice Hamilton led the progressive drives to abolish child labor, protect the health of workers and consumers, and establish day-care centers and birth-control clinics.

V. National Progressivism—Phase I: Roosevelt and Taft

A. *Roosevelt's Path to the White House*

Theodore Roosevelt, who entered the White House in 1901 after an anarchist assassinated William McKinley, became America's first progressive president. A believer in strong executive leadership, Roosevelt enlarged the powers of the presidency, turning the office into both an effective public forum and the center of legislative initiative.

B. *Labor Disputes and Corporate Regulation*

Unlike earlier presidents who used troops to break strikes, Roosevelt, in the coal miners' strike of 1902, induced management and the United Mine Workers Union to submit the dispute to arbitration by a commission that he appointed. The commission granted the miners increased pay and reduced hours.

Roosevelt did not want to attack big business, but he preached that corporate giants must obey the law and serve the public interest. When he believed that firms like the Northern Securities Company had violated the Sherman Anti-Trust Act, he prosecuted them. Despite his trust-busting, he stayed on good terms with big business, which contributed heavily to his 1904 campaign. In that election he easily won a second term over the conservative Democrat Alton B. Parker. In 1906 Roosevelt strengthened corporate regulation when he signed the Hepburn Act, which gave the Interstate Commerce Commission (ICC) the power to set maximum railroad rates and examine railroads' financial records.

C. Consumer Protection and Racial Issues

Responding to public concern generated by Upton Sinclair's *The Jungle,* Roosevelt persuaded Congress to pass the Pure Food and Drug Act and the Meat Inspection Act. On racial matters, Roosevelt's record is much worse. Especially unjust was his summary discharge of a black regiment in the Brownsville, Texas incident.

D. The Conservation Movement

Roosevelt made his most enduring reforms in conservation. Years of exploitation for private gain had damaged and depleted America's natural environment. By the 1890s land use had become a political issue, pitting business interests, preservationists, and conservationists against each other. While entrepreneurs wanted to continue unrestricted development for private enrichment, preservationists such as John Muir and the Sierra Club wished to save large wilderness tracts for their beauty and spiritual worth. Roosevelt's Forest Service chief Gifford Pinchot, father of the conservation movement, sought government scientific management to make the public domain best serve the resource needs of the nation of his day and in the future. Roosevelt used the presidency to popularize both conservation and preservation. He signed the Reclamation Act (1902) and, in cooperation with Pinchot, set aside some 200 million acres of forest and mineral-rich lands for government-managed use rather than for sale to business. Roosevelt approved the Antiquities Act and created new national parks. By 1916 there were thirteen national parks, and Congress, during President Wilson's administration, established the National Park Service to protect and run them.

E. Taft in the White House

With Roosevelt's backing, his secretary of war, William Howard Taft, won the Republican nomination and election as president in 1908 over third-time Democratic nominee William Jennings Bryan. Pledged to continue Roosevelt's square deal, Taft prosecuted more trusts than Roosevelt had, but Taft lacked Roosevelt's activism, flair for publicity, and political skill.

F. A Divided Republican Party

In the fight shaping up between the progressive (Insurgents) and conservative wings of the Republican party, Taft sided with the conservatives. When he signed the tariff-raising Payne-Aldrich bill, backed conservative Speaker of the House Joseph Cannon, and fired conservationist Gifford Pinchot, Taft alienated progressive Republicans. They joined with Theodore Roosevelt, who returned from a trip abroad in 1910, in denouncing the conservatives and campaigning for revived progressive reform.

VI. National Progressivism—Phase II: Woodrow Wilson

A. The Four-Way Election of 1912

In 1912 Theodore Roosevelt challenged Taft for the Republican nomination. When the convention chose Taft, Roosevelt's backers walked out, founded the rival Progressive party, and nominated Roosevelt. The Democrats gave the nod to Woodrow Wilson, reform governor of New Jersey, and the Socialists ran Eugene Debs. Roosevelt campaigned on his New Nationalism program of accepting big business as inevitable but building a powerful, activist fed eral government to regulate the corporate giants. Wilson's New Freedom, on the other hand, rejected big government in Washington and called for return to an economy composed of small, competing enterprises. Roosevelt did well, but the split in Republican ranks gave Wilson and the Democrats control of the White House and Congress.

B. Woodrow Wilson: The Scholar as President

Wilson had been a political science professor and president of Princeton University before becoming New Jersey governor. He could be a skilled and flexible politician, but at other times he was intolerant and self-righteous.

C. Tariff and Banking Reform

Wilson convinced Congress to pass the 1913 Underwood-Simmons Tariff, which reduced import duties, put several items on the free list, and instituted a federal income tax (authorized by the Sixteenth Amendment ratified earlier that year). Also in 1913 he signed the Federal Reserve Act, which kept banking a private enterprise but imposed public regulation over it. The twelve regional Federal Reserve banks were empowered to expand the nation's credit and money supply by issuing Federal Reserve notes under the supervision of the Federal Reserve Board, appointed by the president.

D. Corporate Regulation

Wilson pushed through Congress the Federal Trade Commission law and the Clayton Antitrust Act. The Federal Trade Commission was a federal regulatory agency with the power to uncover unfair methods of business competition and then issue cease and desist orders against their perpetrators. The Clayton Act supplemented the vague and general Sherman Anti-Trust Act by defining and listing specific illegal practices.

E. Labor Legislation and Farm Aid

Wilson endorsed the clause in the Clayton Act exempting union strikes, boycotts, and peaceful picketing from prosecution under the antitrust laws. He signed the Keating-Owen child labor law (later declared unconstitutional), the Adamson Act providing for an eight-hour day for railroad workers, and the Workingmen's Compensation Act for federal employees. Other legislation helped farmers obtain loans at lower interest rates.

F. Progressivism and the Constitution

Wilson nominated to the Supreme Court progressive Jewish attorney Louis Brandeis. Although conservatives and anti-Semites objected, Wilson persuaded the Senate to confirm Brandeis.

G. 1916: Wilson Edges Out Hughes

In 1916 the Democrats renominated Wilson, who ran against Charles Evans Hughes, the candidate of the now reunited Republicans. In a close race Wilson won a second term.

VII. Conclusion

Although some progressive reforms did less good than their backers had hoped, and despite progressivism's repressive and intolerant elements, the movement as a whole left a legacy of government intervention to regulate destructive corporate practices, protect the economically vulnerable, and ameliorate social problems arising from industrialization. It was a precedent on which the New Deal would later build.

VOCABULARY

The following terms are used in Chapter 22. To understand the chapter fully, it is important that you know what each of them means.

pogroms   physical attacks on Russian Jews made by anti-Semitic Russian mobs, often encouraged by the tsarist government

behemoth   huge and powerful institution, person, or beast

capitalism   a system under which the means of production, distribution, and exchange are mostly privately owned and directed

socialism   a system under which the means of production, distribution, and exchange are owned by the community as a whole and administered by the government

pragmatism   the philosophy that truth is not determined by fixed universal laws but by the practical test of what works (it comes from philosopher William James's 1907 book *Pragmatism*)

direct primary   an election in which the registered members of a political party vote on who their party nominees for office should be

initiative   procedure by which a specified number of voters may propose a law and compel a popular vote on its adoption

recall   the right to remove a public official from office by a vote of the people taken upon petition of a specified number of the registered voters

eugenics   the manipulation of reproductive processes to improve the characteristics of a plant or animal species, especially human beings

diatribe   a bitter and violent denunciation

arbitration   the hearing and deciding of a dispute between parties by a person or persons agreed to by the disputing parties

nostrums   patent medicines

workers' compensation law   a law requiring employers to take out an insurance policy on their employees so that if a worker is hurt on the job, the insurance company will pay medical and living expenses until the worker can return to work (in case of the worker's death, the payments are made to his or her dependents)

cease and desist order   an order by a court or government regulatory agency to stop and refrain thereafter from actions that the agency believes are illegal (if the order is complied with, no punitive action is taken)

IDENTIFICATIONS

After reading Chapter 22 you should be able to identify and explain the historical significance of each of the following:

Triangle Shirtwaist fire

International Ladies' Garment Workers' Union

William Haywood and the Industrial Workers of the World

Margaret Sanger and birth control

Eugene Debs and the Socialist Party of America

Jane Addams

Herbert Croly, *The Promise of American Life*, and the *New Republic*

John Dewey

Lincoln Steffens, Ida Tarbell, and the muckrakers

Tom Johnson and the progressive reform mayors

constitutional amendments of the Progressive Era: sixteenth, seventeenth, eighteenth, nineteenth

Robert La Follette

Anti-Saloon League and Woman's Christian Temperance Union

Booker T. Washington in contrast to William Monroe Trotter, Ida Wells-Barnett, W. E. B. Du Bois, and the Niagara Movement

Mary White Ovington, Oswald Garrison Villard, and the NAACP

Carrie Chapman Catt and the National American Woman Suffrage Association

Alice Paul and the Woman's party

Florence Kelley

Theodore Roosevelt and the coal miners' strike of 1902

Northern Securities Company case

Hepburn Act

Pure Food and Drug Act and Meat Inspection Act

Gifford Pinchot and the conservationists

John Muir, the Sierra Club, and the preservationists

Payne-Aldrich Tariff

the Insurgents and Joseph Cannon

Ballinger-Pinchot Affair

New Nationalism and New Freedom

Underwood-Simmons Tariff

Federal Reserve Act, Federal Reserve Board, and Federal Reserve notes

Federal Trade Commission

Clayton Antitrust Act

Louis Brandeis and *Muller* v. *Oregon*

SKILL BUILDING: TABLES

Look at the tables on the elections of 1904 and 1908 in your text. Compare these with the election tables in Chapter 21. What happened to the balance of power between the two major parties between the 1880s and the early 1900s? William Jennings Bryan was the Democratic candidate in the elections of 1896, 1900, and 1908. Using the information in Chapter 21 and the election tables for 1900 and 1908, can you tell in which year he came closest to winning the presidency? Why do you think that was? In many of the elections between 1880 and 1920, the prohibitionists ran a presidential candidate. Judging from the election tables, can you find any evidence that their appeal to the electorate was growing?

Look at the table "Children in the Labor Force, 1880–1930" in your textbook. In what year did the problem of child labor seem to be most severe? Judging from the data in this chart, do you think the progressive movement had any impact on child labor in the United States? Can you offer any other explanations for the percentage differences between 1880 and 1930?

SKILL BUILDING: GRAPHS

Look at the line graph titled "Immigration to the United States, 1870–1930" on page 701 of the text. After studying the graph, you should be able to answer the following questions:

1. During which years did the United States receive the greatest number of immigrants? Was there any year in which more than 1 million persons arrived?

2. During the peak period of immigration, were the majority of newcomers from Western and Northern Europe or from Southern and Eastern Europe?

3. Just from looking at the graph, can you tell what impact the Immigration Act of 1921 had on how many immigrants arrived and where they came from?

4. What were the effects of major economic depressions in the United States (1873–1879, 1893–1897) and of World War I (1914–1918) on immigration to this country?

HISTORICAL SOURCES

If the historian writing about the Progressive Era is to understand why many Americans of the period favored reform, he or she needs to view the problems facing society as citizens living at the time perceived them. In the years 1890–1917 many middle-class people who did not personally experience exploitation learned about it from books, articles, and studies written by reformers. Examples include Florence Kelley's 1905 book *Some Ethical Gains Through Legislation,* dealing with the evils of child labor, and Lincoln Steffens's *The Shame of Cities* (1904), focusing on municipal corruption. Novelists joined in the move to expose social ills, and because they offered plots with adventures and love stories along with their social message, they reached many more readers than Kelley's or Steffens's nonfiction accounts. Muckraking novels of the period include Upton Sinclair's *The Jungle* (1906), Frank

Norris's *The Octopus* (1901), and Theodore Dreiser's *The Financier* (1912). The historian who wants to understand why Americans called for laws to prohibit child labor, protect consumers, regulate railroads and big business, and clean up graft can read these books. While these works make excellent historical sources, can you see any dangers in the historian's reliance on them as the only or main source of information about the period 1890–1917?

Look at "A Place in Time: Hetch Hetchy Valley in 1913." There you will get some sense of the complexity of the issues progressives addressed. The decision to build the dam in the valley pitted two environmentalists, John Muir and Gifford Pinchot, against each other. What position did each take? Why? Historians find the answers to these questions by looking at sources such as the transcripts of the 1913 hearings before the Public Lands Committee of the House of Representatives and the speeches and writings of the two men.

MULTIPLE-CHOICE QUESTIONS

Circle the letter of the item that best completes each statement or answers the question.

1. Theodore Roosevelt's New Nationalism was in part derived from a book written by
    a. Herbert Croly.
    b. Louis Brandeis.
    c. William Jennings Bryan.
    d. Margaret Sanger.

2. The act of Congress that contained a federal income tax provision was
    a. the Hepburn Act.
    b. the Federal Reserve Act.
    c. the Payne-Aldrich Tariff.
    d. the Underwood-Simmons Tariff.

3. "Corporations and combinations have become indispensable in the business world, . . . it is folly to try to prohibit them, but it is also folly to leave them without thorough-going control." This quotation summarizes the position on the big-business question of which politician?
    a. Woodrow Wilson
    b. William McKinley
    c. Theodore Roosevelt
    d. Robert La Follette

4. All of the following were founders of the NAACP *except*
    a. W. E. B. Du Bois.
    b. Booker T. Washington.
    c. Mary White Ovington.
    d. Oswald Garrison Villard.

5. In the coal strike of 1902, Theodore Roosevelt
   a. followed Cleveland's precedent in using federal troops.
   b. refused to intervene.
   c. insisted that labor and management submit the dispute to arbitration.
   d. sided with the employers against the union.

6. The term *muckrakers* refers to
   a. procurers involved in the white slave trade.
   b. journalists and writers who exposed political corruption and corporate wrongdoing.
   c. opponents of Woodrow Wilson.
   d. women who spread mud on the White House grounds to protest being denied the vote.

7. Which of the following was *not* an electoral reform designed to give people a more direct voice in politics and government?
   a. initiative and referendum
   b. Seventeenth Amendment
   c. Eighteenth Amendment
   d. direct primary

8. Which statement about the progressive movement is correct?
   a. Progressives wanted to use the powers of government to restrain big business and protect the economically vulnerable.
   b. Most progressives rejected the capitalist system, preferring one based on cooperation for the good of the whole community.
   c. Like the earlier populist movement, the progressive movement was primarily agrarian based.
   d. Progressives respected civil liberties so highly that they rejected any legislation that dealt with personal morals, such as sexual activities, drinking, and choice of entertainment.

9. Which of the following preached the need for working-class revolution to seize the means of production from the employing class?
   a. Industrial Workers of the World
   b. American Federation of Labor
   c. International Ladies' Garment Workers' Union
   d. Niagara Movement

10. The "Wisconsin Idea" referred to
    a. the new city-manager and commission forms of municipal government.
    b. the attempts of midwestern progressives to limit immigration, stop prostitution, and prohibit sale of liquor.
    c. the municipal ownership of public utilities advocated by Mayor Tom Johnson.
    d. the program of economic and political reforms by state government pioneered by Governor Robert La Follette.

SHORT-ANSWER QUESTIONS

1. Explain the ways in which the populist and progressive reform movements were similar. In what ways were they different?

2. Which groups of people were attracted to the Socialist Party of America and/or the Industrial Workers of the World in the period 1900–1917? Why?

3. Who founded the National Association for the Advancement of Colored People (NAACP)? Why? How did the founders of the NAACP differ in their ideas from Booker T. Washington?

4. What were some of the political and economic-social reforms enacted by state governments under the leadership of progressive governors such as Robert La Follette?

5. Discuss the contributions of Theodore Roosevelt and his U.S. Forest Service chief, Gifford Pinchot, to the conservation movement. Was Roosevelt also a preservationist? Which of his actions indicate he was or was not?

6. Compare and contrast Theodore Roosevelt's New Nationalist platform with Woodrow Wilson's New Freedom.

ESSAY QUESTIONS

1. Discuss the roles played by women in the progressive movement or movements.

2. The author of Chapter 22 states that "on the issue of racial justice," the record of the Progressives was "generally dismal." Do you agree with this statement? Why or why not? (Support your position with as many relevant examples as possible of the actions of various progressives.)

3. In Chapter 22 the author concludes that the "Progressive Era . . . shines forth as a time when American politics seriously began to confront the massive social upheaval wrought by industrialization." But progressivism also "had its repressive, illiberal, and coercive dimensions." Write an essay either agreeing or disagreeing with this assessment. Support your position with as much specific evidence as possible.

4. Explain the reasons for the break between President Taft and the Insurgent (progressive) Republicans. What were the consequences of this break?

5. One historian has written this about progressive reform: "The Roosevelt Era . . . had been a period of beginnings, of a scattering of pioneer legislation. . . . The Wilson Era, building on this foundation, was a period of sweeping achievement." Do you agree with this statement? Why or why not? Support your position with as much specific evidence as possible.

23

World War I

OUTLINE AND SUMMARY

I. Defining America's World Role

A. *The Roosevelt Corollary in Latin America and the Balance of Power in Asia*

Theodore Roosevelt believed that the United States must play an active role in world affairs, protect American interests in Latin America, and preserve the balance of power in Asia. In 1904 he announced the Roosevelt Corollary. It warned European nations not to intervene in the Western Hemisphere to collect debts owed to their citizens. Instead, the United States would act as policeman in Latin America, keeping order there and seeing that finances were handled properly and debts repaid. Citing his corollary, Roosevelt had U.S. officials take over the Dominican Republic's customs service and manage its foreign debt. Roosevelt also mediated an end to the Russo-Japanese War and used his influence to obtain a peace settlement that maintained the balance of power in Asia. Afterward he tried to improve U.S. relations with Japan by negotiating a gentlemen's agreement to limit Japanese immigration and thus cool American prejudice. Discrimination against Japanese immigrants in the western states continued anyway.

B. *Dollar Diplomacy in China and Nicaragua*

Roosevelt's successor, William Howard Taft, concentrated on promoting American commercial interests abroad, a foreign policy referred to as dollar diplomacy. Taft attempted, without much success, to open greater investment opportunities in China for American business. Using the Roosevelt Corollary, Taft sent marines into Nicaragua to protect U.S. investors there and keep in power a government friendly to American business interests. The marines occupied Nicaragua from 1912 until 1933.

C. *Wilson and Latin America*

Despite criticizing Republican expansionism, Democratic president Woodrow Wilson proved just as interventionist in Latin America as Roosevelt and Taft. To keep order and create a favorable climate for American investors, Wilson ordered marines to occupy the Dominican Republic and Haiti. The marines stayed to supervise those governments until 1924 and 1934, respectively. Wilson repeatedly intervened in Mexico during its revolution, trying to bring to power leaders who were liberal, democratic, and friendly to capitalistic enterprise. U.S.

foreign policy in Asia and Latin America between 1900 and 1914 showed that the United States was willing to become involved in foreign affairs to keep order, encourage the kinds of governments the United States approved of, and protect U.S. economic interests. These same tendencies would later pull the country into World War I.

II. War in Europe

A. *The Coming of War*

Colonial rivalries, arms races, aggressive nationalism, suppressed nationalities, a system of rival alliances, and the romantic notion that war brought out the best in men and countries were all underlying causes of World War I in Europe. In 1914 a Serbian nationalist assassinated the heir to the Austrian throne, an event that precipitated the fighting.

B. *The American People's Initial Responses*

As soon as war began in Europe, President Wilson proclaimed U.S. neutrality and asked the American people to be neutral "in thought as well as in action." Most Americans agreed with Wilson that the United States should not fight, but few had neutral feelings. Wilson and the majority of Americans had emotional bonds with England.

C. *The Perils of Neutrality*

Despite his initial proclamation of neutrality, Wilson asked Congress to declare war on Germany in 1917. What accounts for this turnabout? First, Wilson became convinced that, for the United States to shape the postwar settlement, it must participate in the fighting. Second, Wilson's handling of the issue of neutral rights on the high seas pulled the country into a war with Germany. The British violated our rights to trade by mining the North Sea and stopping ships and goods bound for Germany. Wilson's protests were not vigorous enough to prevent the British from ending almost all German-American trade. Germany retaliated with unrestricted submarine warfare. This led to injuries and the deaths of civilians, including Americans, in the sinking of Allied ships such as the *Lusitania,* the *Arabic,* and the *Sussex.* In ever more threatening notes, Wilson warned Germany to stop unrestricted submarine warfare or the United States would break off diplomatic relations. Some Americans—Secretary of State Bryan, the sponsors of the Gore-McLemore Resolution, and the founders of the Woman's Peace party—believed Wilson's abandonment of the "true spirit of neutrality" would pull the country needlessly into the armed conflict. Finally, American citizens between 1914 and 1917 developed a large economic stake in an Allied victory, making neutrality much more difficult. U.S. trade with the Allies increased nearly fourfold, and American investors lent them $2.3 billion to finance these purchases, on which the United States' continued prosperity depended.

D. *Stalemate in the Trenches*

Between 1914 and 1917 the war on the Western Front in Europe degenerated into a bloody stalemate. British propaganda in the United States charged that the Germans were committing atrocities. German counterpropaganda proved ineffective.

E. The Election of 1916

The war was a major issue in the 1916 election. Because the Democrats sensed the American public's desire for peace, Wilson ran for reelection on the slogan, "He kept us out of war." Charles Evans Hughes, the Republican nominee, sometimes called for a tougher stand against Germany and other times criticized Wilson for having been too threatening. Wilson's close victory seemed to indicate that the majority of Americans still hoped to avoid participation in the conflict.

F. The United States Enters the War

Because Germany decided that full use of its submarines would contribute more to its victory than keeping the United States out of the war, it fully unleashed its U-boats on January 31, 1917. In light of his past warnings, Wilson felt he had no alternative but to break off diplomatic relations. During February and March, German U-boats attacked five American ships, and the United States learned of the Zimmermann telegram. On April 2, 1917, Wilson asked Congress to declare war on Germany, which it did after a short, bitter debate. Three important factors produced this declaration: German attacks on American shipping, U.S. economic investment in the Allied cause, and American cultural links to the Allies.

III. Mobilizing at Home, Fighting in France

A. Raising an Army

After declaring war on Germany, Congress passed the Selective Service Act, under which nearly 3 million men were drafted. In addition, more than 11,000 women volunteered for the navy and marines, where they were assigned to noncombat support services.

B. Organizing the Economy for War

To mobilize the economy behind the war effort, the federal government imposed an unprecedented amount of regulation on American business. It did this by creating thousands of special wartime agencies. The most powerful of these, the War Industries Board, allocated scarce materials, established production priorities, and introduced more efficient production practices. The Food Administration encouraged farmers to increase output, while exhorting civilians to conserve food and fiber. The U.S. Railroad Administration consolidated all the privately owned rail lines into one, unified, government-operated system for the duration of the war.

C. With the AEF in France

The American Expeditionary Force (AEF) sent some 2 million soldiers to France in 1917 and 1918. They arrived at a critical time for the Allies. After the Bolsheviks came to power in Russia, that country dropped out of the war, which freed the German armies on the Eastern Front to fight in the west. With these reinforcements Germany launched an offensive in the spring of 1918 that brought its troops within fifty miles of Paris. American soldiers were rushed to the front, where they helped to stop the German advance.

D. *Turning the Tide*

By July 1918 U.S. troops were participating in the Allied counteroffensive that, through the summer and fall, drove the Germans out of much of France. In the often brutal fighting, soldiers lost their illusions about war being a great adventure. An influenza epidemic that swept Europe and the United States in 1918 added to the suffering and death.

E. *African-Americans in the AEF*

More than 260,000 blacks were drafted or volunteered for service in World War I. Fifty thousand went to France. The armed forces were riddled with racism. The army assigned African-Americans to segregated regiments and gave them more than their fair share of menial, heavy-labor duties. The navy used blacks only as messboys, and the marines excluded them entirely. Racist civilians provoked clashes with black troops stationed in Houston and other southern cities. Nonetheless, several African-American regiments served with distinction; one received the French Croix de Guerre.

IV. Promoting the War and Suppressing Dissent

A. *Advertising the War*

Wilson believed that the federal government must promote unanimous support for the war. Secretary of the Treasury William G. McAdoo pioneered in using advertising techniques and propaganda to sell war bonds. With posters, parades, and movie stars as sales promoters, McAdoo was able to sell enough bonds to finance approximately two-thirds of the war costs. The remainder was paid for with increased federal income and other taxes. The main job of popularizing the war fell to George Creel's Committee on Public Information. It created posters, advertisements, news releases, and films and sent seventy-five thousand speakers around the nation.

B. *Intellectuals, Cultural Leaders, and Reformers Present Arms*

Many progressive reformers, muckrakers, teachers, and religious leaders supported the war, echoing Wilson's assertion that we were in a struggle to spread liberalism, democracy, and other American values.

C. *Wartime Intolerance*

The Creel committee's propaganda produced a wave of anti-German hysteria and hatred of anyone who questioned America's participation in the war. As fear and intolerance mounted, German-Americans were victimized, and antiwar radicals were verbally and physically attacked.

D. *Opponents of the War*

Despite all the "patriotic" pressure, some Americans continued to oppose the war. These included some German-Americans and religious pacifists. A minority of women's rights and progressive leaders, such as Jane Addams and Randolph Bourne, pointed out that the war was killing reform and unleashing reaction and intolerance. Many socialists branded the war a crusade to protect capitalists' profits and saw no reason for workers to die to enrich their bosses.

E. Suppressing Dissent by Law

The government attempted to silence these dissenters with the repressive Espionage and Sedition acts. These made it a crime to criticize the war, government, Constitution, or armed forces. Some fifteen hundred people were convicted and jailed; the Socialist Party of America's leader, Eugene Debs, received a ten-year prison term. The Supreme Court upheld the constitutionality of the laws with the "clear and present danger" doctrine.

V. Economic and Social Trends in Wartime America

A. Boom Times in Industry and Agriculture

Stimulated by war, the American economy boomed. The real income of farmers and unskilled workers rose significantly. Thousands of workers streamed into industrial centers to take jobs in war plants. The influx created terrible housing, school, and other shortages in these cities.

B. Blacks Migrate Northward

Reduced immigration and soaring war production created labor shortages in northern industry. From labor recruiters, black-owned newspapers, letters, and word of mouth, southern blacks learned of these new job opportunities. Hoping to escape southern racism and find good jobs, an estimated half a million black people migrated to the North. In northern cities whites resented the black newcomers, who competed for jobs and housing. In places such as East St. Louis, Illinois, race riots broke out.

C. Women and the War

Many women's rights activists hoped that the war would lead to equality for women. During the war thousands of women served in the military and in volunteer organizations. About one million took jobs in industry. Arguing that women should be rewarded for their major contributions to winning the war, the woman-suffrage movement finally got the Nineteenth Amendment added to the Constitution by 1920. Aside from the vote, women lost many of their wartime gains after the armistice. Those holding well-paying jobs in industry generally were replaced by men returning from wartime service.

D. The War and Progressivism

The war strengthened the prohibition movement. The antiliquor forces argued that the "unpatriotic" German-American brewers should be put out of business and that grain used to manufacture whiskey and gin would be better used to feed the armed forces and our allies. In this atmosphere the Eighteenth Amendment, banning the manufacture, transportation, or sale of alcoholic beverages, was ratified by 1919. The war also boosted the Progressive Era antiprostitution campaign and produced a brief flurry of protective labor laws.

VI. Joyous Armistice, Bitter Aftermath

A. Wilson's Fourteen Points

Wilson presented his fourteen-point peace plan in a speech to Congress in January 1918. It included self-determination, impartial adjustment of colonial claims, freedom of the seas, reduced armaments, and a world association of nations, among other proposals. Whether Wilson could get these ideas incorporated in the treaties signed at the end of the war remained to be seen.

B. Armistice

In October 1918 the Kaiser's government asked Wilson for an armistice based on the Fourteen Points. Almost immediately afterward revolutionaries in Germany deposed the Kaiser and proclaimed a republic. Representatives of the new republic signed the armistice with the Allies on November 11, 1918.

C. The Versailles Peace Conference

Wilson personally headed the American delegation to Versailles. He appointed no prominent Republicans to the delegation, a political mistake since a Republican-controlled Senate would have to ratify any treaty signed. At the conference Wilson had to compromise with the Allied leaders, David Lloyd George and Georges Clemençeau, who had no faith in his Fourteen Points. The Treaty of Versailles that they produced contained some of Wilson's points, most importantly the Covenant of the League of Nations, but not all. Overall the treaty was harsh and punitive and aroused resentment and desire for revenge in Germany. Wilson and the Allied leaders also attempted to overthrow the Bolsheviks in Russia and to isolate and weaken that communist-controlled nation.

D. The Fight over the League of Nations

Dismayed at the treaty's punitive features, Wilson concentrated his hopes on the League of Nations part of it. In July 1919 Wilson submitted the Treaty of Versailles to the Senate for ratification. There it ran afoul of Republican reservationists, led by Henry Cabot Lodge, and isolationists. Out of a mixture of partisanship and fear that U.S. participation in the league would embroil the country in future European wars, the Republicans blocked ratification. Had Wilson been willing to accept the modifications (reservations) that Lodge proposed concerning the league, the treaty would have been approved. Wilson, however, refused to compromise his principles any further.

E. Racism and Red Scare

The war-generated intolerance and antiradical hysteria reached a peak in 1919–1920. Lynch mobs killed seventy-six blacks, and race riots broke out in more than twenty-five cities; the bloodiest occurred in Chicago. A rash of postwar strikes and a series of bombing incidents convinced many Americans that the country was on the verge of a communist uprising. To protect against this supposed danger, the Justice Department, under A. Mitchell Palmer, raided the homes and meeting places of suspected radicals and arrested more than four thousand of them, although there was no evidence that they had committed any crime. Aliens suspected of radicalism were deported.

F. The Election of 1920

The election of 1920 came in the midst of the violence and repression. The Democratic nominee, James Cox, was soundly defeated by Republican Warren G. Harding, who appealed to the public with his promise of a return to "normalcy."

VII. Conclusion

World War I brought death to 10 million people worldwide, including 112,000 Americans. The war transformed American society, helped finally to pass the Eighteenth and Nineteenth amendments, and gave the country its first taste of active government regulation of the economy, although the federal supervisory agencies were often run by businessmen friendly to corporate interests. The intolerance and repression that grew during the war, however, arrested further progressive reform.

VOCABULARY

The following terms are used in Chapter 23. To understand the chapter fully, it is important that you know what each of them means.

belligerent   a country at war

contraband   defined in international law as goods that neutrals cannot supply to one belligerent except at the risk of seizure and confiscation by the other; goods imported or exported illegally

liberal   favorable to progress and reform in economic and political affairs and to individual self-expression and liberty; associated with representative government rather than aristocratic, authoritarian, or dictatorial rule

coup   the act of a small group in bringing about a sudden change of government illegally and/or by force

armistice   a truce; a suspension of fighting by agreement of the parties so they can discuss peace terms

dissent   disagreement with the majority opinion and/or that of the authorities, such as the government

sedition   incitement of resistance or rebellion against the government; action or language promoting such resistance

self-determination   the freedom of a people or nationality to decide for itself the form of government it shall have

autonomy   the right of self-government or independence

abdicate   give up power and the right to govern

reparations   compensation in money, material, labor, etc., by a defeated nation for damage done to civilian populations and property during war

mandate or trusteeship a commission given to one nation by an associated group of nations (such as the League of Nations) to administer the government and affairs of a people in a territory judged not yet ready for self-government and independence

IDENTIFICATIONS

After reading Chapter 23, you should be able to identify and explain the historical significance of each of the following:

Roosevelt Corollary

gentlemen's agreement

dollar diplomacy

General John J. Pershing

U-boats and unrestricted submarine warfare

Lusitania

National Security League and preparedness

Jane Addams, Carrie Chapman Catt, and the Woman's Peace party

Sussex threat and pledge

Zimmermann telegram

Bernard Baruch and the War Industries Board

Herbert Hoover and the Food Administration

William G. McAdoo and the U.S. Railroad Administration

American Expeditionary Force

Vladimir Lenin and the Bolsheviks

George Creel and the Committee on Public Information

Randolph Bourne

Espionage and Sedition acts, 1917, 1918

Eugene Debs

Schenck v. *United States* and the "clear and present danger" doctrine

East St. Louis race riot, 1917; Chicago race riot, 1919

Eighteenth Amendment

Nineteenth Amendment

Wilson's fourteen-point peace plan

Council of Four at Versailles

Treaty of Versailles and Covenant of the League of Nations

Henry Cabot Lodge, reservationists, and irreconcilables

Article 10 of the League Covenant

Red Scare, 1919–1920, and the Palmer raids

SKILL BUILDING: MAPS

1. On the world map on the next page, locate the following places and explain how each of them was connected with U.S. foreign policy between 1900 and 1917:

Dominican Republic	Mexico	China	Japan
Haiti	Manchuria	Korea	Russia
Nicaragua			

World Map About 1900

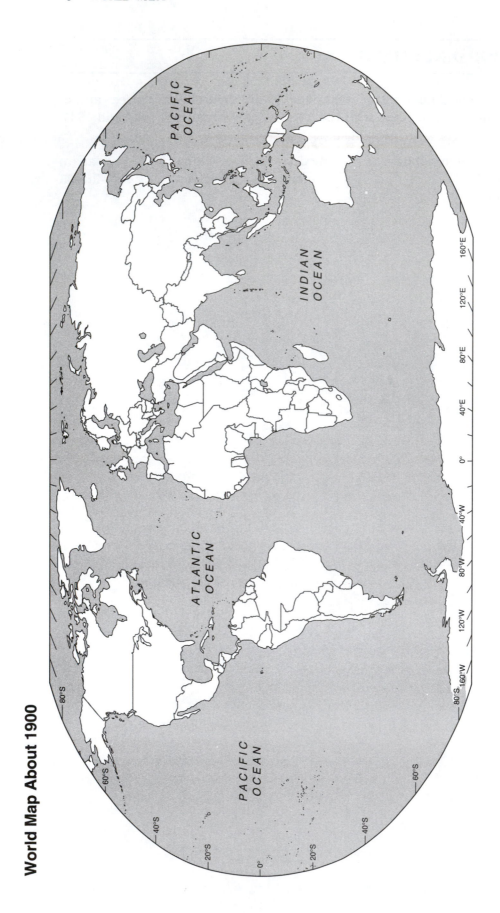

2. On the map of Europe during World War I, (1) indicate the Allied powers, the Central powers, and the neutral countries; (2) indicate the areas and the names of the countries occupied by the Central powers at the time of their greatest success; (3) locate Sarajevo and explain its significance; (4) locate the Marne and Meuse rivers, the Argonne Forest, and Verdun and explain their significance in the war on the Western Front; (5) draw in the Armistice Line of November 11, 1918.

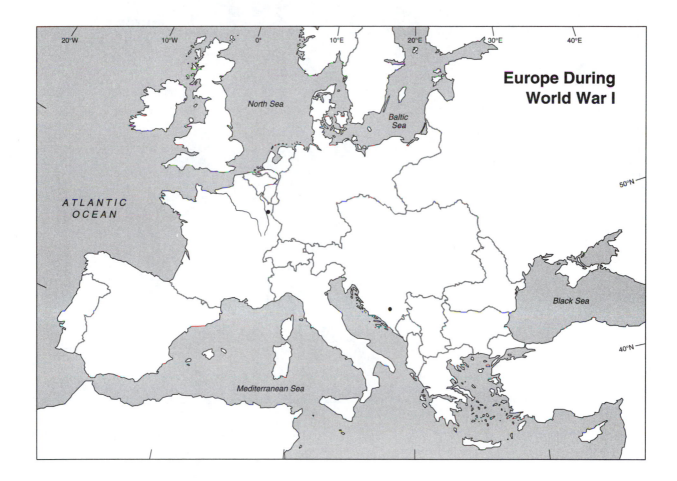

3. On the post–World War I map of Europe, (1) indicate the territories taken from Germany; (2) indicate the territories taken from Russia; (3) indicate the new nations created at the end of the war; (4) show what remained of Austria.

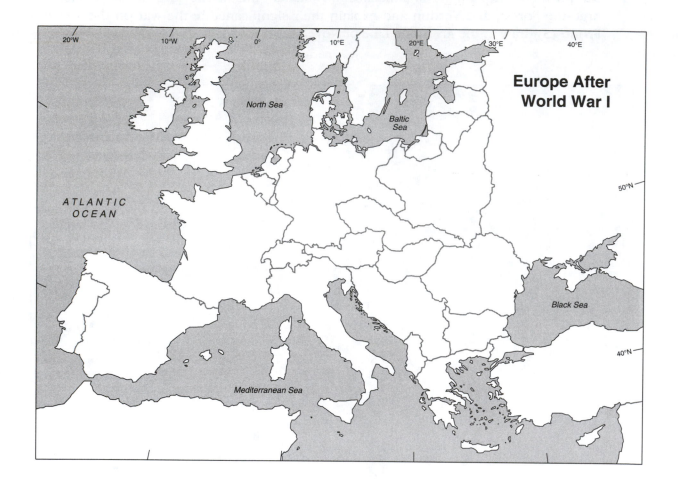

MULTIPLE-CHOICE QUESTIONS

Circle the letter of the item that best completes each statement or answers the question.

1. The Roosevelt Corollary
   a. asserted that the United States had the right to act as policeman in Latin America to keep order and prevent chronic wrongdoing.
   b. was issued to justify the role the United States played in ending the Russo-Japanese War.
   c. reversed that part of the Monroe Doctrine that stated the United States would not intervene in European affairs.
   d. warned the European powers and Japan not to exclude American business interests from China.

2. In the first seventeen years of this century, the United States intervened with military force in all of the following places *except*
   a. Nicaragua.
   b. Mexico.
   c. Jamaica.
   d. Haiti.

3. Secretary of State William Jennings Bryan resigned because
   a. he felt Wilson should have asked for a declaration of war after Germany sank the *Lusitania*.
   b. he believed Wilson's *Lusitania* notes and insistence that Germany stop unrestricted submarine warfare would embroil us in the war.
   c. he wanted Wilson to protest more strongly against British violation of U.S. neutral rights.
   d. he wanted to challenge Wilson for the presidential nomination in 1916.

4. Dollar diplomacy refers to
   a. Woodrow Wilson's allowing U.S. bankers to lend more than $2 billion to the Allies between 1915 and 1917.
   b. William Howard Taft's promotion of U.S. commercial interests in Asia and Latin America.
   c. Theodore Roosevelt's financing of the building of the Panama Canal.
   d. Wall Street's eagerness for the United States to enter World War I.

5. The Zimmermann telegram
   a. pledged that Germany would not sink any more merchant ships without giving warning and saving civilians.
   b. proposed an alliance between Germany and Mexico against the United States; after victory, Mexico would receive New Mexico, Texas, and Arizona.
   c. contained proof that the Germans were committing such atrocities as bayoneting babies.
   d. revealed Germany's designs to conquer and colonize much of Central and South America.

6. The war hastened the approval of two constitutional amendments. These provided for
   a. votes for women and prohibition.
   b. the eight-hour workday and an end to child labor.
   c. equal pay for men and women and votes for black Americans.
   d. direct popular election of U.S. senators and an end to poll taxes.

7. In the case of *Schenck* v. *United States*, the Supreme Court
   a. held that the U.S. Railroad Administration had acted unconstitutionally in taking over privately owned rail lines.
   b. upheld convictions under the Espionage Act on the grounds that free speech could be curtailed when it presented a "clear and present danger" to the country.
   c. ruled that segregated facilities for whites and blacks were acceptable as long as the accommodations were equal.
   d. held that the federal government did *not* have the right to propagandize its own people as George Creel's Committee on Public Information was doing.

8. Which of the following statements is *not* true of the Wilson administration during World War I?
   a. It took over and ran the railroads and imposed greater federal regulation over the economy than ever before in U.S. history.
   b. It set up a federal agency to build public support for the war with news releases, posters, speakers, and other propaganda.
   c. It interned all Japanese-Americans in ten guarded camps until the war was won.
   d. It sold millions of dollars worth of government bonds to Americans through techniques learned from advertising and public relations.

9. The Treaty of Versailles
   a. resembled for the most part Wilson's fourteen-point peace plan.
   b. turned over to Russia large blocks of territory in eastern Europe.
   c. disarmed Germany and stripped her of her colonies.
   d. failed to create an association of nations as Wilson had promised it would.

10. In the two years immediately after World War I, the United States
   a. enjoyed improved relations and cooperation between labor and management.
   b. joined the League of Nations and began to play a larger role in world affairs.
   c. showed a renewed interest in progressive reform and elected an administration promising to carry on Wilson's New Freedom.
   d. experienced heightened racial violence and antiradical hysteria.

SHORT-ANSWER QUESTIONS

---

1. Who were the candidates and what were the major issues in the election of 1916?

2. Discuss the experiences of African-Americans in the U.S. armed forces during World War I.

3. Discuss the people who opposed U.S. entry into World War I. Who were they? Why did they oppose participation?

4. How did World War I help gain passage and ratification of the Eighteenth and Nineteenth amendments?

5. What caused the Red Scare of 1919–1920? What actions did U.S. Attorney General A. Mitchell Palmer take during the scare?

6. Why can the election of 1920 be seen as a repudiation of President Wilson and all he stood for?

ESSAY QUESTIONS

1. In what ways did U.S. policy in Asia and Latin America between 1900 and 1917 foreshadow U.S. intervention in World War I?

2. In 1914 Woodrow Wilson proclaimed U.S. neutrality and asked the American people to be neutral in thought as well as action. In April 1917 Wilson asked Congress to declare war on Germany. What brought about this turnaround in American policy toward World War I?

3. During World War I how did the U.S. government attempt to mobilize the economy, influence public opinion, and silence all dissent?

4. Discuss the impact of World War I on the home front. Include in your answer the effects of the war on business, labor, agriculture, African-Americans, and women.

5. Woodrow Wilson wanted to draw up a liberal settlement at the end of the war that would ensure peace and democracy for generations thereafter. What prevented the realization of his plans?

24

The 1920s

I. A New Economic Order

A. A Decade of Prosperity

Demobilization following World War I disrupted the economy, causing a sharp recession. By 1922 recovery had set in, and for the rest of the decade the economy grew rapidly and prospered. Development of the electrical-appliance (refrigerators, washing machines, vacuum cleaners) and automobile industries contributed to this economic growth and prosperity. Mass production of cars created hundreds of thousands of jobs and stimulated a host of related industries, such as rubber, oil, steel, and highway construction. American business also invested heavily abroad during the 1920s.

B. New Modes of Producing, Managing, and Selling

Introduction of the assembly line and other technological advances brought more than a 40 percent increase in productivity between 1919 and 1929. This led to bigger profits and a wave of corporate mergers. By 1929 one hundred corporations controlled almost half the business done in America. Competition also disappeared as corporations joined together in trade associations to fix prices and divide up markets, and networks of chain stores displaced small, independently owned retail stores. Big business successfully boosted sales and profits by introducing installment buying and relying more heavily than ever on advertising. Business influence and values pervaded all areas of American life in the 1920s: big businessmen became the new cultural heroes, politicians vied to serve business, and organized religion tried to copy its selling techniques.

C. Women in the New Economic Era

The proportion of women working outside the home stayed at about 24 percent throughout the decade. Working women earned less than men holding similar jobs. The growth of large corporations increased the need for secretaries, typists, and filing clerks, and most of these positions were taken by women. Few women, however, broke into management or the professions, other than the traditionally female ones, such as teaching and nursing.

D. Workers in a Business Age

The 1920s were an unsuccessful time for organized labor. Union membership fell from 5 million in 1920 to 3.4 million in 1929. Management discouraged the growth of unions by intimidation, violence, insistence on the open shop, use of scab labor during strikes, and introduction by some companies of benefits such as stock purchase plans. Although the wages of skilled workers and those with strong unions rose during the decade, the majority of unskilled laborers saw little improvement in pay. Southern, black, Mexican-American, recent immigrant, and female workers clustered at the bottom of the wage scale.

E. Ailing Agriculture

American farmers did well during World War I, but after the armistice, both the European and domestic markets contracted, and prices plunged. Farmers, hard-pressed to repay loans and meet mortgage payments, tried to compensate by growing more. This created surpluses that drove down produce prices further. Members of the farm bloc in Congress attempted to help farmers with the McNary-Haugen bill. It provided for government purchase of surplus produce at a fixed price and resale abroad for whatever it would bring. The bill passed Congress twice, but President Coolidge vetoed it each time. Agriculture remained a depressed sector of the economy throughout the decade.

II. Republicans in Power

A. The Harding and Coolidge Years

A conservative-controlled Republican convention in 1920 nominated Warren G. Harding for president. He then won handily over his Democratic opponent, James M. Cox. The Harding administration was riddled with corruption. Veterans' Bureau chief Charles Forbes stole bureau funds. Attorney General Harry Daugherty and his Justice Department underlings sold influence and immunity from prosecution. Secretary of the Interior Albert Fall leased government oil reserves at Elk Hills, California, and Teapot Dome, Wyoming, to favored businessmen in exchange for bribes. On Harding's death, Coolidge assumed the presidency and corruption died down; however, the probusiness attitudes of the Harding years continued. By twice raising the tariff, the government protected domestic manufacturers from foreign competition. Secretary of the Treasury Andrew Mellon convinced Congress to lower federal taxes for the wealthy. Under Chief Justice William Howard Taft, a Harding appointee, the Supreme Court declared unconstitutional the federal child labor law and the minimum wage act for women workers in Washington, D.C.

B. Foreign Policy in an Isolationist Age

Harding's secretary of state, Charles E. Hughes, called an international naval arms conference in Washington, D.C., in 1921. Out of this conference emerged treaties that imposed a ten-year moratorium on battleship construction and pledged the major powers to respect each other's territorial possessions in the Pacific. Other than calling this conference, the Republican administrations of the 1920s followed an isolationist foreign policy, refusing to join both the League of Nations and the World Court. These administrations also insisted that our World War I allies repay a portion of their war debts to us, then made it difficult for them to do so by curtailing their sales in the United States with high protective tariffs.

C. Progressive Stirrings, Democratic Divisions

Progressive reform sentiment did not completely disappear in the 1920s. A coalition of labor and farm groups in 1924 revived the Progressive party and nominated Robert La Follette for president. A Democratic party badly split between its urban and rural wings nominated an unappealing compromise candidate, John W. Davis. With the economy booming, the Republican incumbent, Calvin Coolidge, won the presidency easily.

D. Women and Politics in the 1920s: A Dream Deferred

Ratification of the Nineteenth Amendment granting women the vote had less impact on politics in the 1920s than many women's rights advocates had predicted. During this period the women's movement splintered: some feminists devoted their efforts to the peace movement; others argued among themselves over backing an equal rights amendment.

III. Mass Society, Mass Culture

A. A Nation of Cities, Consumer Goods, and Automobiles

This was the first decade in which the majority of Americans lived in cities. Throughout the 1920s city life-styles and values spread to more and more of the population. Radio, movies, advertising agencies, and popular magazines, and the messages they carried, all emanated from cities. The new consumer goods were most readily available to city dwellers. New electrical appliances transformed household duties, as did the rise of supermarkets and commercial bakeries. Automobiles had the biggest impact on American culture. Traffic jams, parking problems, mounting accidental deaths, reduced parental supervision of young adults, and the spread of suburbs are examples of the changes brought by cars.

B. Soaring Energy Consumption and a Threatened Environment

The mass production and sales of automobiles and electrical appliances took a heavy toll on the environment and natural resources. Generating enough electricity to power the new appliances consumed millions of tons of coal, barrels of oil, and feet of natural gas, but the most voracious users of gasoline were the millions of automobiles. Not only did the nation waste and heedlessly deplete fossil fuels, but cars, power plants, steel mills, and other industries supplying the ever-growing demand for energy polluted the atmosphere. Cars also made it easier for people to visit and settle in former wilderness areas, which were being paved over and disappearing at an accelerated rate. A few groups protested, but Americans on the whole were indifferent to the environmental threat.

C. Routinized Work, Mass-Produced Pleasure

As assembly-line production made work less fulfilling and time-consuming, Americans turned increasingly to mass-produced entertainment for gratification. Popular magazines, such as *Reader's Digest,* built massive circulations. All over America people listened to the same radio programs and watched the same movies, thus producing a more homogeneous national culture.

D. Fads, Celebrities, and Heroes

The mass communication made possible by radio and film created a series of nationwide fads, heroes, and media events. Examples include the mah-jong craze; sports celebrities like Babe Ruth, Gertrude Ederle, and Jack Dempsey; and the wild acclaim showered on Charles A. Lindbergh for his solo flight across the Atlantic.

IV. Cultural Ferment and Creativity

A. The Jazz Age and the Postwar Crisis of Values

In the so-called Jazz Age, some young people rejected the values of their elders on sexual matters, dress, and decorum. The ideas of Sigmund Freud became popular. Women asserted their freedom by discussing sex openly, wearing makeup, smoking, and shortening their skirts and their hair. This upheaval in manners and morals primarily affected the urban middle class. Most farmers, blacks, industrial workers, and recent immigrants were more concerned with economic survival than experimenting with new life-styles.

B. Alienated Writers

The decade saw the emergence of many talented writers, including Sinclair Lewis, Willa Cather, Ernest Hemingway, and F. Scott Fitzgerald. They were often critical of both the narrow-minded, small-town values of prewar America and the materialistic business culture of the twenties. Some felt so uncomfortable with 1920s America that they spent much of the decade abroad, and yet they cared deeply about finding and creating "an authentic" American culture through their works.

In these same years, the growing black population in northern cities, especially New York, stimulated a flowering of African-American creative activity known as the Harlem Renaissance. All-black stage shows played on Broadway, and African-American writers explored the black experience in poems and novels.

C. Achievements in Architecture, Painting, and Music

American cities in the 1920s were filled with skyscrapers, an architectural trend applauded by many and denounced by others. More than ever, American artists painted the American scene, urban and rural, past and present. Some of the most talented were Thomas Hart Benton, Edward Hopper, John Sloan, and Georgia O'Keeffe. New classical composers appeared, such as Aaron Copland, but the unique contribution of America to the musical world was jazz. In the twenties composers and performers such as George Gershwin, Bessie Smith, Louis Armstrong, and Duke Ellington gained national and international recognition.

D. Advances in Science and Medicine

Americans made strides in many areas of science. Arthur H. Compton won the 1927 Nobel Prize for his studies on X-rays; medical researchers found more effective treatments for diphtheria, whooping cough, measles, and influenza, thus increasing life expectancy. Robert Goddard began his work in rocketry.

V. A Society in Conflict

A. Immigration Restriction

The United States, in 1921, 1924, and 1929, passed restrictive laws that drastically cut the total number of immigrants permitted to enter the country and established quotas for each nationality. Reflecting the fears and intolerance of the time, the laws excluded Chinese and Japanese entirely, and Eastern and Southern Europeans received small quotas. This discriminatory, national-origins quota system remained in American law until 1965. The laws did not curtail immigration from Western Hemisphere countries, which continued to be heavy throughout the 1920s.

B. The Sacco-Vanzetti Case

The Sacco-Vanzetti case further illustrates the intolerance and divisions in society in the 1920s. Nicola Sacco and Bartolomeo Vanzetti were Italian immigrants who were convicted of, and finally executed for, robbery and murder. The evidence was circumstantial, but the prosecution probably prejudiced the jury against them by stressing their ethnic origin and political radicalism. Throughout the decade conservatives opposed the attempts of liberals to win a new trial for the pair.

C. The Ku Klux Klan

Another indication of social conflict and intolerance in the twenties was the rise of the Ku Klux Klan. Preaching hatred toward blacks, Jews, Catholics, immigrants, and the new urban values, the Klan grew to an estimated 5 million members. For a time it exerted real political power in a few states, including Oregon and Indiana. It threatened, intimidated, beat, and murdered those it considered dangerous to a "purified" America.

D. The Garvey Movement

Disillusioned to find the North almost as racist as the South, many poor urban blacks in the 1920s became followers of Marcus Garvey and his Universal Negro Improvement Association (UNIA). Garvey preached black pride, black separatism, and a return to Africa. At its peak the UNIA had eighty thousand members and became the first mass movement among African-Americans.

E. Fundamentalism and the Scopes Trial

A number of states passed laws prohibiting the teaching of any scientific theory that contradicted the account of human origin given in the Bible. When John T. Scopes, a high school biology teacher in Dayton, Tennessee, challenged his state's law, the American Civil Liberties Union hired a team of distinguished lawyers, headed by Clarence Darrow, to defend him. William Jennings Bryan assisted the prosecution. Although Scopes was convicted, the fundamentalist religious position was ridiculed in the courtroom and in the national press.

F. Prohibition

Prohibition split Americans. Its supporters were generally native-born, fundamentalist Protestants, especially those in rural areas. Its opponents included liberals, intellectuals, rebellious youths, and big-city immigrants. Enforcement of prohibition broke down almost immediately because many Americans did not believe in it and organized crime was busy supplying the demand for illegal liquor. Prohibition became a big issue in the 1928 election. Democrat Alfred E. Smith called for its repeal; Republican Herbert Hoover praised it as a "noble experiment."

VI. Hoover at the Helm

A. The Election of 1928

Herbert Hoover won the election by a landslide over Alfred Smith. Many rural, fundamentalist Protestants would not vote for Smith because he was a Catholic and a "wet" and he came from New York City, but the biggest reason for Hoover's victory was economic prosperity and Republican promises that things would get even better.

B. Herbert Hoover's Social Thought

Hoover encouraged voluntary cooperation among corporate leaders to raise wages, plan production and marketing, and standardize products. He believed that kind of self-regulation by business, rather than government intervention, would ensure economic growth and a better life for all. After the depression set in, his clinging to voluntarism and reluctance to use government power would greatly handicap his ability to deal with a sick economy.

VII. Conclusion

In the 1920s Americans tried to adjust to the mass production, mass culture, and urban society that had emerged. The decade's political leadership was conservative and backward-looking. Those who found this new world unfamiliar and threatening often reacted with repression and hate, like the champions of prohibition, the fundamentalists, and the Klansmen. Others embraced the new life-styles made possible by radios, cars, movies, and electrical appliances. The social ferment also produced an outpouring of creative energy: the Harlem Renaissance, jazz, and revitalized American literature.

VOCABULARY

The following terms are used in Chapter 24. To understand the chapter fully, it is important that you know what each of them means.

scabs   workers who take strikers' jobs

isolationist   one who favors a policy of nonparticipation in international affairs

taciturnity   disinclination to speak or be social; being given to few words

suffrage   the vote

materialistic   more devoted to accumulating products and possessions than to spiritual needs and considerations

iconoclasm   the attacking of others' cherished beliefs and practices

expatriates   persons who have withdrawn themselves from residence in their native country

cant   insincere statements of goodness or high ideals

eclectic   selected from different sources; selecting and using what is considered best from many different styles or systems

nativism   the policy of protecting the interests or ways of native inhabitants against those of immigrants; prejudice against or dislike for immigrants

charismatic   possessing personal qualities that give an individual influence or authority over large numbers of people

fundamentalism   a movement in American Protestantism that preaches that everything in the Bible is literally true and rejects any historical account or scientific theory that differs from biblical statements

speakeasies   places where liquor was illegally sold and consumed

anachronistic   referring to a thing placed out of its proper time; referring to a hangover from an earlier era

---

IDENTIFICATIONS

After reading Chapter 24, you should be able to identify and explain the historical significance of each of the following:

Henry Ford and *Fordism*

the open shop and the "American Plan"

the farm bloc and the McNary-Haugen bill

Teapot Dome and the other scandals of the Harding administration

Fordney-McCumber (1922) and Smoot-Hawley (1930) tariffs

Andrew Mellon

Charles Evans Hughes and the Washington Naval Arms Conference

Robert La Follette and the Progressive party

Jane Addams and the Women's International League for Peace and Freedom

Alice Paul and the National Woman's party

Oscar DePriest

Charles A. Lindbergh

F. Scott Fitzgerald

Sinclair Lewis

Ernest Hemingway

Willa Cather

Georgia O'Keeffe

Edward Hopper

George Gershwin

Duke Ellington

Harlem Renaissance

Langston Hughes

the Immigration Acts and the national-origins quota system

Sacco and Vanzetti

Marcus Garvey and the Universal Negro Improvement Association

John T. Scopes and the "monkey trial"

Aimee Semple McPherson

Volstead Act, "wets," and "drys"

Alfred E. Smith versus Herbert Hoover

SKILL BUILDING: GRAPHS AND CHARTS

Graphs and charts allow us to convey important historical information and trends in visual shorthand. Look at the graphs and charts in Chapter 24 as examples. First glance at the line graph "Economic Expansion, 1920–1929" on page 772. What does it indicate about industrial production in the 1920s as compared to the prewar years? During which years of the 1920s did the economy go into a short-lived but sharp recession?

Next turn to the pie chart "Women Employed in Professions and Occupations, 1910–1930" on page 775. Did the percentage of employed women in traditionally female occupations (domestic servants, waitresses, beauticians, and so on) change substantially between 1910 and 1930? Did the percentage of employed women working in factories and on farms increase or decrease between 1910 and 1930? Did the percentage of employed women engaged in clerical work increase significantly between 1910 and 1930? What about the percentage in professions?

Next turn to page 783 and look at the line graph "The Automobile Age: Passenger Cars Registered in the United States, 1900–1990." Roughly how many cars were registered in this country in 1910, 1920, 1925, and 1930? Did the number of registered vehicles rise more sharply during the twenties or thirties? How do you account for this?

Finally, look at the table on page 800 dealing with the elections of the 1920s and early 1930s. What does it indicate about American ethnic group voters and the Democratic party? Which was the only ethnic group that did not vote primarily Democratic by 1932? Why do you suppose that was?

HISTORICAL SOURCES

Chapter 24 uses as a source an in-depth community study of Muncie, Indiana, in the 1920s, conducted by two famous sociologists, Robert and Helen Lynd. Their findings, published in

1929 under the title *Middletown,* are referred to on pages 775 and 782–783. What generalizations about American society is the historian making from the findings reported in *Middletown?* Muncie, Indiana, was a medium-sized, midwestern town. Can we be certain that the attitudes, values, and life-styles that the Lynds found there were similar or identical to the ones that prevailed in huge eastern cities such as New York or in small communities in the Far West or Deep South? Does the text claim that a fairly homogeneous national culture emerged in the 1920s?

Look at "A Place in Time: Harlem in the Twenties." Do the attitudes, values, and lifestyles described in this cultural mecca of black America seem at all similar to those that the Lynds found in Muncie, Indiana?

MULTIPLE-CHOICE QUESTIONS

Circle the letter of the item that best completes each statement or answers the question.

1. The decade of the 1920s was the first one in which
   a. farmers drove down agricultural prices by producing a surplus.
   b. the majority of Americans worked in factories rather than on farms.
   c. the majority of Americans lived in cities.
   d. the majority of Americans owned television sets.

2. All of the following contributed to the general prosperity of the 1920s *except*
   a. the development of new consumer-goods industries, especially home electrical appliances.
   b. federal minimum-wage laws that ensured that workers were well paid and thus had additional purchasing power.
   c. the growth of the automobile industry.
   d. a marked increase in productivity due to new technology and industrial techniques, such as the moving assembly line.

3. American foreign policy toward Europe during the 1920s was characterized by
   a. a willingness to forgive and forget the World War I debts owed to the U.S. government by former allies.
   b. a desire to lead and dominate the League of Nations.
   c. isolationism, except for a willingness to enter into a treaty to curtail a naval arms race.
   d. a refusal to participate in the League of Nations but a willingness to join the World Court and abide by its decisions.

4. Which of the following is *not* associated with the Harding administration?
   a. the Teapot Dome scandal
   b. the Washington Naval Arms Conference
   c. probusiness policies such as raising tariff rates
   d. passage of the McNary-Haugen Act to raise farm prices

5. In the election of 1924,
    a. Catholicism and prohibition were the two main issues.
    b. the Democratic nominee, John W. Davis, won by a narrow margin over Republican Calvin Coolidge.
    c. labor, farm, and reform groups revived the Progressive party and ran Robert La Follette for president.
    d. the Democratic party nominated William Jennings Bryan for president for the fourth time.

6. Which of the following was *not* an African-American writer associated with the Harlem Renaissance?
    a. Willa Cather
    b. Langston Hughes
    c. Claude McKay
    d. Jean Toomer

7. The immigration laws passed during the 1920s
    a. favored Eastern and Southern Europeans over Western Europeans.
    b. barred Asian immigration.
    c. barred all Latin Americans from entering the United States.
    d. imposed a limit of 500,000 immigrants each year.

8. Marcus Garvey's Universal Negro Improvement Association
    a. appealed to the small class of black professionals but never to the masses of poor urban blacks.
    b. preached that blacks should remain in the rural South and specialize in farming.
    c. started black-owned business ventures and called for a return to Africa.
    d. gained its main following in the South among sharecroppers.

9. The Sacco-Vanzetti case
    a. pitted fundamentalists against modernists.
    b. indicated that it was difficult for radical immigrants to receive a fair trial in 1920s America.
    c. proved that most Eastern and Southern European immigrants were political radicals.
    d. ended in acquittal for the two Italian immigrants.

10. Which of the following 1920s figures was in many ways a precursor of later television evangelists?
    a. Charles A. Lindbergh
    b. Georgia O'Keeffe
    c. Oscar DePriest
    d. Aimee Semple McPherson

SHORT-ANSWER QUESTIONS

1. Explain why agriculture was economically depressed during the 1920s.

2. What happened to the trade union movement in the 1920s? Why?

3. In what ways did industrial and technological developments in the 1920s increase environmental dangers and the rapid use and waste of natural resources? Was government in the 1920s interested in either conservation or preservation?

4. Explain the economic and social impact of the booming automobile industry on America in the 1920s.

5. How effective was prohibition in reducing excessive drinking? Why wasn't it more successful? What were some of prohibition's socially harmful effects on American society?

6. Discuss Herbert Hoover's social thought. How did his outlook hinder him in fighting the depression that began during his presidency?

ESSAY QUESTIONS

1. What accounts for the economic growth and prosperity of the 1920s? Who benefited most from that prosperity? Who did not share in it and why?

2. Federal policies under presidents Harding and Coolidge reflected the probusiness attitudes of the 1920s. Write an essay discussing and illustrating this statement with specific examples.

3. Discuss the impact of the economic, cultural, and social changes of the 1920s on the lives of American women. Were the changes felt by working-, middle-, and upper-class women?

4. Sharp social conflicts existed in American society in the 1920s. These conflicts produced fear, intolerance, and attempts to "purify" the country by legislation and coercion. Write an essay discussing these conflicts and the attempts of government and private groups to bring back a more traditional and homogeneous America.

5. The 1920s were a time of changing manners and morals and of cultural ferment. Write an essay discussing the changes that took place in popular culture and among artists and intellectuals.

25

Crash, Depression, and New Deal

OUTLINE AND SUMMARY

I. Crash and Depression

A. Black Thursday

In 1928 a wave of wild speculation started. As 9 million Americans played the market in hope of quick profits, they drove stock prices to dangerously inflated levels. Worse yet, they often speculated on borrowed money; that is, they bought on margin. Low taxes for the rich engineered by Secretary of the Treasury Andrew Mellon and the easy-credit policy of the Federal Reserve Board contributed to the speculation. The optimistic buyers ignored warning signs such as the falloff of automobile sales and construction starts. Then, on October 24, 1929, Black Thursday, the speculative bubble burst; stock prices plummeted as panicked shareholders rushed to sell. On the following Tuesday the plunge continued. By mid-November the value of stock had declined by $30 billion. This stock market crash triggered the worst depression in American history.

B. Onset of the Depression

Between 1929 and 1933, the nation sank deeper and deeper into depression. Farm prices declined by 60 percent; more than 5,500 banks failed. Unemployment climbed from 3 percent to 25 percent of the labor force. One of the causes of this depression was maldistribution of wealth. The 40 percent of Americans at the lower end of the economic ladder received only 12 percent of the total national income, whereas most of the wealth generated by technological advances in the 1920s went to the corporate elite. As a result much of the population did not have enough income to keep buying the flow of goods from American factories, and the well-to-do had excess money to speculate with on the stock market. Already by 1929 the automobile, construction, textile, and other industries, with unsold inventories, were forced to cut back and lay off workers. The depressed agricultural sector further weakened the economy. Another cause of the depression was the collapse of European economies under the weight of World War I debt repayments and the unfavorable balance of trade with the United States. This caused our foreign sales to fall sharply.

C. *The Depression's Human Toll*

As banks failed, depositors lost billions in savings. Thirteen million people lost their jobs; millions of others suffered wage cuts and reduced hours. Everywhere banks foreclosed on farmers and homeowners who could not meet mortgage payments. Hospitals and clinics reported a growing number of malnutrition cases. The suicide rate rose by 30 percent.

D. *Hoover's Response*

President Herbert Hoover's ideological commitment to private-sector initiative, limited government intervention, and balanced federal budgets severely handicapped him in dealing with the depression. Hoover asked business leaders not to lay off any more workers or impose further wage cuts. Although businessmen initially agreed, they later broke their pledges because they could not sell their products. Hoover preached that private charity and local government must handle relief for the jobless, but private philanthropy and city and county governments were soon overwhelmed by the numbers needing help. Hoover signed legislation creating the Reconstruction Finance Corporation, which was empowered to lend money to failing business corporations, but he held out until July 1932 against using federal funds to assist the unemployed. He spent reluctantly on public works, fearing that too big a program would unbalance the budget. His pronouncements in favor of self-help made him seem indifferent to the suffering of depression victims.

E. *Mounting Discontent and Protest*

As conditions worsened, protests mounted. Midwestern farmers tried to raise agricultural prices by halting the shipment of food to cities. Destitute veterans marched on Washington demanding immediate cash payment of their bonuses for World War I service. Rather than explain to them why he opposed payment, Hoover ordered the army to remove the "bonus marchers" from the capital. The sight of armed troops expelling peaceful veterans convinced the public of Hoover's callousness.

F. *The Election of 1932*

The Republicans renominated Hoover, who stuck by his failed antidepression measures. The Democrats nominated Franklin D. Roosevelt. How he would fight the depression was not clear. Nonetheless, the anti-Hoover sentiments of the people carried FDR and the Democrats to lopsided victories in the presidential and congressional elections.

II. The New Deal Takes Shape

A. *New Beginnings*

The promise of government action and the mood of optimism in FDR's inaugural address lifted people's spirits. The relief, recovery, and reform measures that followed, known as the New Deal, were forged by many contributors. A circle of Roosevelt advisers called the "brain trust" devised broad "programs of federal economic planning." Eleanor Roosevelt and her social-worker and women-reformer friends pushed for legislation to assist the economically disadvantaged and minority groups. Secretary of Agriculture Henry A. Wallace advocated measures to aid hard-pressed farm owners. Old-time progressives, university professors, and able young lawyers joined the Roosevelt administration to contribute ideas and administer new programs.

B. The Hundred Days

Between March 9 and June 16, 1933, the administration introduced and Congress passed an unprecedented volume of legislation. These laws had the overall effect of greatly increasing federal involvement in the economy. The Federal Deposit Insurance Corporation (FDIC) insured bank accounts up to $5,000. The Civilian Conservation Corps (CCC) employed jobless young men on conservation projects. The Home Owners Loan Corporation and the Farm Credit Administration refinanced mortgages and thus saved the homes and farms of millions of Americans. Other important laws imposed regulation on the stock market and established the Tennessee Valley Authority (TVA) and the Public Works Administration (PWA). Washington entered the field of relief with the creation of the Federal Emergency Relief Administration (FERA). The Agricultural Adjustment Act (AAA) and the National Recovery Administration (NRA) aimed at reviving agriculture and business. The former guaranteed parity prices for agricultural produce and paid farmers for not growing crops that were in surplus. The NRA helped business draft and enforce codes to eliminate cutthroat competition, price-cutting, and other ruinous practices in exchange for management promises to bargain with unions chosen by their employees.

C. The NRA Bogs Down

After a brief upturn in the summer of 1933, the economy again slumped, and complaints about the NRA mounted. Management resented government encouragement of unions. Small businesses claimed that the codes helped only the big firms. The NRA bogged down in supervising code making in every possible industry. In 1935 a case challenging the constitutionality of the NRA reached the Supreme Court, and in a unanimous decision the justices struck it down.

D. Troubled Agriculture

Drought and the AAA reduced price-depressing surpluses, and as a consequence overall farm income rose by 50 percent between 1933 and 1937. However, the AAA did nothing for landless farm laborers, and it hurt tenants and sharecroppers. Landlords kicked many tenants and sharecroppers off their property and pocketed the government subsidy checks for withdrawing the land from production. Poor farmers also fell victim to the vast dust storms that rolled over the Upper South and Great Plains, destroying the crops in their paths. Ruined by nature and the AAA, many poor farmers, tenants, and sharecroppers headed for California, where they struggled to survive as migratory farm laborers. Between 1933 and 1935 New Dealers were split between whether the government should concentrate on pulling up the agricultural sector as a whole or on helping the rural poor. It was not until 1935 that legislation aiding farm laborers, tenants, and sharecroppers was passed.

E. Controversy over Relief Strategy

Harold Ickes, the careful PWA administrator, thoroughly checked each project to be underwritten by his agency. As a result the projects eventually built with PWA funds were enduring. In the short run, however, the PWA was slow to get work under way and slow to put money into the hands of the unemployed. Harry Hopkins, the less meticulous head of the FERA, quickly dispensed millions of dollars to the destitute. President Roosevelt, anxious for fast economic recovery, relied more and more heavily on Hopkins, transferring funds from the PWA to Hopkins's FERA and its work projects arm, the Civil Works Administration (CWA). Even after the CWA was terminated in the spring of 1934, Hopkins rather than Ickes dominated federal relief policy-making.

F. The New Deal in Midstream: Popularity and Problems

Although the first phase of FDR's New Deal did not end the depression, the president and his policies gained enthusiastic support from most Americans. This was demonstrated in the 1934 midterm congressional elections when, in contrast to the usual pattern in which the party in power lost seats, the Democrats greatly increased their majorities in the House and Senate.

III. The New Deal Changes Course

A. Introduction

Roosevelt, after receiving overwhelming endorsement from the people in the 1934 elections, took a swing to the left. In 1935 he proposed to Congress a new package of relief and reform measures known as the Second New Deal.

B. Challenges from Right and Left

One reason that FDR launched his Second New Deal was to combat the challenge to his administration from opponents on the political Right and Left. Certain big-business leaders and conservative Democrats and Republicans formed the American Liberty League in 1934. It denounced Roosevelt as a dictator who was leading the country down the path to socialism. Demagogic extremists, such as Charles E. Coughlin, Francis E. Townsend, and Huey Long, also were attacking the New Deal and proposing instead various panaceas for ending the depression. In 1934 and 1935 they were attracting thousands of followers. In addition, FDR embarked on his Second New Deal because the measures passed earlier, while bringing some improvement, had not lifted the economy out of the depression. The frustration with continued hard times showed itself in a wave of strikes, labor unrest, and protests, often led by communists and socialists.

C. The Second New Deal: Expanding Federal Relief

At Roosevelt's request Congress in 1935 passed the Emergency Relief Appropriation Act, granting nearly $5 billion for expanded work-relief programs. The largest part of the money went to the newly created Works Progress Administration (WPA), headed by Harry Hopkins. Between 1935 and 1943 the WPA spent $11 billion and employed more than 8 million people in a variety of construction, clerical, professional, and arts endeavors. Some of the appropriations also went to the National Youth Administration, which helped students support themselves with part-time jobs. Ickes's PWA shared in the money, too, using it for major construction projects. The large amount spent on these work-relief programs caused mounting federal budget deficits. According to British economist John Maynard Keynes, such deficit spending was a positive way to pump funds into the economy and combat the depression. Roosevelt never endorsed Keynesian economics, but he tolerated deficit spending as a short-term necessity to relieve suffering.

D. The Second New Deal: Turning Leftward

The massive relief programs and other laws of the Second New Deal were not intended to please all social classes. They openly aimed at serving the needs of labor and the rural and urban poor. The Resettlement Administration, created in May 1935, resettled and/or made loans to small farmers, tenants, and sharecroppers to turn them into farm owners on productive land. Although the Resettlement Administration aided the rural poor, agriculture as a whole suffered a blow when the Supreme Court in 1936 declared the AAA unconstitutional. The pro-union National Labor Relations (Wagner) Act of July 1935 stimulated the growth of organized labor. It required employers to recognize and bargain with their employees' unions and established the National Labor Relations Board to act as watchdog in labor-management relations. The Social Security Act of 1935 provided for old-age pensions, survivors' benefits for families of deceased workers, unemployment insurance, and aid to dependent mothers and children and the handicapped. Taxes imposed on employers and deductions withheld from employees' salaries financed the old-age and survivors' benefits. The Revenue Act of 1935 (which the wealthy called the "Soak the Rich" law) boosted taxes on corporations and upper-income Americans. These and other Second New Deal laws went a long way toward reducing the appeal of extremist demagogues and saving the capitalist system "by reforming its excesses and addressing some of its less desirable social consequences."

E. The Election of 1936: The New Deal at High Tide

The Republicans nominated Alfred Landon of Kansas to run against Roosevelt, whom the Democrats enthusiastically renominated. Roosevelt swept every state but Maine and Vermont, and the Democrats increased their large majorities in Congress.

F. The New Democratic Coalition

The victories resulted from a new Democratic coalition that had emerged, consisting of the South, urban immigrants, industrial workers, farmers, African-Americans, and women. Black voters were attracted to the Democratic party by Roosevelt's aid to the poor and his stepped-up appointments of blacks to responsible government positions. The Roosevelt administration also made careful efforts to cultivate women's votes.

G. The New Deal and the Environment

The New Deal achieved an impressive record in conservation. The CCC built hiking trails and fire lookout stations and planted thousands of trees. The Departments of Agriculture and the Interior taught farmers soil-conservation practices and stopped overgrazing on public lands. The TVA's dams controlled earth-eroding floods and harnessed the region's resources to serve the needs of its people. Congress created three more national parks, and the president heeded the lobbying of the Wilderness Society, established in 1935, by setting aside more than 7.5 million acres for wildlife refuges. The New Deal did not worry much about problems of atmospheric pollution, overpopulation, and dwindling global resources.

IV. The New Deal Draws to a Close

A. FDR and the Supreme Court

In February 1937 FDR proposed a court-reform bill that would allow the president to appoint a new Supreme Court justice to serve alongside each member of the Court who had reached seventy years of age and would not retire. Roosevelt requested this change because the aging, conservative majority on the Supreme Court had been declaring reform and recovery laws such as the NRA and AAA unconstitutional and seemed likely to invalidate the Social Security and Wagner acts that would soon be brought before it in test cases. Congress killed the president's "court-packing plan" and thereafter defied him on other matters as well. FDR did, however, influence a number of the elderly, conservative judges to modify their views or retire. The Supreme Court upheld the Wagner Act, and between 1937 and 1939 Roosevelt was able to fill four Court vacancies with liberal New Dealers.

B. The Roosevelt Recession

Roosevelt suffered another blow when the economy turned sharply downward in August 1937. The causes of this so-called Roosevelt recession included (1) a reduction in consumer spending power because of social-security deductions and (2) cutbacks, to try to balance the budget, in New Deal work and relief programs. Faced with rising unemployment and slumping industrial output, Roosevelt had to ask Congress for new appropriations to revive and expand the PWA, WPA, and other programs, which restarted economic recovery.

C. The End of the New Deal

In Roosevelt's second term, Congress passed only a few reforms. These included the National Housing Act; the Fair Labor Standards Act; the 1937 Farm Tenancy Act, which replaced the Resettlement Administration with the Farm Security Administration; and a second Agricultural Adjustment Act, similar to the first except for the processors' tax to which the Supreme Court had earlier objected. A coalition of conservative, southern Democrats and Republicans blocked further reform. Roosevelt attempted to break up this anti–New Deal coalition by asking voters to defeat conservatives in the 1938 elections. The people instead elected more conservatives. Thereafter, FDR switched his attention to foreign affairs and proposed no additional domestic reform, and the New Deal ended.

V. Conclusion

The New Deal chalked up impressive accomplishments in relief and reform, although it did not bring about full recovery. That would take World War II. Whereas business interests dominated Washington in the 1920s, in the 1930s government became more responsive to the needs of farmers, organized labor, and other interest groups. The New Deal left behind a permanently expanded and strengthened federal government and presidency.

VOCABULARY

The following terms are used in Chapter 25. To understand the chapter fully, it is important that you know what each of them means.

buying stock on margin   purchasing stock partly with one's own money and partly with money borrowed from a bank or broker specifically for the purpose of buying the stock

gross national product   the market value of the nation's total output of goods and services

foreclosure   the legal action by which a bank repossesses the house or farm of a borrower for failure to keep up regular payments on the mortgage

ideology   the doctrines believed by an individual or a group, often influencing their political and social actions

dark-horse candidate   a little-known or unlikely political figure who unexpectedly wins nomination

pump-priming   government spending (often to the point of creating a budget deficit) for the purpose of stimulating the economy

demagogue   an unprincipled political leader; one who leads people by playing on their prejudices, passions, and fears

panacea   a remedy for all ills; a cure-all

anti-Semitic   prejudiced against or intolerant of Jewish people

deficit spending   government expenditure in excess of its tax receipts and other revenues

collective bargaining   negotiation between employers and union representatives concerning wages, hours, and conditions of work

sacrosanct   sacred; not to be violated

disingenuous   not sincere; lacking in candor or frankness

IDENTIFICATIONS

After reading Chapter 25, you should be able to identify and explain the historical significance of each of the following:

Reconstruction Finance Corporation

bonus marchers

brain trust

Frances Perkins

Harold Ickes and the Public Works Administration

the Hundred Days

Civilian Conservation Corps

Federal Deposit Insurance Corporation

Federal Emergency Relief Act

Harry Hopkins

Tennessee Valley Authority

Agricultural Adjustment Acts, 1933, 1938

National Recovery Administration and Section 7a

Federal Securities Act and the Securities and Exchange Commission

Southern Tenant Farmers' Union

dust bowls and "Okies"

"fireside chats"

Second New Deal

Charles E. Coughlin, Francis E. Townsend, and Huey Long

Works Progress Administration

National Youth Administration

John Maynard Keynes and Keynesian economics

Resettlement and Farm Security administrations

National Labor Relations (Wagner) Act

Social Security Act

Revenue Act of 1935 ("Soak the Rich" law)

Mary McLeod Bethune and the "black cabinet"

Molly Dewson

National Housing Act, 1937

Fair Labor Standards Act, 1938

SKILL BUILDING: MAPS

On the map of the United States on the following page, locate each of the places listed below:

the seven-state region covered by the Tennessee Valley Authority

the areas affected by the dust storms (dust bowls) of the 1930s

Olympic National Park

Shenandoah National Park

Kings Canyon National Park

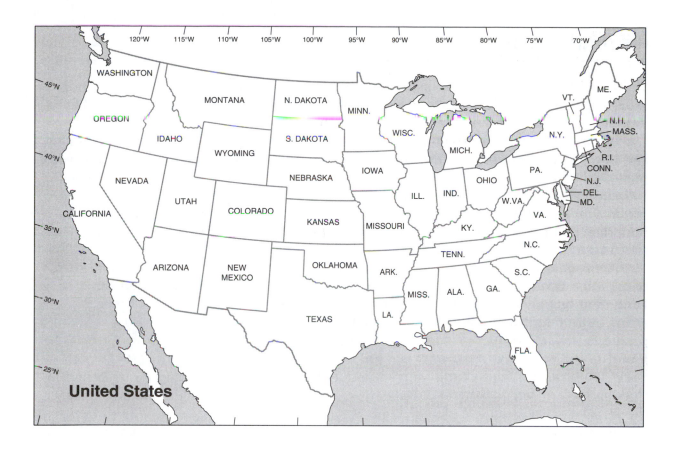

United States

SKILL BUILDING: GRAPHS

Look at the line and bar graphs on page 811, under the title "The Statistics of Hard Times." From these you should be able to learn the answers to many questions about the Great Depression and the New Deal. For example:

1. Judging from the statistics on personal income, unemployment rate, stock prices, and building construction, did the New Deal succeed in reviving the economy to 1929 levels at any point prior to the United States' 1941 entry into World War II?

2. What was the impact of World War II on economic recovery?

3. Judging from all of the statistics shown in the graphs, which was the worst year of the depression?

4. Herbert Hoover, during his presidency, kept predicting that prosperity was just around the corner. Is there anything in these graphs that would support his forecast? The Roosevelt administration claimed that it had made considerable headway in improving the economy by 1939. Do the graphs confirm that assertion?

HISTORICAL SOURCES

The sources of information that historians use to learn about the personalities, feuds, hopes, fears, and intentions of the men and women who wield power in each presidential administration are the memoirs, diaries, and histories those individuals write. Find the places in Chapter 25 that discuss Hugh Johnson, Frances Perkins, Eleanor Roosevelt, Harry Hopkins, and Harold Ickes. Part of what the historian knows about them comes from books that each published: Hugh Johnson, *The Blue Eagle from Egg to Earth*; Frances Perkins, *The Roosevelt I Knew*; Eleanor Roosevelt, *This I Remember*; Harry Hopkins, *Spending to Save*; and *The Secret Diary of Harold L. Ickes*. Why are such books good historical sources? Why is it important that historians check any "facts" they obtain from these memoirs, diaries, and histories against several other sources before relying on them?

On page 832 of the text and in "A Place in Time: Cimarron County, Oklahoma—Heart of the Dust Bowl," the author refers to pictures taken by Dorothea Lange and other New Deal photographers. In the 1930s the Farm Security Administration employed Lange, Walker Evans, Arthur Rothstein, and other talented photographers to compile a visual record of rural America: its people, problems, and poverty. A selection of these photographs can be found in the book *The Years of Bitterness and Pride: FSA Photographs, 1935–1943* (New York, 1975). Find a copy of this volume, and look at photographs 76 and 83 by Rothstein. Both show dust storm–battered Oklahoma in 1936. In what ways do the pictures enhance the verbal descriptions in "A Place in Time"?

Historians suggest that these dust storms were not unavoidable acts of nature; human use and misuse of the land contributed. How? What actions did the New Deal take to try to remedy the environmental damage?

MULTIPLE-CHOICE QUESTIONS

Circle the letter of the item that best completes each statement or answers the question.

1. In 1932 President Hoover used the army to expel which of the following protest groups from Washington, D.C.?
    a. farmers demanding that government support agricultural prices
    b. women demanding equal treatment from relief officials
    c. World War I veterans demanding immediate payment of their bonuses
    d. blacks demanding passage of a federal antilynching law

2. Who hoped to be elected president in 1936 by building a huge following for his "Share Our Wealth" scheme (confiscate the great private fortunes and redistribute the money to the poor)?
    a. Harold Ickes
    b. Henry Wallace
    c. Francis E. Townsend
    d. Huey Long

3. Which of the following best characterizes Herbert Hoover's handling of the depression?
   a. He followed the advice of Secretary of the Treasury Andrew Mellon to do nothing and wait for economic recovery to occur naturally.
   b. His efforts were limited by his fears of unbalancing the federal budget and concentrating too much power and responsibility in Washington.
   c. He refused to have the federal government help failing business corporations.
   d. He initiated vast new programs to employ the jobless, control farm surpluses, and regulate banking and the stock exchange.

4. The leader of Franklin Roosevelt's "black cabinet" was
   a. Hugh Johnson.
   b. Frances Perkins.
   c. Mary McLeod Bethune.
   d. Harold Ickes.

5. Two reforms passed during Roosevelt's second term were the
   a. Fair Labor Standards Act and National Housing Act.
   b. National Industrial Recovery Act and Agricultural Adjustment Act.
   c. Social Security Act and Wagner Act.
   d. SEC and WPA.

6. During the New Deal, which interest group exercised less influence over the federal government than it had in the 1920s?
   a. organized labor
   b. farmers
   c. business
   d. social workers

7. Which federal programs created during the Hundred Days were later declared unconstitutional by the Supreme Court?
   a. NRA and AAA
   b. FDIC and HOLC
   c. FERA and CCC
   d. TVA and PWA

8. Which of the following agencies was created during Hoover's administration to help failing business corporations and continued to be active through the New Deal years?
   a. Federal Emergency Relief Administration
   b. Tennessee Valley Authority
   c. Federal Deposit Insurance Corporation
   d. Reconstruction Finance Corporation

9. John Maynard Keynes's economic theory
   a. suggests that deficit spending by the government can stimulate economic recovery.
   b. was closely followed by Franklin Roosevelt and his New Deal.
   c. stresses the importance of a government's maintaining a balanced budget at all times.
   d. was proved wrong by America's experiences in the 1930s.

10. The "Okies"
    a. founded the American Liberty League.
    b. were farmers displaced by dust storms, depression, and the AAA who migrated to California.
    c. were the main followers of Dr. Townsend, who demanded a pension for elderly farmers and laborers.
    d. founded the first union for ranch hands, cowboys, and country-music performers.

SHORT-ANSWER QUESTIONS

1. What caused the huge stock market boom in 1928–1929 and its subsequent crash in October 1929? How did the practice of buying on margin contribute to both boom and bust?

2. Compare the New Deal's attitudes toward urban Democratic political machines and bosses with those of the earlier progressive reformers.

3. Which groups made up the new Democratic coalition that reelected Roosevelt by a landslide in 1936? Why was each group attracted to the New Deal?

4. Discuss the record of the New Deal on conservation and the environment.

5. Describe Roosevelt's court-packing plan. Why did he propose it? Did he win or lose the fight to remake the Supreme Court? Why?

6. What caused the "Roosevelt recession"? What did the New Deal do to combat it?

7. What brought about the end of the New Deal in 1939?

ESSAY QUESTIONS

1. Discuss the causes of the depression of the 1930s.

2. Compare and contrast President Hoover's and President Roosevelt's attempts to deal with the depression and its victims. Why did each president follow his particular course?

3. Discuss how the Roosevelt administration affected the lives of women and blacks. How much progress was made in raising each group to full political and economic equality with white males?

4. One historian has written, "When Franklin D. Roosevelt faced the newly elected Congress in 1935, the result promised to be a fresh outburst of reform and recovery legislation which would surpass even that of the Hundred Days." Explain what movements and events in America in 1934 and 1935 were pushing Congress and Roosevelt toward this new "outburst of reform."

5. Compare and contrast the legislation and programs of the first and second New Deals. In what ways was the second merely a continuation of the first? In what ways did the second represent a leftward shift, a significant change in direction? How successful was each in reviving the economy?

26

American Life in a Decade of Crisis at Home and Abroad

OUTLINE AND SUMMARY

I. The American People in the Depression Decade

A. *The Plight of a People*

The depression imposed tremendous suffering. Even with all the New Deal programs, the unemployment rate never fell much below 14 percent during the thirties. A quarter of all farm families had to accept relief to survive, as did 1 million elderly citizens. The hard times brought both physical and emotional distress to millions. According to one historian, much of the generation that lived through the depression carried with it thereafter an "invisible scar."

B. *Industrial Workers Unionize*

In 1933 fewer than 3 million workers belonged to unions. Management in the steel, automobile, textile, and other mass-production industries had defeated all previous attempts to organize their employees. In the 1930s the combination of hard times and the prolabor attitude of government revived interest in unions. At first the American Federation of Labor, committed to protecting the narrow interests of its skilled craft-union affiliates, failed to grasp the new opportunities. But some of its more activist leaders, including John L. Lewis and Sidney Hillman, in November 1935 established the Committee for Industrial Organization (later renamed the Congress of Industrial Organizations, CIO) and sent hundreds of organizers to the steel, rubber, car, and textile factories to sign up members in industrywide unions. In March 1937 Lewis convinced U.S. Steel to sign a contract recognizing the steelworkers' union and granting pay increases and a forty-hour workweek. When General Motors refused to negotiate, Walter and Victor Reuther and other United Automobile Workers (UAW) officials led sit-down strikes that halted all production for six weeks. President Roosevelt and the governor of Michigan refused to use the army or militia to dislodge the strikers, and the occupiers beat back the attacks of local police. Thus General Motors had no alternative but to sign a contract recognizing the UAW.

Henry Ford and Tom Girdler, leader of Republic and other "Little Steel" companies, refused to deal with unions and fought them with violence, as in the Battle of the Overpass and the Memorial Day Massacre. Even they, however, finally recognized and bargained with

133

unions by 1941. The textile workers of the South; agricultural laborers; domestics; and most women, black, and recent immigrant workers remained unorganized. Nonetheless, the labor movement in the thirties scored a major breakthrough, raising union membership to more than 8 million. Powerful corporations gave in to unionization because of workers' militance, management's fear of labor violence and sabotage, and above all the refusal of the New Dealers to put the power of government on the side of business against strikers.

C. Mixed Blessings for Women

During the depression women workers suffered about a 20 percent unemployment rate; were often displaced by men in teaching, social work, and librarianships; were usually paid less than men; and were often told that if they married, they would be dismissed. Some women workers were helped by unions and by the Fair Labor Standards Act, but many of the occupations in which women predominated were not covered by either. Despite all these disadvantages, the proportion of women, including married women, in the labor force continued to grow.

D. Blacks, Hispanic-Americans, and Native Americans Cope with Hard Times

The depression slowed the movement of rural African-Americans to cities and to the North. In 1940, 77 percent of the 12 million African-Americans still lived in the South. Blacks in agriculture and industry had even higher rates of displacement and unemployment than whites, and they were often denied equal protection of the law, as demonstrated by lynchings and the case of the Scottsboro boys. Blacks organized and protested as best they could.

The depression was equally hard on more than 2 million Hispanics. Many of the Mexican immigrants were migratory farm laborers who competed for jobs with the "Okies" arriving in the Southwest. With a surplus of farm workers, employers and relief officials put pressure on Hispanics to return to Mexico, and half a million did during the 1930s. Those who remained either drifted to the barrios of southwestern cities or worked for miserably low wages on large farms. Mexican-Americans occasionally struck for better pay.

The 170,000 Indians were the poorest of all Americans. By 1933 they had lost to whites two-thirds of the land they had owned in 1887, the year the ill-conceived Dawes Act was passed. John Collier, a reformer, became Roosevelt's commissioner of Indian affairs. He used CCC and WPA labor and money to create jobs and build much-needed facilities on Indian reservations. He also proposed legislation to end the Dawes Act, stop all further sale of Indian lands, grant self-government to the tribes, and encourage revival of Native American culture. After much opposition from both land-hungry whites and some Native Americans, Collier saw part of his program embodied in the 1934 Indian Reorganization Act, which did at least reverse the steady loss of Indian lands. After the New Deal, however, Collier resigned and federal protection of Native Americans evaporated.

E. Family Life and Population Trends

Hard times brought changes in family life and population trends. Marriage rates and birthrates declined, while desertion increased. Population and urban growth slowed. The shift of people westward across the continent, however, continued. If the depression broke up some families, it produced in others greater solidarity and promoted a spirit of coopera-tion among people. The poor shared what little they had with those even poorer.

II. The American Cultural Scene in the Thirties

A. *The Golden Age of Radio*

Listening to the radio was an extremely popular activity in the 1930s. The comedy of Jack Benny and George Burns and Gracie Allen and the melodrama of the soap operas gave peo-ple an escape from bleak economic reality. Mass culture became even more standardized than it had been in the twenties.

B. *The Silver Screen*

Movies, too, were enormously popular. A few documentaries and some dramas dealt with contemporary social problems. But most Hollywood films offered escape from a troubled world. Americans flocked to see gangster movies like *Little Caesar,* musicals like *Gold Dig-gers of 1933,* and the Marx Brothers comedies. Hollywood films of the thirties presented most characters as stereotypes.

C. *The Literature of the Early Thirties*

Fiction in the early thirties was somber in tone and radically "challenged the fundamental premises of American ideology." James T. Farrell's *Studs Lonigan,* John Dos Passos's *U.S.A.,* and Nathanael West's *Miss Lonelyhearts* are examples. Radical novelists and playwrights such as Jack Conroy, Josephine Herbst, and Clifford Odets often dealt with exploitation of labor and class struggle in their works.

D. *The Later Thirties: The Popular Front and Cultural Nationalism*

Writers and artists in the latter half of the 1930s found much to admire in America's history and its people, though not necessarily in its capitalist economic system. Several things account for this upsurge in cultural nationalism: (1) the rise of aggressive fascism abroad threatened all the democratic and humanitarian values our country claimed to uphold; (2) the communists, between 1935 and 1939, praised New Deal America and advocated a Popular Front of all left-wingers and liberals against fascism: the Loyalists' struggle against Francisco Franco's fascist rebels in the Spanish Civil War (1936–1939) especially awakened American liberals and intellectuals to the fascist menace; (3) the WPA art projects encour-aged appreciation of America's heritage. John Steinbeck's *The Grapes of Wrath* and James Agee's and Walker Evans's *Let Us Now Praise Famous Men* paid tribute to the endurance of America's rural poor. Composers Aaron Copland and George Gershwin used American folk-tales and racial minorities in their works. American jazz and swing blossomed. Regional writers, such as Zora Neal Hurston and William Faulkner, and painters, such as Thomas Hart Benton, depicted their home sections of the nation. American folk art and historical muse-ums and novels became popular.

E. *The Age of Streamlining*

The look of material objects surrounding Americans in the 1930s began to change as business, hoping to boost sales, adopted the industrial design known as streamlining. Corporate attempts to show the public that capitalism could bring the nation a prosperous, modern, streamlined future reached a high point at the New York World's Fair of 1939.

F. *Undercurrents of Apprehension*

If Americans felt more positive about their society in the late thirties, they also experienced growing apprehension about the gathering war clouds. That may be why so many people overreacted to Orson Welles's 1938 radio dramatization of *War of the Worlds*.

III. The United States in a Menacing World

A. *Introduction*

While Americans struggled with the depression at home, aggressive, militaristic fascist regimes came to power in Italy, Germany, and Japan. The United States reacted to these developments abroad "with ambivalence," torn between dislike of fascism and "an even stronger desire for peace."

B. *FDR's Nationalism and the Good Neighbor Policy*

In his first inaugural address, Roosevelt pledged the United States to be a "good neighbor" in the family of nations. His administration applied this policy in Latin America by supporting the Montevideo declaration that "no state has the right to intervene in the internal or external affairs of another." FDR withdrew U.S. troops from Haiti, reduced American domination over Panama and the Canal Zone, and refrained from using force against left-wing governments in Cuba and Mexico. The administration did, however, apply economic pressure to influence events in those two countries.

C. *The Rise of Fascism in Europe and Asia*

Benito Mussolini and his Fascist followers took control of Italy in 1922. In 1933 the Nazi leader Adolf Hitler became chancellor of Germany. Preaching racism, aggressive nationalism, and anti-Semitism, Hitler quickly established an absolute dictatorship over Germany, began persecuting the Jews, and embarked on military buildup and conquest. In 1936 his troops reoccupied the Rhineland; in 1938 they annexed Austria. Meanwhile, Mussolini invaded Ethiopia. Germany grabbed the Sudetenland from Czechoslovakia without firing a shot when, in 1938, at the Munich Conference, the British and French agreed to the transfer to appease Hitler. On the other side of the world, Japanese imperialists seized the Chinese province of Manchuria, renaming it Manchukuo, and in 1937 began a war of conquest to take over all of China. In 1936 the three aggressors signed an alliance.

D. *The American Mood: No More War*

Americans disliked these actions but were determined not to be pulled into another war. The majority in this country now viewed our participation in World War I as a mistake. The revelations of the Nye Committee about the roles played by bankers and weapons suppliers in that war reinforced that belief. In the thirties students held antiwar protests; novelists and playwrights condemned war in their works; and Congress passed the Neutrality Acts, prohibiting the United States from making loans or selling arms to belligerents.

E. Hesitant Response to the Fascist Challenge

Some Americans admired Hitler and Mussolini, or at least found them preferable to communist leaders. Others saw them as comic rather than dangerous figures. Still other Americans from 1933 on warned of the menace that fascism and its leaders posed to freedom and peace. Almost all agreed, however, that the United States should not go to war against them. Roosevelt, whatever his personal sentiments, hesitated to buck this strong antiwar feeling. Aside from refusing to recognize the puppet government that Japan set up in Manchuria and extending modest loans to China, Roosevelt did little against fascist aggression.

F. 1938–1939: The Gathering Storm

In 1939 Hitler seized the remainder of Czechoslovakia, threatened to attack Poland, and signed the Nazi-Soviet Non-Aggression Pact to ensure Soviet neutrality during the planned German invasion of Poland. Meanwhile, Mussolini sent Italian troops into Albania. These events in Europe intensified the debate in the United States about the role this country should play. Though deploring the aggression, some continued to argue against American intervention, recalling that our participation in World War I had killed the progressive reform movement and had led to repression at home. This time, they thought, we should concentrate on saving reform and democracy in the United States.

On the other hand, many Americans grew alarmed and preached that the United States must take a more active role. FDR agreed. After the fascist conquest of Czechoslovakia and Albania, the president sent messages to Hitler and Mussolini asking them to pledge not to invade any other nation. The two dictators responded with ridicule. Roosevelt also asked Congress to appropriate much more money to build up American defenses.

G. America and the Jewish Refugees

Throughout the thirties German persecution of the Jews intensified. In 1935 the Nazis enacted the Nuremberg Laws, stripping German Jews of citizenship and rights. On *Kristallnacht* in 1938 the Nazis unleashed a wave of violence against Jews, attacking them and their homes, synagogues, and businesses. As the outrages and threats increased, tens of thousands of European Jews fled, seeking countries that would admit them. Sixty thousand entered the United States between 1933 and 1938. Among them were distinguished musicians, architects, writers, and scholars who enriched the cultural life of their adopted nation. Such refugee physicists as Leo Szilard and James Franck played key roles in developing the atomic bomb for the United States.

Congress would not amend discriminatory immigration laws, however, to offer a haven to the hundreds of thousands of additional Jews desperately needing a safe home, nor would Roosevelt exert pressure on the lawmakers to do so. The majority of Americans opposed letting in more Jews, apparently because of isolationist, anti-immigrant, and anti-Semitic attitudes. In 1939 the United States even stopped the *St. Louis,* a ship carrying nine hundred Jewish refugees, and forced it to return to Europe. There the countryless refugees were soon murdered by the Nazis.

IV. Conclusion

The thirties opened on the heels of the stock market crash and closed on the brink of war. Between these bleak events, the decade "brought bright moments of political creativity, social advance, and cultural achievement." Millions of industrial workers became unionized. The NAACP and other organizations continued their fight against discrimination, laying the groundwork for later gains. Writers and artists depicted American life, including its rich regional cultures, in their novels, plays, photographs, and paintings. And all the while, in Europe and Asia, fascism, Nazism, and militarism grew more threatening.

VOCABULARY

The following terms are used in Chapter 26. To understand the chapter fully, it is important that you know what each of them means.

militance   aggressiveness, combativeness

urbanization   growth of cities and towns; movement of population from rural areas to cities and towns

barrios   Hispanic urban neighborhoods

repatriation   the bringing or sending back of a person to his or her own country

assimilation   the process of absorbing or incorporating a minority group into the majority culture or society; the process of making the minority resemble or become like the majority

demographic   pertaining to social statistics such as the births, deaths, marriages, movements, growth, and so on, of populations

proletariat   the industrial working class

totalitarian   of or pertaining to a centralized government that attempts to control all institutions in its society and permits no opposition parties or opinions

streamlining   eliminating all extraneous design features in favor of smoothly flowing surfaces (ones that are often teardrop shaped and offer the least resistance in passing through the air)

appeasement   making concessions to pacify, quiet, or satisfy the other party

IDENTIFICATIONS

After reading Chapter 26, you should be able to identify and explain the historical significance of each of the following:

John L. Lewis

Sidney Hillman

Committee for Industrial Organization, later Congress of Industrial Organizations (CIO)

Walter Reuther, the United Automobile Workers, and the sit-downs

Henry Ford, Harry Bennett, and the Battle of the Overpass

Tom Girdler, "Little Steel," and the Memorial Day Massacre

Scottsboro boys

Richard Wright

John Collier and the Indian Reorganization Act, 1934

Pare Lorentz, "The River" and "The Plow That Broke the Plains"

Marx Brothers

Stepin Fetchit

James T. Farrell, *Studs Lonigan*

John Dos Passos, *U.S.A.*

Nathanael West, *Miss Lonelyhearts*

fascism and Nazism

Popular Front

Francisco Franco, Spanish Loyalists, and the Spanish Civil War

Ernest Hemingway, *For Whom the Bell Tolls*

Nazi-Soviet Pact, 1939

John Steinbeck, *The Grapes of Wrath*

James Agee and Walker Evans, *Let Us Now Praise Famous Men*

Benny Goodman, Count Basie, and Glenn Miller

Zora Neal Hurston, *Their Eyes Were Watching God*

William Faulkner

Good Neighbor policy

Benito Mussolini

Adolf Hitler, *Mein Kampf*

Munich Conference, 1938

Nye Committee hearings

Neutrality Acts

Nuremberg Laws, *Kristallnacht*, and the "final solution"

St. Louis

SKILL BUILDING: MAPS

1. On the map of Europe and North Africa in the 1930s on the following page, locate each of the following and explain its significance in the coming of World War II:

   Spain

   Soviet Union

   Italy

   Germany

   Rhineland

   Ethiopia

   Austria

   Sudetenland

   Munich

   Czechoslovakia

   Albania

   Poland (area occupied by the Soviet Union; area occupied by Germany under the terms of the Nazi-Soviet Pact)

**Europe and
North Africa, 1930s**

2. On the map below of Asia in the 1930s, locate each of the following and explain its significance in the coming of World War II:

Japan

Manchuria (Manchukuo)

China (areas occupied by Japan as of 1939)

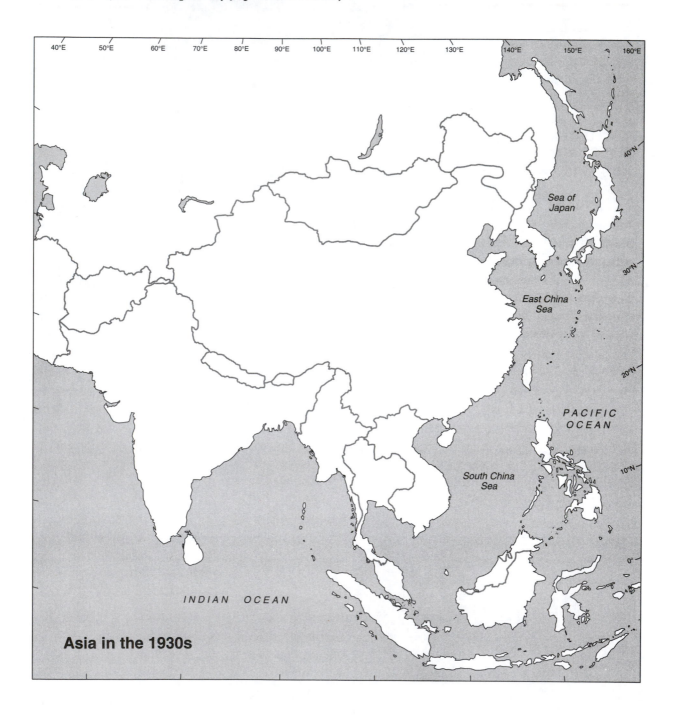

Asia in the 1930s

HISTORICAL SOURCES

In Chapter 26 of the text, the author has used, among others, two types of sources that have proved helpful in the study of modern history: oral-history interviews and public-opinion polls. Equipped with tape recorders and/or notepads, historians have interviewed a broad cross section of people, from the famous and powerful to ordinary men and women, who have lived through a variety of experiences and events, such as immigrating to the United States, coping with the depression, and participating in sit-down strikes. Recordings and/or transcripts of some of these interviews have been placed in oral-history archives, such as the one at Columbia University, which are available to scholars. Others have been published in books. One of the best collections of interviews about life in the 1930s is Studs Terkel's *Hard Times*. The recollection of the automobile worker of the 1936–1937 sit-down strike on page 839 comes from that book. You will find other oral-history accounts on pages 838–840, 842, and 845–846. Why has the author used each of these recollections? Although oral-history interviews are an excellent source, they often contain inaccurate information. Why do you suppose that is so?

On pages 842, 857, and 863 the author cites the findings of public-opinion polls. In each case, what is this information meant to show? Social scientists and statisticians first started taking these polls in a formal, "scientific" way in the 1930s. In 1935 George H. Gallup founded the best known of these poll-taking organizations, the American Institute of Public Opinion. Are the findings of public-opinion polls always accurate? Why or why not?

Look at "A Place in Time: The Los Angeles Barrio in the 1930s." This is an example of ethnic history. The field of ethnic and immigrant history has received increased attention from scholars since the 1960s, as we have come to appreciate fully the fact that America has always been composed of a variety of peoples. To comprehend our nation's past, we must study what each of its ethnic groups contributed to and experienced in that past. What does this account of Mexican-Americans in the depression illustrate about the impact of hard times on various groups and on the ways that government officials reacted to depression problems?

MULTIPLE-CHOICE QUESTIONS

Circle the letter of the item that best completes each statement or answers the question.

1. The Scottsboro boys were
   a. black teenagers sentenced to death by an all-white jury for allegedly raping two white women.
   b. one of the most popular swing bands of the 1930s.
   c. the main characters in Clifford Odets's play about labor unrest and a strike, *Waiting for Lefty*.
   d. young, unemployed Mexican-American farm workers who were forced by relief officials to return to Mexico.

2. Commissioner of Indian Affairs John Collier proposed to
   a. encourage Native Americans to leave reservations and seek jobs in the cities.
   b. stop the further sale of Indian lands, grant tribal self-government, and revive Native American cultures.
   c. end segregated schools for Native Americans, enroll their children in white schools, and thus speed up Indian assimilation.
   d. terminate all special government programs and protection for Native Americans because he believed that they kept Indians dependent and demoralized.

3. Which company agreed to recognize and bargain with the union its workers had joined after the workers occupied its plants in a six-week sit-down strike?
   a. Ford Motor Company
   b. Republic Steel
   c. General Motors
   d. U.S. Steel

4. The protagonist in which of these novels goes to Spain to help the Loyalists fight against Franco and fascism?
   a. James T. Farrell's *Studs Lonigan*
   b. Ernest Hemingway's *For Whom the Bell Tolls*
   c. Richard Wright's *Native Son*
   d. William Faulkner's *Absalom, Absalom!*

5. Which of the following did *not* occur during the depression?
   a. Birthrates and marriage rates declined.
   b. Urbanization and population growth slowed.
   c. Immigration into the United States from Europe and Mexico increased greatly.
   d. High school enrollment increased sharply.

6. All of the following were popular pastimes during the depression *except*
   a. going to the movies.
   b. watching television.
   c. listening to the radio.
   d. listening to swing played by the big bands of Benny Goodman, Count Basie, and Glenn Miller.

7. Women in the 1930s were
   a. excluded from the UAW and other industrial unions.
   b. encouraged by Secretary of Labor Frances Perkins and other New Dealers to pursue good jobs and careers along with being wives and mothers.
   c. concentrated in industries where unionization made the least headway.
   d. driven out of the paid labor force almost entirely.

8. Which of the following statements is true about American attitudes in the 1930s?
    a. The majority of Americans believed that married women had as much right to work at gainful employment as married men.
    b. The majority of Americans still disapproved of going to the movies and considered it to be sinful behavior.
    c. The majority of Americans favored liberalizing U.S. immigration laws to admit more Jewish refugees.
    d. The majority of Americans believed that the United States should have stayed out of World War I.

9. All of the following took strong anti-Nazi positions in the 1930s *except*
    a. Ambassador Joseph P. Kennedy.
    b. journalist Dorothy Thompson.
    c. poet Archibald MacLeish.
    d. cultural critic Lewis Mumford.

10. Which of the following helped convince Americans that U.S. participation in World War I was a mistake that should not be repeated by getting involved a second time?
    a. the Ludlow Amendment
    b. Roosevelt's "Quarantine the Aggressors" speech
    c. the Nye Committee hearings
    d. the *St. Louis* incident

SHORT-ANSWER QUESTIONS

1. What was the Good Neighbor Policy, and how closely did the Roosevelt administration adhere to it?

2. What aggressive actions on the international scene did Fascist Italy and militarist Japan take during the 1930s?

3. In what ways did Hitler defy the terms of the Treaty of Versailles and commit acts of aggression between 1933 and 1939?

4. Explain what the Popular Front was. Who was attracted to the idea? When and why did the Popular Front idea collapse?

5. How did British prime minister Neville Chamberlain and French premier Edouard Daladier attempt to appease Hitler at the 1938 Munich Conference? Did President Roosevelt approve of the agreement they made at Munich? Did Munich bring "peace in our time," as Chamberlain predicted?

6. What was the 1939 Nazi-Soviet Pact? How did it open the door to Hitler's invasion of Poland and World War II? How did American liberals react to it?

7. How did the United States respond to Jewish refugees from Nazi Germany? Why?

ESSAY QUESTIONS

1. One social history of the 1930s is titled *The Invisible Scar*. Is this an appropriate title for a book about the depression decade? Why or why not?

2. In 1933 fewer than 3 million workers belonged to unions; by 1941 more than 8 million did. How and why did this "unionization of vast sectors of America's industrial work force" come about? Which workers were still almost totally unorganized in 1941?

3. Discuss the impact of the depression on the lives of women, blacks, Hispanics, and Indians.

4. Discuss American culture in the 1930s. How did popular culture and the fine arts respond to the political and economic events and conditions of the depression decade?

5. Discuss the reactions of the American public and the U.S. government in the 1930s to the rise of aggressive fascist regimes in Italy, Japan, and Germany. How do you explain these reactions?

27

Waging Global War, 1939–1945

OUTLINE AND SUMMARY

I. Into the Storm, 1939–1941

A. *Storm in Europe*

World War II began on September 1,1939, when Hitler attacked Poland. Britain and France, committed by treaty to defend Poland, declared war on Germany. Soon after, the United States revised the Neutrality Acts to permit sales of weapons to belligerents on a cash-and-carry basis. Most Americans favored this move as a way to help Britain and France without having to fight. In April 1940 German armies turned on Denmark and Norway; in May they conquered the Netherlands and Belgium; by mid-June France capitulated. The Germans then began terror bombing raids over the cities of England. During this Battle of Britain, Prime Minister Winston Churchill appealed to President Roosevelt for help. The majority of Americans favored stepped-up weapons shipments to bolster Hitler's one remaining opponent, but an articulate minority feared that such aid would weaken U.S. defenses and needlessly pull us into war.

B. *The Election of 1940*

Because of the menacing situation in Europe, Roosevelt decided to run for a third term. His Republican opponent, Wendell L. Willkie, held foreign-policy views similar to Roosevelt's. During the campaign Roosevelt underlined his interventionist position by signing an executive agreement with Winston Churchill to give Britain fifty overage U.S. destroyers in exchange for leases on air and naval bases in British possessions in the Western Hemisphere. In protest, isolationists organized the America First Committee, which preached that we must not give any aid to belligerents or become involved in the struggle against Hitler. However, in apparent support of Roosevelt's actions, the voters elected him to an unprecedented third term.

C. *From Isolation to Intervention*

When FDR learned that Britain was running out of dollars to buy the war supplies she desperately needed, he proposed the Lend-Lease bill. It would permit the president to lend or lease military equipment to any country whose defense he thought vital to American security. Although this would certainly be an unneutral act, the majority of the public favored it, and Congress passed it in March 1941. When Hitler attacked the U.S.S.R. in June 1941, Roosevelt gave lend-lease aid to the Soviets as well as to the British. Unfortunately, the supplies often ended up at the bottom of the Atlantic because of the constant sinkings by German submarines. To prevent such losses the United States began convoying British ships as far as Iceland, tracking German submarines, and notifying the British of their location. These actions inevitably led to conflict between German and American vessels. By the fall of 1941 the two countries were engaged in an undeclared naval war. Meanwhile Roosevelt and Churchill moved closer to an alliance when they met off the coast of Newfoundland in the summer of 1941 and issued the Atlantic Charter. Still, Roosevelt hesitated to ask Congress for a formal declaration of war against Germany.

D. Toward Pearl Harbor

With Europe at war, Japan expanded its aggression from China to the resource-rich British, Dutch, and French colonies in Southeast Asia. Japan's drive to replace Western imperialists and alone dominate the Far East clashed directly with the Open Door policy of the United States. Though not wanting a war, the Roosevelt administration attempted to change Tokyo's course by applying economic pressure. In July 1940 Washington prohibited the sale of aviation gasoline to Japan. When Tokyo occupied northern Indochina and signed the Tripartite Pact with Germany and Italy, Roosevelt placed an embargo on all metals, chemicals, and machine parts. In July 1941, in response to Japan's seizure of the rest of Indochina, Washington froze Japanese assets in the United States, ending all trade. Japanese prime minister Hideki Tojo decided to make a last-ditch effort to persuade Washington to reopen trade and recognize Japan's conquests. If that failed, Japan would attempt to destroy the U.S. Pacific fleet with a surprise attack on Pearl Harbor, leaving the United States too weak to thwart Japan's imperial dreams. Washington knew its refusal would provoke an attack somewhere in the Pacific. Nonetheless, the Roosevelt administration would not yield and sent warnings to all base commanders. On December 7, 1941, the Japanese struck Pearl Harbor, and the next day Congress recognized that a state of war existed with Japan. On the eleventh Japan's two allies, Germany and Italy, declared war on the United States, and we reciprocated.

E. On the Defensive

In the months after Pearl Harbor the United States faced a bleak situation. Nazi submarines prowled off our east coast and took a heavy toll on Allied ships. Hitler's armies had pushed to the outskirts of Leningrad and Moscow and were launching new offensives in the Crimea and Caucasus. Other German armies landed in North Africa and headed toward the vital Suez Canal. Japan followed the raid on Hawaii with conquests of the Philippines, Malaya, Thailand, Hong Kong, Guam, Wake, Singapore, the Dutch East Indies, and most of the island chains in the Western Pacific.

II. America Mobilizes for War

A. Organizing for Victory

To mobilize the economy Roosevelt established hundreds of special wartime agencies, such as the War Production Board, which allocated scarce materials, limited manufacture of civilian goods, and awarded military production contracts. In 1943 FDR appointed James F. Byrnes head of the Office of War Mobilization, which coordinated the efforts of the many government agencies, private industry, and the military. Under this government direction the United States produced more armaments than Germany, Italy, and Japan combined. Cost-plus-fixed-fee contracts guaranteed handsome profits to the giant corporations that received most of the defense contracts. Federal authority and the federal budget grew rapidly, as did the influence of the military and big corporations on American life.

B. A War Economy

Between 1941 and 1945 the U.S. government spent nearly twice as much as it did from 1788 through 1940. Fueled by this expenditure, the economy boomed. During the war farm income doubled, corporate profits climbed by 70 percent, and unemployment vanished as 17 million new jobs were created. Many of the poor moved into the middle class. Most labor leaders gave no-strike pledges, but John L. Lewis led his miners on repeated work stoppages. An increasingly conservative Congress retaliated with the antilabor Smith-Connally Act. To curb inflation the Office of Price Administration imposed price controls and rationing. As a result the cost of living during World War II rose 28 percent, compared to a 62 percent increase during World War I. The government raised the huge sums needed to fight the war with the sale of bonds, which provided half the money, and with steeply increased federal taxes, which provided the rest.

C. Science and the War

The government also employed thousands of scientists in the drive for victory. The secret Manhattan Project to beat the Germans in the race to develop nuclear weapons was the greatest of the government-sponsored scientific endeavors. Led by physicist J. Robert Oppenheimer, the Manhattan Project spent some $2 billion. On July 16, 1945, it catapulted the world into the atomic age when it tested the first nuclear bomb over the New Mexico desert.

D. Propaganda and Politics

To unify Americans and prevent dangerous security leaks, Roosevelt established the Office of War Information and the Office of Censorship. They interfered less with freedom of speech and the press than similar World War I agencies had.

Full employment and prosperity led to a politically conservative trend. More Republicans and conservative Democrats were elected to Congress in 1942. They cut welfare programs, abolished New Deal agencies, and halted any further reforms.

III. War and American Society

A. The New Mobility

More than 15 million Americans left their homes to serve in the armed forces. Another 15 million moved from one location to another for family and economic reasons. Poor whites, blacks, and Chicanos left rural areas to seek jobs in war-production centers in the North and West. Terrible shortages of housing and other facilities developed in these cities, contributing to urban blight and to conflicts between newcomers and older residents. These vast internal migrations also produced a more uniform national culture and broadened the horizons of many.

B. Education and Entertainment

High school enrollment dropped as more teenagers quit to take full-time jobs. On the other hand, the armed forces sent nearly a million people to college campuses for special training. Americans went to the movies to watch films that entertained them. Films often presented the enemy as fiends and the Allies, including the Soviets, in a highly favorable light. The public gobbled up war news from periodicals such as *Life* and from the reports of radio correspondents Edward R. Murrow, Eric Sevareid, and others.

C. Women and the Family

Drawn by high wages, patriotism, and government encouragement, millions of women went to work in defense plants. By 1945 women constituted over one-third of the labor force. They took on such formerly male-dominated work as welding, riveting, operating cranes, and running lathes, although they earned only about 65 percent of what men received in the same fields. More than one-third of the women had children under fourteen years of age. Because there were few day-care centers, youngsters were often left on their own. Juvenile delinquency increased alarmingly. Marriage, birth, and divorce rates also soared. Some 300,000 women joined the armed forces. After 1945 most women left these wartime occupations but the experience gave them a new sense of their own capabilities.

D. African-Americans and the War

During World War II African-Americans demanded that the nation fight racism at home as well as abroad. The NAACP and the Congress of Racial Equality led the struggle for civil rights. To forestall a massive march on Washington organized by A. Philip Randolph, FDR in 1941 signed an executive order prohibiting racial discrimination in hiring and promotion by government agencies and defense contractors. The Fair Employment Practices Commission he created had little power, but wartime labor shortages opened many new jobs to blacks. Roughly 1 million blacks served in the armed forces, generally in segregated outfits commanded by white officers. They experienced other forms of discrimination as well. In civilian life, tensions developed between blacks demanding equality and resistant whites. Race riots erupted in Detroit and dozens of other places. More than 700,000 blacks left the South to settle in cities of the North and West. The move opened up greater opportunities and potential political power for African-Americans.

E. Native Americans, Mexican-Americans, and Jews in Wartime

Twenty-five thousand Native Americans served in the armed forces; another seventy-five thousand left reservations to work in defense industries. With assimilation impeded by prejudice against them, most Native Americans returned to their reservations after the war. Conditions there had deteriorated badly because Congress had slashed appropriations for Indian programs.

Hundreds of thousands of Mexicans entered the United States, legally and illegally, during the war to work on the big farms in the western states. At the same time many Mexican-Americans left migratory farm labor to seek better jobs in cities. In Los Angeles Anglo-American prejudice against Mexicans exploded in the zoot-suit riot. Some 350,000 Mexican-Americans served in the armed forces, and as with African-American and Native American veterans, they emerged from the experience with a heightened consciousness and demands for equality.

Despite America's condemnation of Nazi persecution of the Jews, anti-Semitic attitudes continued in the United States. These attitudes partly explain why this country refused to admit most refugees and was slow to organize other rescue efforts to save European Jews. By 1945 the Nazis had killed 6 million Jews and several million gypsies, Poles, communists, and homosexuals.

F. The Internment of Japanese-Americans

The government's treatment of Japanese-Americans during World War II was the one glaring exception to its otherwise good civil-liberties record. In an atmosphere of hysteria over Pearl Harbor, fear of Japanese invasion of the mainland, and traditional prejudice against Asian-Americans, the government uprooted 112,000 Japanese-Americans living on the West Coast and locked them in internment camps in remote interior regions. Unwilling in wartime to question claims of military necessity, the Supreme Court in 1944 upheld the constitutionality of evacuation. In the 1980s the government finally admitted that its actions had been unjustified, apologized to Japanese-Americans, and agreed to pay compensation to them for the property losses they suffered when they were detained.

IV. The Battlefront, 1942–1944

A. The Allied Drive in Europe

The British and Americans concentrated on beating Hitler first, Japan afterward. Stalin pressed his two allies to launch an invasion of Europe across the English Channel as quickly as possible. Churchill convinced Roosevelt they should postpone this second front and land instead in North Africa, where by May 1943 they had defeated large German and Italian armies. Meanwhile the Soviets turned the tide of battle in the east by winning at Stalingrad, holding out at Leningrad, and attacking the German invaders along a thousand-mile front. Again postponing the cross-channel invasion, the British and Americans captured Sicily and started a slow march up the Italian peninsula. There they encountered stiff opposition from German troops that were rushed in after Mussolini was deposed and the Italian government surrendered. In 1944–1945 the Soviets cleared the Germans out of the U.S.S.R. and pursued them across Eastern Europe. The British and Americans finally landed on the beaches of Normandy in June 1944 and fought their way toward Germany. The Nazis temporarily stopped the Allied drive in the Battle of the Bulge, but by early 1945 the Americans and British had reached the Rhine.

B. The War in the Pacific

The Japanese advances in the Pacific were first halted in the spring and summer of 1942 at the Battles of the Coral Sea and Midway. Thereafter, the U.S. Navy and Army assaulted

Japanese strongholds in the Solomon, Gilbert, Marshall, and Mariana islands. General Douglas MacArthur, earlier driven from the Philippines, retook Manila by 1945, and the U.S. Navy largely destroyed what was left of the Japanese fleet at the Battles of the Philippine Sea and Leyte Gulf. Despite its devastating losses, Japan showed no inclination to surrender.

C. The Grand Alliance

The Grand Alliance of Britain, the U.S.S.R., and the United States was forged out of military necessity, but the three had different goals for the postwar period. Roosevelt wanted to defeat fascism and establish a new world order strong enough to keep the peace, open trade, and protect national self-determination. Churchill hoped to keep the British colonial empire and maintain a balance of power in Europe against the Soviets. Stalin intended to weaken Germany permanently and to protect his country against any future attacks from the west by imposing Soviet domination over Eastern Europe. FDR attempted to reconcile and paper over these differences with personal diplomacy. He held top-level wartime conferences with other Allied leaders at Casablanca, Cairo, and Tehran. At Tehran, the first meeting of Churchill and Roosevelt with Stalin, details of the Normandy invasion were worked out and other military and political problems discussed.

D. The Election of 1944

Roosevelt had to divert his attention from wartime diplomacy long enough to win reelection in 1944. The Democrats nominated him for a fourth term but dropped Vice President Henry Wallace in favor of Harry S Truman. The Republicans nominated Thomas E. Dewey. In November Roosevelt won an unprecedented fourth term by the smallest margin of his career.

V. Triumph and Tragedy, 1945

A. Introduction

Roosevelt, Churchill, and Stalin conferred for the last time at Yalta in February 1945. Since the Red Army occupied most of Eastern Europe at that point and the United States wanted to secure Soviet help in defeating Japan, Roosevelt and Churchill had to make concessions to Stalin. In return for Stalin's promise that the U.S.S.R. would declare war on Japan shortly after Germany's surrender, the Western leaders agreed to Russia's regaining the territory Japan had wrested from it in 1905. Roosevelt and Churchill settled for Stalin's vague promise to allow free elections in Poland and other Eastern European nations. Stalin endorsed plans for the United Nations founding conference in April 1945 and recognized the anticommunist Jiang Jieshi as ruler of China rather than the communist Mao Zedong.

B. The Defeat of Germany

In April 1945 American and Russian troops met at the Elbe River, and Hitler committed suicide. On May 2, Berlin fell to the Soviets, and on May 8, Germany unconditionally surrendered. In the last phase of the fighting, the Allies liberated the German concentration camps, revealing the scope and horror of Nazi-perpetrated genocide. Roosevelt did not live to see V-E Day. On April 12 he died suddenly, bringing Harry S Truman to the presidency.

C. A New President

Truman distrusted the Soviets and soon accused them of breaking their Yalta promise to allow free elections in Poland. Stalin responded angrily and tightened his hold on Eastern Europe. By the time Truman, Churchill, and Stalin met at Potsdam in July, the Grand Alliance had disintegrated so badly that the three could agree on little.

D. The Atomic Bombs

The fighting in the Pacific continued. In 1945, after suffering heavy casualties, the United States captured Iwo Jima and Okinawa. In July the United States successfully tested an atomic bomb at Alamagordo, and Truman and Churchill issued the Potsdam Declaration, calling on Japan to surrender unconditionally or face "prompt and utter destruction." When Japan rejected that warning, Truman ordered use of the nuclear bombs. On August 6 the first fell on Hiroshima; on the eighth the second hit Nagasaki, following which Japan surrendered. Since then historians and others have probed the United States' motives and debated whether it was justified in dropping atomic bombs on Japanese cities.

VI. Conclusion

Fourteen million fighting men and 25 million civilians died in World War II. Vast areas of Europe and Asia lay in ruins. The United States, much changed socially and economically, emerged physically unscathed and militarily powerful. Almost immediately it locked horns with the Soviet Union in a Cold War and a spiraling atomic arms race that threatened global destruction.

VOCABULARY

The following terms are used in Chapter 27. To understand the chapter fully, it is important that you know what each of them means.

blitzkrieg   lightning war; swift waging of war by use of aircraft, tanks, and other powerful weapons, as practiced by Hitler's armies between 1939 and 1941

executive agreement   an agreement made between the president of the United States and the head of a government of another country; it is binding only on the president who makes it but does not require ratification by the Senate as a treaty does

convoying   using destroyers or other armed naval vessels and/or planes to escort and protect cargo ships and troop transports

embargo   a prohibition of commerce by government order

braceros   Mexican farm laborers brought into the United States under contract for seasonal work who are then expected to return to their country

acculturation   the process and result of adopting the cultural traits of another group

the Holocaust   the name given to the systematic effort of the Nazis to annihilate all European Jews

genocide   the planned extermination of a national, racial, or religious group

IDENTIFICATIONS

After reading Chapter 27, you should be able to identify and explain the historical significance of each of the following:

"phony war"

Battle of Britain

Henry L. Stimson

Henry Wallace

Wendell L. Willkie

isolationists and the America First Committee versus the interventionists

lend-lease

Atlantic Charter

Greater East Asia Co-Prosperity Sphere versus the Open Door policy

Tripartite Pact of the Axis powers

Hideki Tojo

Office of Price Administration (OPA)

James F. Byrnes and the Office of War Mobilization

Smith-Connally War Labor Disputes Act

Manhattan Project and J. Robert Oppenheimer

Servicemen's Readjustment Act (GI Bill of Rights)

"Rosie the Riveter"

A. Philip Randolph and the March-on-Washington Movement

Executive Order 8802 and the Fair Employment Practices Commission

pachucos, sailors, and the Los Angeles zoot-suit riot

Korematsu case (1944)

the Declaration of the United Nations

the Second Front

Dwight D. Eisenhower

Operation Torch and Operation Overlord

Battle of the Bulge

Battles of the Coral Sea and Midway

Chester Nimitz

Douglas MacArthur

Jiang Jieshi (Chiang Kai-shek) versus Mao Zedong (Mao Tse-tung)

Tehran and Yalta conferences

Potsdam Conference and Potsdam Declaration

SKILL BUILDING: MAPS

1. On the map of the European theater of war, 1939–1945, on page 156, locate and explain the military and/or political importance of each of the following:

Warsaw and Lublin, Poland

areas overrun by the German offensive between April and June 1940 (Denmark, Norway, Netherlands, Belgium, Luxembourg, France)

English Channel

Dunkirk

Iceland

areas of Eastern Europe and the Soviet Union held by the Germans as of spring 1942

Leningrad

Moscow

Stalingrad

Crimean Peninsula (Yalta)

Caucasus Mountains

North African campaign (Mediterranean Sea, Egypt, Suez Canal, Morocco, Algeria, Tunisia, Libya, Allied landing areas)

Sicily

Casablanca

Cairo

Rome

Eastern European countries occupied by the Soviet Union in 1944–1945 (Romania, Bulgaria, Yugoslavia, Hungary, Czechoslovakia)

Tehran, Iran

Normandy

Paris

Ardennes Forest (Battle of the Bulge)

Rhine River

Berlin

Vienna

Elbe River

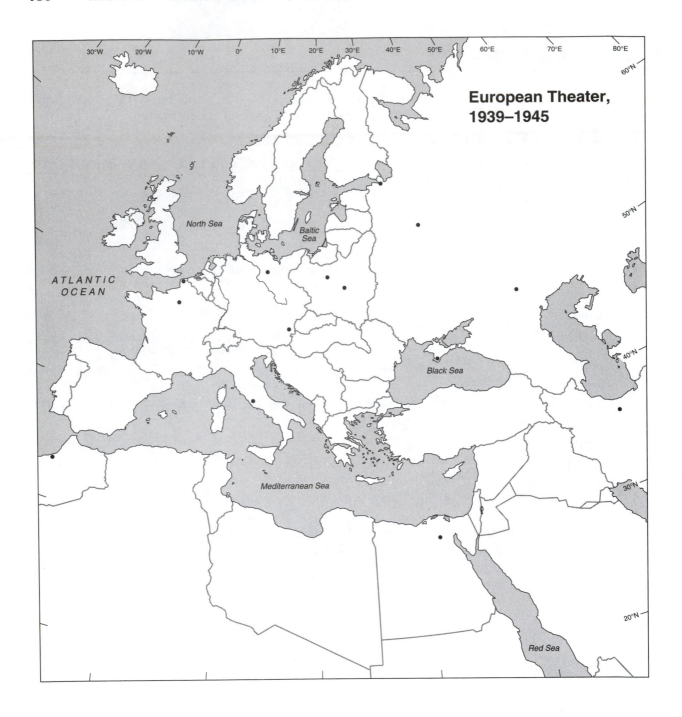

European Theater, 1939–1945

ATLANTIC OCEAN

North Sea

Baltic Sea

Black Sea

Mediterranean Sea

Red Sea

2. On the map of the Far Eastern theater of war, 1941–1945, which appears on the following page, locate and explain the military and/or political importance of each of the following:

areas attacked and/or occupied by Japan prior to or on December 7, 1941 (Manchuria, parts of China, Indochina, Thailand, Pearl Harbor)

Dutch East Indies

Burma and the Burma Road

Malaya

Philippines (Manila)

Java

Guam

Wake

Gilbert Islands

Battle of the Coral Sea

Battle of Midway

Solomon Islands (Guadalcanal)

Marshall Islands

Mariana Islands

Battle of the Philippine Sea

Leyte Gulf

Iwo Jima

Okinawa

Hiroshima and Nagasaki

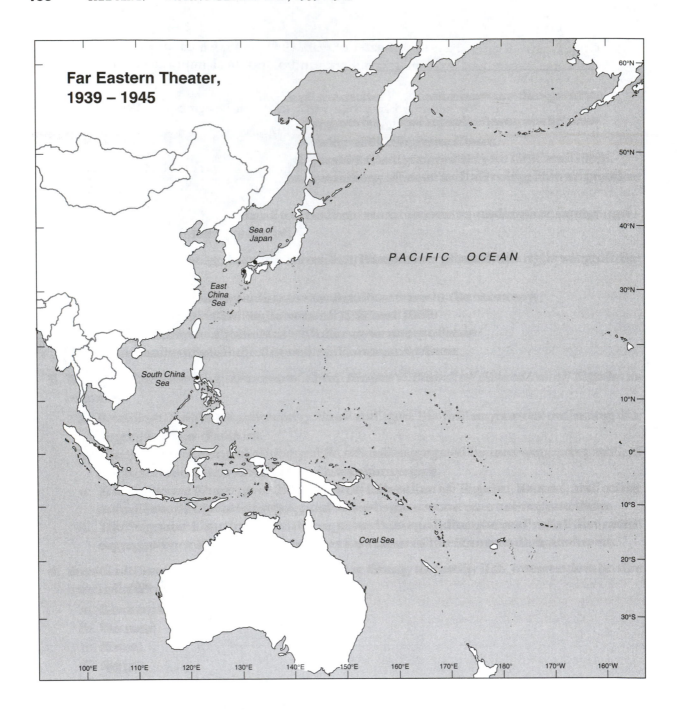

**Far Eastern Theater,
1939 – 1945**

Sea of
Japan

PACIFIC OCEAN

East
China
Sea

South China
Sea

Coral Sea

100°E   110°E   120°E   130°E   140°E   150°E   160°E   170°E   180°   170°W   160°W

60°N

50°N

40°N

30°N

10°N

0°

10°S

20°S

30°S

HISTORICAL SOURCES

Look at the discussions of the decisions made at the wartime conferences held at Casablanca, Cairo, Tehran (p. 892), Yalta (pp. 893–894), and Potsdam (pp. 894–895). How do historians know what was said and done at these conferences? Surely Roosevelt, Churchill, and Stalin did not announce to the world as they left Tehran that they had agreed to an Allied landing in France in May or June 1944 to coincide with a Soviet offensive on the Eastern Front. The historian learns what secret decisions were made at which diplomatic conferences some years later (the wait can be twenty-five years or more) when the records from those meetings, held in the archives of the U.S. State Department and the foreign-service offices of other countries, are opened to researchers. In the United States in recent decades, historians have been able to shorten the wait occasionally by bringing court cases under the Freedom of Information Act to force government agencies to declassify secret documents. In other instances secret diplomatic deals have been exposed within a few years because the archives of a defeated nation have been captured by the winner and then published. For example, the agreement between Hitler and Stalin in the 1939 Nazi-Soviet Pact to conquer and divide Poland became public knowledge when the United States captured German records in 1945 and quickly published them to embarrass the Soviet Union. What other sources can the historian use to double-check the accuracy of archival records? What additional sources can the historian consult to find out why the participants in these conferences said and agreed to certain things?

Sometimes discovering why governments follow certain courses of action on the domestic scene can be equally challenging to historians. Look at "A Place in Time: Wartime Hawaii." There we learn that the 160,000 Nisei and Issei living in the islands were not interned in camps as those residing in the Pacific coast states were. The army and the president apparently were less worried about the possible security threat from the large Japanese minority in Hawaii, which had suffered a devastating attack, than from the smaller Japanese population in California, Oregon, and Washington, where no hostilities had occurred. How can we explain the difference in attitude?

MULTIPLE-CHOICE QUESTIONS

Circle the letter of the item that best completes each statement or answers the question.

1. Which of the following sequences of events is correct?
   a. United States sends aid to Britain and the Soviet Union; Japan attacks Pearl Harbor; United States declares war on Japan; Germany and Italy declare war on the United States.
   b. United States declares war on Germany; Japan attacks Pearl Harbor; United States declares war on Japan; United States sends aid to Britain and the Soviet Union.
   c. United States declares war on Japan; Japan attacks Pearl Harbor; Germany and Italy declare war on the United States; United States sends aid to Britain and the Soviet Union.
   d. Germany, Italy, and Japan declare war on the United States; Japan attacks Pearl Harbor; United States declares war on the Axis; United States sends aid to Britain and the Soviet Union.

2. Lend-lease
   a. was favored by isolationists as a way to prevent the United States from having to fight in World War II.
   b. favored the Germans because they were considered better credit risks than the British and Soviets.
   c. was extended to both Britain and the Soviet Union to help them defeat the Nazis.
   d. was one of the most unpopular policies of the Roosevelt administration because it was pulling the country into a war the majority of Americans wished to avoid.

3. Which of the following was unique about the presidential elections of 1940 and 1944?
   a. A candidate was elected president for a third term and a fourth.
   b. The Democratic incumbent ran with no real opposition from the Republicans.
   c. The contests were both so close that the winner had to be decided by a House of Representatives vote.
   d. They were the first two elections in which women voted for president.

4. The United States assisted European Jews threatened by Nazi extermination by
   a. admitting millions of Jewish refugees to the United States.
   b. convincing the British to allow millions of refugees into Palestine.
   c. offering the Nazis trucks and other war supplies in exchange for Jewish concentration-camp inmates.
   d. establishing the War Refugee Board.

5. The United States and Britain launched the long-delayed second front with the
   a. capture of Iwo Jima and Okinawa.
   b. landing in North Africa.
   c. landing in Normandy.
   d. seizure of Sicily and southern Italy.

6. The battle that ended the Japanese offensive and forced her to revert to defending what she had earlier occupied was the
   a. Battle of Midway.
   b. Battle of the Bulge.
   c. Battle of the Philippine Sea.
   d. battle for Iwo Jima.

7. The text states that the main reason for United States' use of atomic bombs against Hiroshima and Nagasaki was
   a. the desire to frighten the Soviets into being more reasonable in Eastern Europe.
   b. America's racist attitudes toward Japan.
   c. the hope of ending the war in the Pacific before the Soviet Union had a chance to get into the conflict.
   d. the reliance of American leaders on technology to win the war with the least sacrifice of American lives.

8. Which of the following did *not* occur during World War II?
   a. The federal government imposed wage and price controls and rationing to combat inflation.
   b. The federal government took over many industries and strictly limited the profits of others.
   c. The federal government raised the income tax and introduced the payroll-deduction system to collect it more efficiently.
   d. Farm income soared, unemployment disappeared, and real wages increased.

9. Which of the following happened during World War II?
   a. Marriage, birth, and divorce rates rose rapidly.
   b. Women were denied the right to serve in the armed forces.
   c. High school and college attendance increased greatly because families had the money to keep their youngsters in school.
   d. The majority of preschool-age children were placed in child-care centers as their mothers worked in defense-industry jobs.

10. A. Philip Randolph's call for a massive march on Washington led to
    a. an executive order permitting the military to evacuate and intern Japanese living on the West Coast.
    b. an executive order prohibiting employment discrimination and creating a Fair Employment Practices Commission.
    c. passage of the Smith-Connally Act restricting union strikes and protests.
    d. prosecution of the sailors involved in the zoot-suit riot against the pachucos.

SHORT-ANSWER QUESTIONS

1. What caused the outbreak of war in Europe in September 1939?

2. Discuss the debate between the isolationists and the interventionists between 1939 and 1941 over the role the United States should play in the war in Europe.

3. What was U.S. policy toward Jewish refugees during World War II?

4. Outline the major strategy and campaigns of the United States and its allies in the European war theater between 1942 and 1945.

5. Outline the major strategy and campaigns of the United States in the Asian war theater between 1942 and 1945.

6. Explain the issues discussed, the controversies that arose, and the decisions made at the Tehran conference.

7. Explain the issues discussed, the controversies that arose, and the decisions made at the Yalta conference.

ESSAY QUESTIONS

1. Discuss the conflicts between the United States and Japan that led to the Japanese attack on Pearl Harbor.

2. Discuss the effects of World War II on American business, labor, and government.

3. Discuss the effects of World War II on African-Americans, Mexican-Americans, Native Americans, and Japanese-Americans.

4. Discuss the impact of World War II on American women, marriage, and the family.

5. Discuss the formation of and strains in the Grand Alliance of the United States, Britain, and the Soviet Union during World War II. How was the second-front controversy related to those strains?

6. Why did the United States drop atomic bombs on Hiroshima and Nagasaki? What explanations have been offered? Do you feel the United States' actions were justified? Why or why not?

28

Cold War America, 1945 – 1952

OUTLINE AND SUMMARY

I. The Postwar Political Setting

A. Introduction

Harry S Truman, who became president in April 1945, had been a hardworking senator and a supporter of President Roosevelt's programs, though not a "committed New Dealer." Once in the White House, he replaced liberal cabinet members with moderates, but he also urged Congress to continue and expand New Deal reforms. During his presidency Truman had to contend with a revived Republican party, a divided Democratic party, and a Congress resentful of the great powers that had accrued to the executive branch during the Roosevelt years.

B. Demobilization and Reconversion

In response to popular demand, the Truman administration rapidly demobilized the armed forces. Predictions of a postwar depression did not come true. Instead, the reconversion years began a quarter-century of expanding prosperity. The money the government gave to veterans for education, homes, and businesses under the GI Bill of Rights stimulated the economy. With most of its industrial rivals weakened by the war, the United States enjoyed a favorable position in world trade. Further, wartime advances in science and technology made possible the growth of whole new industries, such as electronics and synthetic materials. Consumers, who had accumulated some $140 billion in savings between 1941 and 1945, went on a postwar buying spree, grabbing up homes, cars, electrical appliances, and televisions.

C. Truman's Troubles

There was little support after World War II for resuming New Deal reform. Congress passed the watered-down Employment Act in 1946 but balked at Truman's other domestic-reform proposals. With the OPA and price controls terminated, inflation soared. Escalating prices led to an unprecedented number of strikes in 1946 as workers demanded higher wages to keep up with the cost of living. Truman wavered between getting tough with strikers and giving in to their demands. Shortages of housing and consumer goods continued as reconverting industries struggled to catch up with consumer purchases. Americans blamed

Truman for inflation, strikes, and shortages, and in November 1946 they elected Republican majorities to Congress for the first time since 1928.

II. Anticommunism and Containment

A. Confrontation and Polarization

After defeating their common enemy Hitler, the United States and the Soviet Union began to argue over Eastern Europe, especially Poland. To secure his nation against future attacks from the west, Stalin insisted that friendly communist governments must be installed on the Soviet borders. While the Red Army occupied these countries, Stalin broke his Yalta promise to allow free elections and saw to it that communist regimes came to power in Poland, Bulgaria, Hungary, and Romania. President Truman would not accept Soviet domination of Eastern Europe because it violated the principles of national self-determination that the United States had espoused in the Atlantic Charter and Yalta Declaration. Further, Truman believed the spread of communism threatened American economic interests in Eastern Europe and elsewhere. Also, he realized that opposition to Soviet intervention would be popular at home with conservatives and voters of Eastern European extraction.

B. The Cold War Begins

Truman's denunciation of Soviet actions induced Stalin to tighten his grip on Eastern Europe. Nonetheless, the president became more convinced that he should "get tough with the Russians," and he received encouragement. George F. Kennan, a State Department expert on the U.S.S.R., advised that the United States should apply "long-term, patient, but firm and vigilant containment of Russian expansive tendencies." Former British prime minister Winston Churchill, in his iron curtain speech, condemned Stalin's behavior, called for an anticommunist alliance of the English-speaking peoples, and cautioned against sharing atomic know-how with the Soviets. Truman followed Churchill's nuclear advice and threatened to use American naval and land forces if Stalin did not withdraw his troops from Iran. In their emerging Cold War, the United States and the Soviet Union would use economic pressure, nuclear threats, propaganda, and subversion against each other, but they would not engage in direct military combat.

C. European Crisis, American Commitment

In March 1947 Truman asked Congress to appropriate millions of dollars to help the Greek and Turkish governments fight communist rebel movements in their countries. The president declared that this was part of a new American commitment to support peoples all over the world who were threatened by Soviet aggression and/or internal communist uprisings. The Republican-controlled Congress endorsed this Truman Doctrine when it voted to appropriate the money in May. Truman and his secretary of state, George C. Marshall, also worried about the situation elsewhere in Europe. Postwar economic collapse was causing impoverished Western Europeans to vote for Communist party candidates. To curtail the appeal of communism, Marshall and Truman proposed massive U.S. assistance to rebuild European economies. Congress appropriated $17 billion for this Marshall Plan. By 1952 that money had revived Western Europe economically. Communist popularity there had waned, and American business boomed with increased sales to now prosperous European customers.

D. Confrontation

In 1947–1948 Stalin broadened his sphere of influence in Eastern Europe as communist regimes took over Hungary and Czechoslovakia. When the United States, Britain, and France announced that they would unite their zones of occupation in Germany into a rearmed West German state, including the Western-occupied parts of Berlin, the Soviets reacted with the Berlin blockade. Stalin prevented all ground movement of goods and people between West Germany and West Berlin. He hoped to halt establishment of the West German republic or at least force the Western powers out of Berlin. Instead Truman instituted the Berlin airlift. In May 1949 Stalin ended his unsuccessful Berlin blockade, and the West German Federal Republic (West Germany), including West Berlin, was established. Also that year the United States joined with ten European nations and Canada in an anticommunist military alliance called the North Atlantic Treaty Organization (NATO). The Soviets responded by establishing the German Democratic Republic (East Germany), developing their atomic bomb, and in 1955 joining with their satellites in the Warsaw Pact military alliance. Thus the two super-powers divided Europe into rival armed camps.

E. The Cold War in Asia

The United States and the U.S.S.R. also contended for economic and military influence in Asia. The United States pulled a rebuilt Japan into its economic orbit, occupied much of Japan's former Pacific island empire, and crushed a communist movement in the Philippines. But American military and economic assistance to Jiang Jieshi did not save his unpopular Nationalist government from overthrow by Mao Zedong. In 1949 communist takeover of China and Soviet testing of an atomic bomb led to hysteria in the United States and a search for disloyal elements at home to blame for these events. Stung by Republican charges that it was responsible, the Truman administration decided to develop the hydrogen bomb and recommended great increases in military spending. The Soviets built hydrogen bombs, too, and the thermonuclear terror increased.

F. The Korean War

In 1945 the U.S.S.R. and the United States liberated Korea from Japanese rule. The Soviets set up a communist-governed People's Democratic Republic of Korea north of the thirty-eighth parallel; the United States helped create the pro-Western Republic of Korea to the south. Eager to reunite Koreans under its rule, the People's Republic invaded the South in 1950. Truman, without consulting Congress, sent American forces under General Douglas MacArthur to South Korea to repel the invasion. The United Nations also dispatched a token army to fight under MacArthur. U.S., U.N., and South Korean troops soon pushed the North Koreans back to the thirty-eighth parallel, but Truman and MacArthur decided to conquer the North and place it in the hands of the South Korean government. When MacArthur's armies neared the Yalu River, the boundary between North Korea and China, Mao Zedong warned that he would not "stand idly by." MacArthur, ignoring the threat, was caught off guard by the thirty-three Chinese divisions that hurled his troops deep into South Korea.

After months of bloody fighting, MacArthur's forces again reached the vicinity of the thirty-eighth parallel. Truman then ordered the general to hold that position while the United States sought to negotiate a settlement. MacArthur protested, swearing that he could achieve total victory if only Truman would allow him to atomic-bomb and blockade China. When the general would not desist, the president removed him from command to uphold the principle of civilian control over the military. By the time the truce talks concluded in 1953, the border between the two Koreas was set in nearly the same place it had been before 1950, and the United States had expended some fifty-four thousand lives and $54 billion. Between 1950 and 1953 defense spending climbed from one-third to two-thirds of the entire federal budget. The United States also began aiding France against an independence revolt in Indochina, and it created an anticommunist military alliance with Australia, New Zealand, and other countries in Asia.

III. The Truman Administration at Home

A. *The Eightieth Congress*

The Republican-controlled Congress refused to pass further reforms and began to undo the New Deal. Over Truman's veto it passed the Taft-Hartley Act, which was far less favorable to unions than the Wagner Act had been. Truman courted liberal, labor, and Jewish votes for the next election by condemning the reactionary Congress and recognizing the new state of Israel.

B. *The Politics of Civil Rights*

In 1946 Truman created the President's Committee on Civil Rights to investigate racism and suggest ways to protect minorities. The committee recommended that Congress pass anti-lynching, anti–poll tax, and other civil-rights bills. When Truman encountered strong resistance from southern Democrats, he failed to submit specific proposals to the lawmakers. At the 1948 Democratic National Convention, liberals and urban politicians, who needed the northern black vote, forced the party to adopt a strong civil-rights plank, committing Truman to press for the measures recommended by his civil-rights committee. This platform induced many southern Democrats to found the rival States' Rights Democratic (Dixiecrat) party and nominate South Carolina segregationist J. Strom Thurmond for president.

C. *The Election of 1948*

The Democrats ran Truman; the Republicans, Governor Thomas E. Dewey. Truman's defeat seemed likely because of the Dixiecrat split and the defection of some left-wing Democrats to Henry A. Wallace, nominee of the new Progressive party. During the campaign Truman secured the northern black vote by issuing executive orders against discrimination in government employment and segregation in the armed forces. With the support of northern blacks and most of the Roosevelt New Deal coalition, Truman scored an unexpected victory. Neither Thurmond nor Wallace had drained off enough Democratic votes to hurt him.

D. The Fair Deal

Truman then asked Congress to pass a package of social and economic reforms he called the Fair Deal. The Eighty-first Congress extended several older New Deal programs, such as increasing the minimum wage and social-security benefits and undertaking slum clearance and public-housing construction. But a conservative coalition of southern Democrats and Republicans blocked all civil-rights and most Fair Deal measures. Truman increasingly turned his attention from domestic reform to the Cold War and the Korean War.

IV. The Politics of Anticommunism

A. Loyalty and Security

Truman, concerned by Republican accusations that he was not protecting internal security, established the Federal Employee Loyalty Program in March 1947. It provided for checks on all government workers to root out any disloyal personnel. Between 1947 and 1951 more than three thousand persons were fired or forced to resign, often because they had espoused unpopular ideas, not because they had committed unlawful acts.

B. The Anticommunist Crusade

The loyalty program stimulated more fear of subversion. Magazines published stories about the "red" menace. Thirty-nine states passed laws requiring their employees to take loyalty oaths. Teachers, union leaders, and public officials hesitated to advocate reform lest they be suspected of being pro-communist. In 1947 the House Un-American Activities Committee (HUAC) began hearings on communist influence. Witnesses who refused to testify about their own and other people's past political activities and views were cited for contempt of Congress and lost their jobs. After HUAC investigated the entertainment industries, Hollywood studios and radio networks blacklisted employees they considered left-wing, and they turned out a wave of anticommunist films and programs. The Truman administration prosecuted the leaders of the Communist party for conspiracy to preach the overthrow of the government, and the Supreme Court upheld the convictions on the grounds that First Amendment freedoms may be restricted to protect national security. All of this ignored the fact that danger from the thirty thousand American Communists was minimal.

C. Hiss and the Rosenbergs

In 1950 former State Department official Alger Hiss was convicted of perjury for lying about providing classified documents to the Soviets. This case heightened public alarm, as did the Rosenberg trial. Ethel and Julius Rosenberg were found guilty of conspiracy to commit espionage as part of a spy ring that had stolen atomic secrets for the Soviets. The Rosenbergs insisted they were innocent, but the judge, reflecting anticommunist hysteria, imposed the death sentence. Republicans claimed these cases proved that the Democratic administrations had been honeycombed with communist traitors.

D. McCarthyism

Of all Republicans, Senator Joseph McCarthy exploited the theme of communist traitors among the Democrats most blatantly. Without supporting evidence, McCarthy loudly accused Democratic senators, members of the Truman administration, and other public officials of either being or harboring communist agents. He won a following among insecure and/or discontented groups, and he frightened political leaders into rigid anticommunist stances on complex issues that required open minds and discussion. Witnesses suspected of being subversive were cited for contempt of Congress by lawmakers eager to prove their own loyalty. Congress also passed the repressive McCarran Internal Security Act and the McCarran-Walter Immigration and Nationality Act.

E. The Election of 1952

The Democrats nominated Adlai Stevenson for president; the Republicans, the popular military hero Dwight D. Eisenhower. McCarthyist labeling of the Democrats as the party of treason, public frustration over the stalemate in Korea, and Eisenhower's pledge to go to that country to end the war all combined to win the Republicans control of the White House and Capitol Hill.

V. Conclusion

The election of 1952 marked the close of the early postwar era, a time of prosperity and nearly full employment. It was also a period of "bitter partisanship," unsettling nuclear fears, and "suspicion and repression." The civil-rights movement and the involvement in Vietnam that reached full bloom in the 1960s sprouted between 1945 and 1952.

VOCABULARY

The following terms are used in Chapter 28. To understand the chapter fully, it is important that you know what each of them means.

polarization   moving to opposite or contrasting positions

subversion   working to undermine or overthrow existing institutions, such as the government, especially by secret means

intransigence   unwillingness to compromise

insurgent   one who engages in armed resistance to the established government; a rebel or revolutionary

oligarchy   a form of government in which power is vested in a few or in a dominant class or clique; the members of that class or clique

protectorate   country dependent on the authority of another nation; a state under the guidance of a more powerful state

insubordination   refusal to submit to higher authority

coterie   a group of persons who associate closely; a clique or circle

closed shop   a factory or other workplace in which new workers must join the union before they can be employed

fulminations   explosive outbursts of criticism or denunciation

espouse   advocate or embrace, as a cause

scurrilous   grossly or indecently abusive

recalcitrant   not compliant; uncooperative

red herring   something to divert attention

IDENTIFICATIONS

After reading Chapter 28, you should be able to identify and explain the historical significance of each of the following:

GI Bill of Rights (Servicemen's Readjustment Act of 1944)

Bretton Woods Agreement, International Monetary Fund, and World Bank

Employment Act of 1946 and the Council of Economic Advisers

Yalta Declaration of Liberated Europe

George F. Kennan and the containment policy

James F. Byrnes

Winston Churchill's iron curtain speech

Atomic Energy Act and the Atomic Energy Commission

Truman Doctrine

George C. Marshall and the Marshall Plan

Berlin blockade and airlift

North Atlantic Treaty Organization and Warsaw Pact

General Douglas MacArthur

National Security Council and NSC-68

Edward Teller, J. Robert Oppenheimer, and the hydrogen bomb

Taft-Hartley Act

To Secure These Rights

J. Strom Thurmond and the Dixiecrats

Henry A. Wallace and the Progressive party

Thomas E. Dewey

the conservative coalition in Congress

House Un-American Activities Committee

Federal Employee Loyalty Program

Smith Act and *Dennis* v. *United States*

Alger Hiss, Whittaker Chambers, and Richard M. Nixon

Ethel and Julius Rosenberg

Joseph R. McCarthy and McCarthyism

McCarran Internal Security Act

McCarran-Walter Immigration and Nationality Act

Adlai Stevenson

SKILL BUILDING: MAPS

1. On the map of Europe on the following page, locate and explain the historical significance, during the period 1945–1952, of each of the following:

   communist-bloc nations of Eastern Europe (Soviet Union, Bulgaria, Hungary, Romania, Albania, Yugoslavia, Poland, and Czechoslovakia)

   Iran

   Black Sea

   Greece and Turkey

   Mediterranean Sea

   Berlin

   German Federal Republic (West Germany)

   German Democratic Republic (East Germany)

   North Atlantic Treaty Organization members in Europe

   Warsaw Pact members

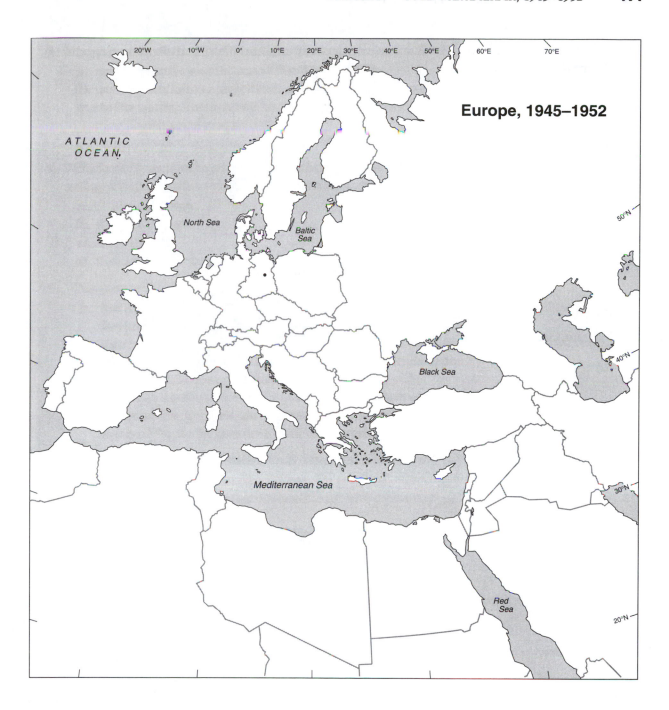

Europe, 1945–1952

ATLANTIC OCEAN.

North Sea

Baltic Sea

Black Sea

Mediterranean Sea

Red Sea

2. On the map of Asia that follows, locate and explain the historical significance, during the period 1945–1952, of each of the following:

Japan

Manchuria

People's Democratic Republic of Korea (North Korea)

Republic of Korea (South Korea)

thirty-eighth parallel

Seoul

Yalu River

Philippines

French Indochina (Cambodia, Laos, and Vietnam)

Taiwan (Formosa)

People's Republic of China

Marshall Islands

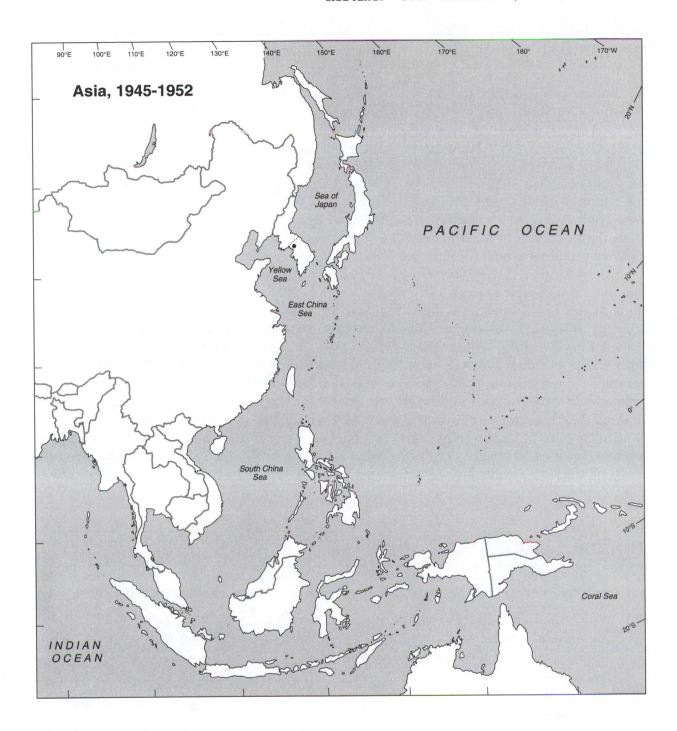

Asia, 1945-1952

Sea of Japan

PACIFIC OCEAN

Yellow Sea

East China Sea

South China Sea

Coral Sea

INDIAN OCEAN

HISTORICAL SOURCES

In Chapter 28 the author has used as historic sources three significant public speeches: (1) Winston Churchill's iron curtain speech delivered at Westminster College in Fulton, Missouri, in March 1946 (p. 907); (2) President Truman's address to a joint session of Congress in March 1947, in which he announced the Truman Doctrine (p. 908); (3) Secretary of State George C. Marshall's commencement address at Harvard University in June 1947, in which he suggested what is now known as the Marshall Plan (pp. 908–909). The historian can find the contents of these speeches in the *Congressional Record* and in newspapers such as the *New York Times,* which published the full text. How does the author use these speeches? What does he learn from them about the thinking that shaped U.S. foreign policy? What do they tell about the origins of the Cold War?

The historian writing about postwar history has available particularly valuable source material in movies and television. Television and motion-picture cameras recorded for millions of viewers the images of "the rumpled" Whittaker Chambers and "the elegant" Alger Hiss (pp. 922–923). Millions watched as the House Un-American Activities Committee questioned film directors, screenwriters, movie stars, and other "friendly" and "unfriendly" witnesses about their political views (p. 922). Today the historian can read the printed transcripts of these hearings and also view the film footage. How does the author use these printed and visual records in Chapter 28? Do visual images from television and movie cameras tell their own story, or must the historian still interpret what he or she sees?

In "A Place in Time: Los Angeles Confronts the Atomic Age," the historian also refers to a scene recorded by television cameras. What is the scene? What does it show about the concerns of Americans in the late 1940s and early 1950s? What role did government play in fanning these fears?

MULTIPLE-CHOICE QUESTIONS

Circle the letter of the item that best completes each statement or answers the question.

1. Who held up a laundry list and claimed, "I have here in my hand a list of 205 names known to the Secretary of State as being members of the Communist party and who nevertheless are still working and shaping policy"?
   a. Richard M. Nixon
   b. George C. Marshall
   c. Joseph R. McCarthy
   d. Whittaker Chambers

2. Which of the following was accomplished during Truman's presidency?
   a. The armed forces were desegregated.
   b. A national health-insurance system was started.
   c. Labor unions were strengthened by government backing for the closed shop.
   d. A federal antilynching law was enacted.

3. In which of these cases did the Supreme Court rule that Congress could curtail freedom of speech to protect national security?
    a. the *Rosenberg* case
    b. the Alger Hiss trial
    c. *Morgan* v. *Virginia*
    d. *Dennis* v. *United States*

4. The term *Fair Deal* refers to
    a. Harry S Truman's domestic social- and economic-reform programs.
    b. Franklin D. Roosevelt's programs to give labor and farmers more lenient treatment by the federal government.
    c. Joseph R. McCarthy's complaints that communist traitors got better treatment from the Democrats than loyal, hard-working ordinary Americans.
    d. none of the above

5. Which of the following people did *not* agree with and encourage Truman's "get tough with Russia" policy in the late 1940s?
    a. Winston Churchill
    b. Henry A. Wallace
    c. George F. Kennan
    d. Senator Arthur Vandenberg

6. Truman was able to stage an upset victory in the election of 1948 because
    a. he gave in to southern wishes and ran on a weak civil-rights platform.
    b. he chose the staunch anticommunist Richard M. Nixon as his running mate.
    c. he re-created the old New Deal coalition and won an even greater percentage of the black vote than Roosevelt had.
    d. he wooed the left wing of the Democratic party with promises to reach an accord with the U.S.S.R. and to drop the Federal Employee Loyalty Program.

7. NSC-68
    a. was rejected by Truman as prohibitively expensive.
    b. called for negotiations with the Soviet Union to reach a verifiable nuclear disarmament treaty.
    c. was a secret Soviet plan to foment a communist uprising in the United States by 1968.
    d. called for a massive U.S. military buildup to counter the U.S.S.R.'s aggressive intentions.

8. In which of these conflicts did American and Soviet troops clash on the battlefield?
    a. the Korean War
    b. the efforts to get supplies to Berlin despite the Russian blockade
    c. the Indochinese war in which Ho Chi Minh's communists tried to oust the French
    d. none of the above

9. Alger Hiss was accused of
   a. giving, in the 1930s, secret State Department documents to an agent working for the Soviet Union.
   b. preaching the overthrow of the U.S. government by force and violence.
   c. helping the Communists come to power in China in 1949 by sending them information on Jiang Jieshi's secret military plans.
   d. opposing American development of the hydrogen bomb in the early 1950s because of his communist sympathies.

10. The Korean War
   a. ended Soviet occupation of the Korean peninsula.
   b. reunited North and South Korea.
   c. set a precedent for U.S. participation in undeclared wars not approved by Congress.
   d. permanently moved the border of South Korea to the Yalu River.

SHORT-ANSWER QUESTIONS

1. Why did the U.S. economy enjoy a boom after World War II rather than slide back into depression?

2. Explain why the president expounded the Truman Doctrine to Congress. What was Truman proposing? Why did Congress go along with the doctrine?

3. Why did the Soviet Union impose the Berlin blockade, and how did President Truman respond to it?

4. Why were the communists able to take over China in 1949? How did some Republicans explain communist success in China?

5. Who supported Senator Joseph McCarthy and McCarthyism, and why?

6. What accounts for the victory of Eisenhower and the other Republicans in the election of 1952?

ESSAY QUESTIONS

1. One historian has argued that President Truman was at least partly responsible for McCarthyism and the popular obsession with communist subversion that gripped the United States in the late 1940s and 1950s. Discuss your reasons for either agreeing or disagreeing with that charge.

2. Another historian observed, "If the Truman years represent an era of progress, however limited, in civil rights [for black Americans], they represent an era of retrogression in civil liberties [free exercise of the rights guaranteed in the First Amendment]." Discuss the statement and support or refute it with specific evidence from Chapter 28.

3. Discuss the origins of the Cold War.

4. What was the containment policy? How did the Truman administration implement it in Europe and Asia?

5. Discuss the differences between President Truman and General Douglas MacArthur on how to conduct the Korean War. Was the president justified in firing the general? Why or why not?

29

America at Midcentury

OUTLINE AND SUMMARY

I. The Eisenhower Presidency

A. *The General as Chief Executive*

Popular as the World War II commander of Allied forces in Western Europe, Dwight Eisenhower became president of the United States in 1953. He exercised executive authority with restraint; seldom took a public, forceful role in lawmaking; and delegated much responsibility to subordinates.

B. *"Dynamic Conservatism"*

Eisenhower called his approach to governing "dynamic conservatism" or "modern Republicanism." He staffed his administration with corporate executives and expected them to run it with business efficiency. He resisted right-wing pleas to dismantle the New and Fair Deals but tried to restrain further growth of federal activities. Eisenhower's pragmatism led him, despite his dislike of unbalanced budgets, to increase federal spending to combat economic recessions in 1953 and 1957. He also signed the Interstate Highway Act of 1956, which authorized the most expensive public-works program in American history. The forty-one thousand miles of national highway speeded the growth of suburbs, decay of central cities, decline of railroads, dependence on cars and trucks, demand for gasoline, and pollution of the air. In 1956 Eisenhower was renominated by the Republicans and again beat his Democratic opponent, Adlai Stevenson.

C. *The Downfall of Joseph McCarthy*

Although Eisenhower hated McCarthy, the president did not speak out against him and his reckless accusations. Senator McCarthy's 1954 televised hearings, during which he accused the army of protecting communist spies, finally led to his downfall. The Senate censured him, and thereafter the media and public officials ignored him. Fears of internal subversion remained, however, as the House Un-American Activities Committee continued its endless hunt for communists. Right-wing groups such as the John Birch Society warned against the "creeping socialism" of Truman and Eisenhower.

D. The Warren Court

Conservatives were especially upset at the liberal direction Supreme Court decisions started to take after 1953, when Earl Warren became chief justice. Not only did the Court reverse the convictions of some Communist party leaders under the Smith Act, but in 1954 in *Brown* v. *Board of Education*, it ruled that racially segregated schools violated the Fourteenth Amendment. Eisenhower's failure to back the *Brown* decision and his regret at having appointed Warren encouraged southern resistance. White Citizens Councils, the Ku Klux Klan, and congressional signers of the Southern Manifesto all fought school integration.

E. The Laws of the Land

Southern defiance of the *Brown* ruling reached a high point in September 1957 when mobs of angry whites and the Arkansas National Guard, under orders from Governor Orval E. Faubus, blocked the entry of nine African-American students into Little Rock's all-white Central High School. Eisenhower eventually ordered the U.S. Army into Little Rock to enforce federal authority and protect the black students. Resistance elsewhere continued so fiercely that by 1960 fewer than 1 percent of black students in the Deep South attended integrated schools. Still, Eisenhower's use of troops, no matter how reluctant, raised black hopes and won approval from 90 percent of northern whites. Eisenhower also signed the Civil Rights Acts of 1957 and 1960, which did little to protect the right of blacks to vote but did establish a permanent federal civil-rights commission with broad investigative powers.

II. The Cold War Continues

A. Truce in Korea

The Eisenhower administration signed an armistice that ended the fighting in Korea in July 1953. The settlement left Korea divided between communist North and anticommunist South near the same thirty-eighth parallel border that had existed prior to hostilities.

B. Ike and Dulles

Right-wing Republicans were not satisfied with simply containing the spread of communism. To placate them, Eisenhower appointed the aggressive John Foster Dulles secretary of state. Dulles advocated liberating the Eastern European countries from communism and insisted the West should risk war rather than back down in a crisis. Eisenhower ignored Dulles's advice, however, and essentially continued the containment policy.

C. Waging Peace

Eisenhower tried to achieve "peaceful coexistence" with the U.S.S.R. by meeting Soviet leaders at the 1955 Geneva summit conference. The gathering produced no nuclear-arms-control plan, but subsequently the two powers independently stopped their atmospheric atomic tests. Meanwhile, the United States relied increasingly on its nuclear weapons to deter Soviet aggression, and Dulles committed the United States to defending many Third World military dictators against all uprisings.

D. The Clandestine CIA

In its effort to secure anticommunist regimes, the Eisenhower administration relied more and more on covert actions by the Central Intelligence Agency (CIA), led by Allen Dulles. During the 1950s the CIA helped install pro-Western autocratic governments in Iran, the Philippines, and Guatemala.

E. Conflict in Vietnam

The CIA carried on its most extensive secret operations in Vietnam. After the Vietnamese overthrew French rule, the CIA blocked elections to unify the country and pushed into power the dictatorial Ngo Dinh Diem in South Vietnam. Eisenhower claimed Diem had to remain in office to prevent Vietnam's fall to the Communists, which would be followed by Communist takeovers in all of the surrounding countries.

F. Antiwesternism in the Middle East

When England, France, and Israel invaded Egypt in 1956 to reclaim the Suez Canal from Gamal Abdel Nasser, Eisenhower demanded that they withdraw because they had not consulted with the United States in advance. He feared the Suez expedition might lead to a war with the Soviets, who were backing Egypt. After the aborted Suez venture, the president committed the United States to keeping communism out of the Middle East with his 1957 Eisenhower Doctrine, and the United States continued to view Arab nationalism as "communist inspired."

G. Frustrations Abroad

Eisenhower's support for pro-Western dictators led to anti-U.S. demonstrations in Latin America and Japan and hostility from the new revolutionary government led by Fidel Castro in Cuba. The president's hope for improving Soviet-American relations with a 1960 summit conference was dashed when the U.S.S.R. shot down an American U-2 reconnaissance plane that had been spying on Soviet military installations.

H. The Eisenhower Legacy

President Eisenhower ended the fighting in Korea, kept the peace thereafter, and initiated small steps toward relaxing Soviet-American tensions. On the other hand, he speeded up the nuclear-arms race, expanded the Cold War, and gave the CIA the go-ahead to subvert foreign governments that the United States disliked. At home Eisenhower followed a middle-of-the-road course that pleased neither right-wingers nor liberals. Liberals criticized his failure to denounce McCarthy and racism. Conservatives faulted him for not repealing the New and Fair Deals. Eisenhower will be remembered for his farewell warning about the growing influence of the "military-industrial complex" over American society.

III. The Affluent Society

A. Introduction

In the 1950s the United States enjoyed a broad-based, unprecedented level of prosperity. By 1960, 60 percent of American families owned homes and 75 percent had cars. The prosperity was slightly marred by three brief recessions and worry over a mounting national debt.

B. The New Industrial Society

Greatly increased government expenditures partly accounted for the prosperity and the national debt. Some of the federal money financed public-works and other domestic programs, but the majority of it (about 10 percent of the GNP) went into military buildup. The government also underwrote much scientific research, as did large corporations. New technology from this research fueled the growth of industry, made possible increasing automation, and supplied a host of consumer products. The availability of abundant, cheap petroleum also contributed to economic growth and prosperity.

C. The Age of Computers

The development of computers was one of the most important parts of the postwar technological revolution. Starting with the Mark I calculator in 1944, the manufacturing of ever more complex electronic computers became a billion-dollar business, and the devices transformed the nature of many jobs.

D. Concentration and Consolidation in Industry and Agriculture

Technological advances accelerated the long-term trend toward fewer and larger economic enterprises controlling the United States' industry and agriculture. A new middle class of professionals and administrators arose to manage these corporate giants. The big corporate farms increased their yields and profits by heavy use of chemical fertilizers, herbicides, and pesticides. Until the 1962 publication of Rachel Carson's *Silent Spring,* most Americans ignored the dangers of these toxic substances to the environment. Not until the 1960s and 1970s did states and the federal government begin to ban the use of DDT.

E. Blue-Collar Blues

Union membership and power reached its peak in the early 1950s. The AFL and CIO merged into a single federation in 1955 and won for some of the 36 percent of nonagricultural workers who were unionized benefits such as guaranteed annual wages and health-care plans. Thereafter, the union movement declined, as its successes quieted labor militance; the number of blue-collar laborers fell; and the growing portion of workers in public, white-collar, and service employment proved difficult to organize.

F. Prosperity, Suburbanization, and Mobility

Rising purchasing power, expanding credit, and burgeoning advertising stimulated avid consumerism. During the 1950s Americans purchased 58 million cars, which improved mobility but contributed to increased highway fatalities, air pollution, and the movement of whites to the suburbs. Government highway building, loans, and tax credits also made it possible for former city dwellers to purchase homes in suburbia. The construction industry, adopting mass-production techniques, built 13 million new homes, 85 percent of them in suburbs. While millions of poor blacks and Hispanics moved from rural areas into cities, 18 million mostly white, middle-class Americans left, so that by 1960 the suburban population of the United States equaled that of the central cities. People and industry also moved increasingly from the Northeast to the Sun Belt states of the South and West.

IV. Consensus and Conservatism

A. Togetherness and the Baby Boom

In the 1950s Americans married younger and produced more babies than the previous generation had. The increased birthrate and medical advances that cut infant mortality resulted in the largest population growth of any decade in U.S. history.

B. Domesticity

In the midst of this baby boom, educators, psychologists, and the media all delivered the message that women were most contented when they fulfilled their "natural" roles of wife, mother, and homemaker. Women accounted for a smaller percentage of college students than in the 1920s and 1930s, but they did not all leave the workplace. By 1960 almost 40 percent of women held full- or part-time jobs, and of those some 40 percent had school-age children. Most women, however, worked in poorly paid sales and office positions. There was little protest because the organized feminist movement was at a low ebb.

C. Religion and Education

There were signs of renewed interest in religion in the 1950s, such as the popularity of films and books with religious themes, growing church attendance, and the inclusion of the words *under God* in the Pledge of Allegiance. School and college enrollments reached all-time peaks in the 1950s, but much of the education promoted social and psychological adjustment rather than math, science, and other academic subjects.

D. Affirmation and Anxiety: The Culture of the Fifties

American fiction of the fifties slighted social issues in favor of exploring the personal yearnings of alienated characters. The most significant novels tended to be by southern, black, and Jewish writers, such as William Faulkner, Eudora Welty, James Baldwin, and Philip Roth. Hollywood films, portraying Americans as white and middle class, generally "glorified material success and romantic love." Women were usually shown as "cute, cozy helpmates" or sexy "dumb blondes." Moviegoing declined as Americans watched more television.

E. The Message of the Medium

By the early 1960s, 90 percent of all households owned at least one television, and the industry both reflected and influenced the values and perceptions of the nation. Programs catered to the tastes of a mass audience and nurtured consumerism, conformity, complacency, and racial and gender stereotypes. The television image of political candidates often mattered more than what they really said or did.

V. The Other America

A. Poverty and Urban Blight

Few white, middle-class Americans realized that more than one-fifth of their compatriots still lived below the poverty line. The poor included the elderly, tenant farmers, sharecroppers, and migratory agricultural workers. Native Americans, Appalachian whites, blacks, and Hispanics concentrated in city slums. With their tax base shrinking as well-off whites fled to suburbia, cities were unable to provide adequate schools, housing, public transportation, and social services.

B. Blacks' Struggle for Justice

The struggle of southern blacks for social justice entered a new phase of nonviolent, direct action with the 1955 Montgomery bus boycott, sparked by Rosa Parks and led by Martin Luther King, Jr. After their success in Montgomery, King and other black ministers organized the Southern Christian Leadership Conference to continue the campaign against discrimination.

C. The Hispanic-American and Native American Predicament

Hispanics and Indians were among the poorest and most discriminated against minorities in the 1950s. Nearly 1 million Puerto Ricans migrated from the island to northeastern city slums. Mexican-Americans, many of them "undocumented aliens," filled migratory-labor, construction, light manufacturing, and domestic-service jobs in the Southwest and faced the constant threat of deportation. In the fifties the government terminated all special federal services for Indians and encouraged breakup of the reservations. These policies resulted in the transfer of more than 500,000 acres of Indian land to whites and the further impoverishment and demoralization of Native Americans.

VI. Seeds of Disquiet

A. Sputnik

Russia's launching of Sputnik in 1957 shook American confidence and complacency. In a rush to catch up, the United States created the National Aeronautics and Space Administration (NASA), launched its own missiles, and greatly increased federal spending on education, with an emphasis on turning out more engineers, scientists, and mathematicians to put us ahead of the Soviet Union in the Cold War of arms research and development.

B. A Rebellion of Youth

Many teenagers expressed mild cultural rebellion in their manner of dress, choice of film idols, and enthusiasm for rock and roll and its most popular performer, Elvis Presley.

C. Portents of Change

By the late 1950s the first signs of the "youth movement that would explode in the 1960s" could be seen in the emergence of the Beat writers, such as Allen Ginsberg and Jack Kerouac, and in college student protests against the House Un-American Activities Committee, racial segregation, and the nuclear-arms race.

VII. Conclusion

On the whole Americans in the 1950s were conformist and complacent and enjoyed their great economic prosperity. They largely ignored the persistence of poverty and discrimination in their midst as well as the dangerous concentration of power in the military-industrial complex. But by the end of the decade many felt a sense of uneasiness about the arms race, U.S. foreign-policy commitments, and unsettling social and technological changes.

VOCABULARY

The following terms are used in Chapter 29. To understand the chapter fully, it is important that you know what each of them means.

pragmatic   concerned with or guided by the practical consequences of a given action

junta   a small, governing council or committee (often of military leaders)

demur   to take exception to; to object

autocratic   acting like a dictator; exercising absolute, unchecked power

automation   operating or controlling a mechanical process by highly automatic means, such as electronic devices

oligopoly   situation in which a few large companies dominate a whole industry

conglomerates   huge business corporations created by the merger or takeover of many companies in unrelated fields of industry

Jim Crow   practice or policy of racial segregation

mores   customs of central importance accepted without question and embodying the fundamental moral views of a group, people, or social class

IDENTIFICATIONS

After reading Chapter 29, you should be able to identify and explain the historical significance of each of the following:

"dynamic conservatism" or "modern Republicanism"

Interstate Highway Act, 1956

Adlai Stevenson

"new conservatives" or radical right

Earl Warren

Brown v. *Board of Education of Topeka*, 1954

Orval E. Faubus and the Little Rock desegregation fight

Civil Rights Acts of 1957 and 1960

John Foster Dulles and "brinksmanship"

"peaceful coexistence" and the "spirit of Geneva"

Third World

Allen Dulles, the Central Intelligency Agency, and covert action

Ho Chi Minh, the Vietminh, and the National Liberation Front

the "domino theory" in Asia

Ngo Dinh Diem

Gamal Abdel Nasser

Eisenhower Doctrine

military-industrial complex

Rachel Carson, *Silent Spring*

George Meany, Walter Reuther, and the AFL-CIO

Sun Belt

baby boom

Rosa Parks, Martin Luther King, Jr., and the Montgomery bus boycott

Southern Christian Leadership Conference

House Concurrent Resolution 108, termination, and relocation

National Aeronautics and Space Administration (NASA)

Elvis Presley and rock and roll

the Beats

SKILL BUILDING: MAPS

1. On the map of Asia, locate and explain the historical significance of each of the following in U.S. foreign policy at midcentury:

North Korea

South Korea

thirty-eighth parallel

Philippines

North Vietnam

South Vietnam

seventeenth parallel

Thailand

Burma

Indonesia

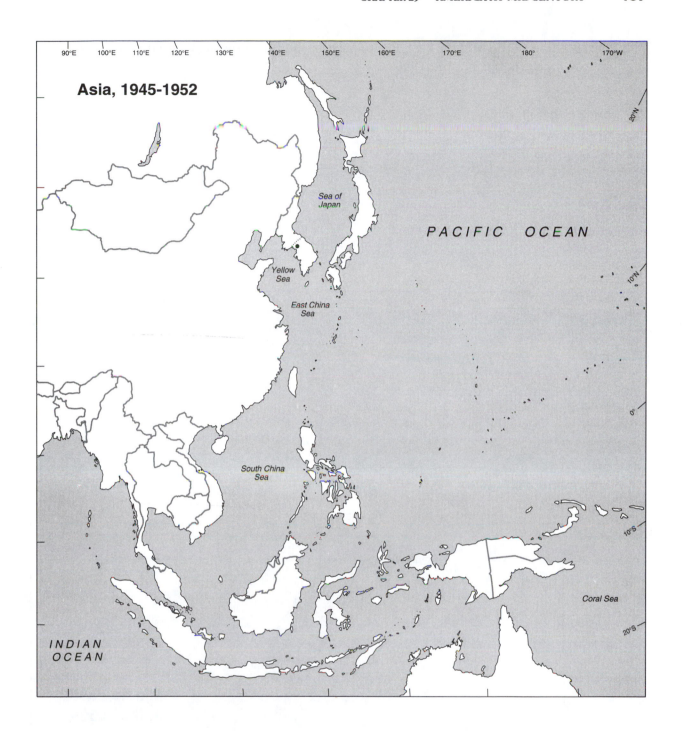

Asia, 1945-1952

Sea of Japan

PACIFIC OCEAN

Yellow Sea

East China Sea

South China Sea

Coral Sea

INDIAN OCEAN

2. On the map of the Middle East, locate each of the following and explain its significance in U.S. foreign policy in the 1950s:

Egypt

Suez Canal

Mediterranean Sea

Gulf of Suez

Israel

Syria

Jordan

Lebanon

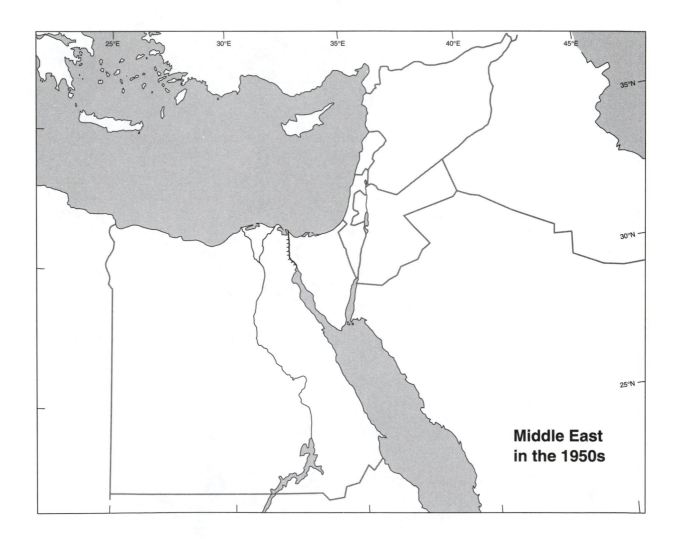

Middle East in the 1950s

SKILL BUILDING: GRAPHS AND CHARTS

Look at the pie charts under the title "Urban, Suburban, and Rural Americans, 1940–1960" on page 945. These charts indicate some of the most significant population shifts in those years. After studying them, you should be able to answer the following questions:

1. Between 1940 and 1960 which area of the United States—cities, suburbs, or rural small towns—declined in its percentage of total population?

2. What happened to the percentage of Americans living in suburbs during that period?

3. Historians tell us that most of the population growth in suburbs came from white, middle-class families moving out of central cities. Yet the pie charts show the central cities containing slightly less than one-third of the population in 1940, 1950, and 1960. Who was moving into the central cities to replace the white middle class migrating to the suburbs?

HISTORICAL SOURCES

In Chapter 29 the author has learned much about the recent past by looking at items of popular culture and entertainment: television programs, Hollywood films, hit songs, most admired movie and rock stars, and the best-selling books of the period. On page 949 the author describes some of the most watched television shows. On pages 947, 948, and 957 the author discusses such 1950s box-office successes as *The Tender Trap, The Robe, Ben Hur, The Wild One,* and *Rebel Without a Cause* and such favorite movie stars as Sandra Dee, Marilyn Monroe, and James Dean. There is a section devoted to Elvis Presley and reference on page 957 to Dick Clark's *American Bandstand.* On pages 946–947 the author discusses the book that sold more copies than any other but the Bible in the 1950s: Benjamin Spock's *Baby and Child Care.* How does the author use each of these examples of popular culture? In each case what does the author claim it shows about American society and values at mid-century? Using the same sources, could you come to different conclusions about 1950s America?

The author also has gathered material from the works of a number of social scientists who described and analyzed post–World War II America. A few examples are John Kenneth Galbraith's *The Affluent Society,* David Riesman's *The Lonely Crowd,* and Michael Harrington's *The Other America.* What are some of the observations about prosperity, poverty, and conformist values that the author draws from these sources?

Look at "A Place in Time: Levittown, U.S.A." This is a capsule history of the post–World War II home-construction industry and one particular company. What does it illustrate about the reasons for the move to the suburbs and the benefits and problems that the population shift has caused?

MULTIPLE-CHOICE QUESTIONS

Circle the letter of the item that best completes each statement or answers the question.

1. President Eisenhower once said "the biggest damn fool mistake I ever made" was
   a. appointing Earl Warren as chief justice of the Supreme Court.
   b. not denouncing Joseph McCarthy and McCarthyism publicly in 1952 and 1953.
   c. appointing John Foster Dulles as secretary of state and allowing him to practice "brinksmanship."
   d. giving the CIA a free hand to conduct covert actions to undermine foreign governments it didn't approve of.

2. Which of the following actions of President Eisenhower pleased the right wing of the Republican party?
   a. his resort to deficit spending to combat downturns in the economy
   b. his signing of the Civil Rights Acts of 1957 and 1960
   c. his appointment of John Foster Dulles as secretary of state
   d. his refusal to abolish the Council of Economic Advisers

3. Which of the following statements about *Brown* v. *Board of Education of Topeka* is correct?
   a. President Dwight Eisenhower praised and gave his full support to enforcing the Supreme Court decision.
   b. The Supreme Court ruled that public schools segregated by race were acceptable if the facilities made available to each race were equal.
   c. The Supreme Court gave the Board of Education of Topeka, Kansas, and other school boards operating segregated school systems one year to integrate them.
   d. The Supreme Court rejected the separate-but-equal doctrine and ruled that racial segregation violates the equal-protection clause of the Fourteenth Amendment.

4. President Eisenhower advanced his domino theory to justify U.S. intervention in the internal affairs of
   a. Guatemala.
   b. Vietnam.
   c. Korea.
   d. Egypt.

5. Which of the following statements about women in the 1950s is correct?
   a. Women generally married later and had fewer children than they had in the 1930s and 1940s.
   b. Women constituted a smaller percentage of college students and received fewer advanced degrees than they had in the 1920s and 1930s.
   c. The proportion of married women who were employed declined.
   d. A greater proportion of women became involved in the feminist movement than ever before.

6. The 1950s government policies of termination and relocation proved disastrous for
   a. Native Americans.
   b. African-Americans.
   c. Mexican-Americans.
   d. Puerto Ricans.

7. Which of these statements about literature in the 1950s is correct?
   a. Novelists were primarily concerned with societal problems, such as poverty, racism, and labor exploitation.
   b. Almost no literature of lasting value was written during this complacent, conformist decade.
   c. Most literature celebrated America's good life of cars, televisions, and suburban homes.
   d. Southern, black, and Jewish writers produced much of the decade's most outstanding literature.

8. Which did *not* occur in the 1950s?
   a. The total number of farms declined as large-scale agribusinesses increasingly dominated farming.
   b. Fewer than 1 percent of American businesses earned more than half of all corporate profits.
   c. The portion of the labor force belonging to unions increased from roughly one-quarter to almost one-half.
   d. More than half of the federal budget each year went to finance military preparedness.

9. About what portion of the American people lived in poverty during the prosperous 1950s?
   a. one-third
   b. one-fifth
   c. one-half
   d. one-tenth

10. The Beats were
   a. a popular rock group in the 1950s.
   b. an anticommunist, paramilitary organization.
   c. a group of nonconformist writers who rejected the materialism and conformity of American society.
   d. CIA agents specially trained to carry out covert actions in Third World countries.

SHORT-ANSWER QUESTIONS

1. What brought about the downfall of Joseph McCarthy? Did his eclipse end excessive fears of communist subversion?

2. Explain the roles in U.S. foreign policy of Secretary of State John Foster Dulles and his brother, CIA director Allen Dulles.

3. What did President Eisenhower mean when he warned Americans to be wary of the military-industrial complex?

4. Describe the economic changes that occurred in American agriculture in the 1950s. What impact did those changes have on the environment?

5. Why in the second half of the 1950s did union membership and influence decline?

6. Describe at least three major demographic changes that occurred in America in the 1950s. What social and political impact would these developments have on the nation?

7. What were the reasons for growing urban blight in the prosperous America of the 1950s?

8. What were the effects on American life of Russia's launching of *Sputnik*?

ESSAY QUESTIONS

1. "Balance and moderation . . . characterized Eisenhower's domestic record. But his middle-of-the-road policies pleased neither liberals nor conservatives." Write an essay either agreeing or disagreeing with this assessment. Back up what you say with as many specific facts as possible.

2. Discuss the Eisenhower legacy in foreign policy. How successful was he in keeping the peace and easing tensions with the Soviets? In what ways did his policies expand the Cold War and accelerate the nuclear-arms race?

3. "A booming, broad-based prosperity made the 1950s a period of economic abundance without historical parallel." Explain the developments and circumstances that produced the prosperity and abundance. What role did government policies play in encouraging economic activity?

4. The section of Chapter 29 dealing with American society and culture in the 1950s is titled "Consensus and Conservatism." Is this an apt title? Discuss major trends in American family life, religion, education, the arts, and entertainment during the fifties to illustrate why this is or is not an appropriate title.

5. Discuss "the other America." What does the term refer to? Which groups made up the other America in the 1950s? Why were they shut out of the unprecedented economic prosperity of that decade?

30

The Turbulent Sixties

OUTLINE AND SUMMARY

I. Introduction

Starting in February 1960, in Greensboro, North Carolina, a wave of sit-ins to desegregate lunch counters and other public places swept through the South. The courage of the black students who initiated these demonstrations emboldened their elders and energized the struggle for racial equality. It also broke the conservative complacency of the 1950s, paving the way for crusading authors like Michael Harrington, Ralph Nader, and Betty Friedan to arouse the nation to the plight of the poor, the dangers to the consumer, and the pervasive sexism. The rhetoric of John Kennedy's New Frontier and Lyndon Johnson's Great Society attracted young, progressive Americans with their promise of an end to these wrongs. But assassinations of key leaders, widespread racial strife, and escalation of the war in Vietnam produced a white, conservative backlash and curtailed social reform. The decade closed in discord and disillusionment.

II. The New Frontier, 1960–1963

A. *The Election of 1960*

Richard M. Nixon, the Republican presidential nominee, identified himself with the still popular Eisenhower and his "middle way," although liberals never forgot Nixon's McCarthyist background. John F. Kennedy, the lesser-known Democratic candidate, challenged his opponent to a series of televised debates. The four debates enhanced the popularity of the telegenic Kennedy and marked the beginning of television's domination in American presidential politics. Kennedy won in the closest contest since 1888.

B. *"To Get America Moving Again"*

Unlike Eisenhower, whose cabinet was top-heavy with businessmen, Kennedy surrounded himself with technocrats and academics. He appointed his closest confidant and adviser, his brother Robert Kennedy, as attorney general. The president gave his administration a cultural tone by inviting artists and writers to the White House, and he used television to broaden his popular appeal. Knowing little of his personal weaknesses, Americans responded warmly to JFK's carefully crafted public image.

C. Kennedy's Domestic Record

Despite Kennedy's call for a New Frontier, he pushed little reform legislation through Congress. Rather than press the fight with Congress, the president concentrated on promoting economic growth through increased military spending and tax incentives to business. At the time of Kennedy's assassination, the economy was indeed booming, but corporate profits had risen faster than personal income, spending on social welfare lagged, and thanks to Rachel Carson's *Silent Spring* and other warnings, Americans were beginning to worry about the polluted environment. In response Congress passed the 1963 Clean Air Act.

D. Kennedy and Civil Rights

Kennedy initially sought to avoid the civil-rights issue because he knew it would divide the Democratic party. The intensity of protests against segregation and the answering fury of southern racists, however, forced the president's hand. Kennedy finally sent federal marshals into the South after white mobs in Anniston, Birmingham, and Montgomery, Alabama, savagely attacked Congress of Racial Equality (CORE) freedom riders who were defying the unconstitutional segregation imposed on interstate travelers. It took still more freedom rides to convince the president that the Interstate Commerce Commission would have to enforce the Supreme Court ruling against segregated interstate transportation. Racist violence also eventually brought Kennedy to dispatch federal troops to the University of Mississippi campus to protect James Meredith, the first black student enrolled there.

E. The African-American Revolution

To expose the viciousness of southern racists and compel Kennedy to act, Martin Luther King, Jr., in 1963 led marches, sit-ins, and pray-ins in Birmingham, Alabama. Police chief Eugene "Bull" Conner, in front of television cameras, sent his police with electric cattle prods, high-pressure water hoses, and attack dogs against the peaceful demonstrators. The televised brutality aroused international indignation and prompted Kennedy, behind the scenes, to convince Birmingham's leaders that they must desegregate stores and upgrade black employees. The concessions won in Birmingham encouraged "Freedom Now!" protests in hundreds of other southern towns and cities. Kennedy began to realize that if the federal government did not commit the nation to "peaceful and constructive" reform of race relations, blacks in their frustration might follow leaders who preached the need for violence. Therefore, the president quickly forced segregationist governor George Wallace to allow two black students to enter the University of Alabama, and in June 1963 Kennedy proposed a broad civil-rights bill. On August 28, 1963, Martin Luther King, Jr., addressed a throng of 250,000 who had marched on Washington to persuade Congress to pass the measure. Unfortunately, the legislation remained bottled up on Capitol Hill, and southern white terrorism continued.

III. New Frontiers Abroad, 1960–1963

A. Introduction

Kennedy tripled overall nuclear capabilities; increased conventional weapons strength; formed the Green Berets to fight pro-communist guerrilla movements; and augmented economic and technical assistance to Third World countries with the Agency for International Development, the Food for Peace program, the Alliance for Progress, and the Peace Corps.

B. Cold War Activism

Kennedy approved a plan formulated under Eisenhower to help anticommunist Cuban exiles in the United States who wanted to invade the island and overthrow Fidel Castro. The Bay of Pigs landing failed miserably, but Kennedy persisted in backing plots to assassinate or depose Castro. Kennedy also took a tough line with the U.S.S.R. in defense of Western occupation rights in Berlin. Unable to dislodge U.S. forces from West Berlin, the Soviets walled it off from their zone.

C. To the Brink of Nuclear War

In October 1962 the Soviet Union and the United States came to the verge of nuclear war over the Cuban missile crisis. Kennedy and U.S.S.R. premier Nikita Khrushchev stepped back from the brink at almost the last moment with an agreement that the Soviets would remove the rockets they had installed in Cuba in exchange for Kennedy's promise not to invade that country. After this brush with disaster, the United States and the Soviet Union moved toward détente, a determination on both sides to avoid direct, armed conflict in settling their differences. A "hot line" was installed between the White House and the Kremlin to facilitate communication. The two powers signed a treaty banning atomic tests in the atmosphere and the oceans. But the nuclear- and conventional-arms races escalated, and the rivalry for influence over the Third World widened.

D. Kennedy and Indochina

In July 1962 Kennedy accepted a compromise that restored a neutralist premier to power in Laos but left communist influence in the countryside intact. Determined to give no further ground to communism in Indochina, the president sent ever more military advisers to South Vietnam to aid in the struggle against the National Liberation Front, or Vietcong. Nonetheless, successive American-backed regimes seemed incapable of winning popular support. By the time of Kennedy's assassination, it was becoming clear that the United States would either have to send in many more combat troops or seek a compromise settlement with the pro-communist Vietcong. We do not know which course Kennedy would have taken had he lived.

E. The Thousand-Day Presidency

On November 22, 1963, in Dallas, Texas, Lee Harvey Oswald shot President Kennedy to death, bringing Vice President Lyndon Baines Johnson to the Oval Office. Kennedy passed on to his successor a mixed legacy. The slain leader had favored social revolution in Latin America but had not promoted it sufficiently with funds. He had compromised in Laos but intensified U.S. entanglement in Vietnam. While praising disarmament and détente, he had pushed a massive arms buildup. In domestic matters also the New Frontier proved more promise than accomplishment. Congress had not acted on the majority of Kennedy's reform proposals, and his administration spent more on missiles and the space race than it did on human welfare. His idealistic rhetoric aroused the hopes of reformers, the poor, and African-

Americans, but he also left behind a hopeless entanglement in Vietnam that would make the fulfillment of rising domestic expectations next to impossible.

IV. The Great Society

A. Toward the Great Society

Johnson urged Congress to approve Kennedy's tax-cut and civil-rights proposals as a memorial to the fallen president. In February 1964 taxes were sliced by $10 billion, and the resulting increase in consumer spending and employment brought in more revenue, thus reducing the federal deficit. The 1964 Civil Rights Act outlawed segregation in public facilities; strengthened federal powers to combat racial disfranchisement and school segregation; and created the Equal Employment Opportunity Commission to intervene in cases of job discrimination based on race, religion, national origin, or gender. Inspired by Michael Harrington's *The Other America*, Johnson and Congress declared war on poverty with the Economic Opportunity Act of 1964, which founded the Office of Economic Opportunity, the Job Corps, VISTA, Head Start, and the Community Action Program. As the 1964 election approached, Johnson said his purpose with these measures and more to come was to create the Great Society, free from poverty and racial injustice.

B. The Election of 1964

The Democrats nominated President Johnson. Conservatives thoroughly disliked his Great Society promise of more federal spending on domestic welfare. Southern segregationists and some white industrial workers resented Johnson's backing of the civil-rights movement. At the Republican convention, these forces and other right-wing elements gained control, nominating ultraconservative Senator Barry Goldwater of Arizona. Goldwater, repudiating moderate Republicanism, advocated ending the graduated income tax, the Tennessee Valley Authority, and "compulsory" social security. He hinted that he might use nuclear weapons against Cuba and North Vietnam to bring them into line with U.S. wishes. Johnson won a landslide victory and brought with him huge Democratic majorities on Capitol Hill. The stage seemed to be set for completing the liberal agenda.

C. Triumphant Liberalism

During 1965 Johnson sent to Congress a steady stream of social-welfare and reform proposals and got most of them enacted. These included Medicare and Medicaid, federal assistance to education, the Voting Rights Act, a liberalized immigration law, the establishment of the Departments of Transportation and Housing and Urban Development and funding of major programs for them to run, creation of the National Endowments for the Arts and the Humanities, additions to and protection of the national parks, and tougher antipollution and highway beautification measures. But by 1966 the president's attention and more and more of the nation's resources were diverted from building the Great Society to fighting the war in Vietnam. The dashed hopes of liberals, blacks, and the poor produced urban race riots and anger at LBJ. The riots, in turn, alienated white, middle-class Americans. Democratic losses in the 1966 congressional elections reflected the disappointment and ended most reform efforts.

D. *The Warren Court in the Sixties*

With Johnson's appointment of Abe Fortas and Thurgood Marshall, the first black justice, to the Supreme Court, the already liberal Warren Court became even more liberal. In the 1960s it handed down decisions banning prayer in public schools, limiting press and film censorship, and requiring equal-size election districts and due process for persons accused of crimes. Liberals applauded. Conservatives railed that the judges were legislating instead of interpreting the law; they were undermining law and order.

V. The Changing Struggle for Equality, 1964–1968

A. *The Voting Rights Act of 1965*

In 1964 the Student Nonviolent Coordinating Committee (SNCC) and CORE organized the Mississippi Freedom Summer Project, sending thousands of college-student volunteers into the South to run freedom schools and register blacks to vote. Their efforts were stymied by the violence of the Ku Klux Klan and local police officials. To dramatize the problem of continuing disfranchisement, Martin Luther King, Jr., organized mass demonstrations in Selma, Alabama. When a national television audience saw Sheriff Jim Clark and his troopers viciously attack peaceful protestors, the public demanded federal action. President Johnson urged Congress to pass a voting-rights law. The resulting Voting Rights Act of 1965 authorized federal examiners to register qualified voters and suspend discriminatory literacy tests. Poll taxes were abolished by Supreme Court decision and the ratification of the Twenty-third Amendment. For the first time since Reconstruction, African-Americans, through the ballot box, came to have significant power in southern politics.

B. *The Long, Hot Summers*

The summers of 1965 through 1968 saw the outbreak of race riots in cities around the country, causing some $200 million worth of property damage, seven thousand injuries, and two hundred deaths. The Kerner Commission, appointed by President Johnson to investigate, found the causes of the trouble to be persisting "white racism" that had subjected blacks to poverty, slum housing, poor education, and police brutality. The Kerner report recommended programs to create more jobs and public housing and an end to de facto segregation in northern schools. However, Johnson and Congress, noting the white backlash against further federal assistance to African-Americans, did not act on the proposals.

C. *"Black Power"*

The Black Power movement, influenced by the teachings of Malcolm X, emerged from the civil-rights campaign in 1966. Its leaders, such as Stokely Carmichael and H. Rap Brown, preached race pride and self-determination, rejected Martin Luther King, Jr.'s nonviolence, and questioned the value of integration.

D. *Native American and Chicano Power*

The civil-rights and Black Power movements set an example for Native Americans and Mexican-Americans. They began to organize to raise group pride and fight for redress of their grievances, with both nonviolence and threats of force. Native Americans occupied

Alcatraz Island and founded the American Indian Movement (AIM). César Chávez attempted to unionize agricultural laborers in his United Farm Workers, and Chicanos joined such militant societies as the Alianza and La Raza Unida.

E. A Second Feminist Wave

The growing unhappiness of middle-class white women with the 1950s emphasis on maternity and domesticity was articulated by Betty Friedan in *The Feminine Mystique* (1963). Founded in 1966, the National Organization for Women (NOW) grew rapidly and began to lobby for full economic and social equality. Meanwhile younger women, disillusioned by the sexism they had encountered in the civil-rights and peace movements, joined the revived feminist crusade. They established women's liberation consciousness-raising sessions, health collectives, and day-care centers and demonstrated for equal rights and legal abortions.

VI. The Lost Crusade in Vietnam, 1964–1968

A. The Gulf of Tonkin Resolution

Johnson, who believed in the domino theory and did not want to give the Republicans grounds for accusing him of being soft on communism, stepped up U.S. involvement in Vietnam. In February 1964 he had the military prepare plans for air attacks on communist North Vietnam, which was supplying the Vietcong with weapons. In August, claiming that North Vietnamese patrol boats had fired on two U.S. destroyers in the Gulf of Tonkin, Johnson persuaded Congress to pass a resolution authorizing the president to "take all necessary measures to . . . prevent further aggression."

B. Americanization of the War

In 1965 Johnson started sustained bombing of North Vietnam and by 1968 had dropped three times more tonnage on it than the United States had used against all its enemies in World War II. Nonetheless, Hanoi sent more men and supplies to the Vietcong. Therefore, the president took the fateful step of ordering American combat troops to South Vietnam. Some 485,000 draftees were fighting there by 1967, thus Americanizing the war. Still victory eluded us, and the Joint Chiefs of Staff called for a larger U.S. force.

C. Opposition to the War

The Vietnam War polarized the United States as no event since the Civil War had done. Mounting numbers of college students and faculty, intellectuals, clergymen, and liberal Democrats resisted the draft, conducted teach-ins, spoke out, and demonstrated against this escalation. They denounced U.S. meddling in an internal struggle in Indochina. They pointed out that the more than $20 billion that this nation was spending annually on the war was draining almost all revenue from Great Society programs and that the draftees sent to fight and die were primarily the poor and disadvantaged. Television coverage of the carnage further eroded support for Johnson's war. On the other hand, "hawks" demanded that the president win a quick and total victory by hitting the Vietnamese with everything we had.

VII. Conclusion

Much was accomplished in the turbulent sixties. The civil-rights movement and the legislation it induced the federal government to enact ended legally enforced segregation, disfranchisement, and discrimination. Black self-respect was bolstered by the effort, and other formerly suppressed groups—Chicanos, Native Americans, and women—took courage to fight for equality. Johnson's Great Society reforms, at their peak in his first two years in the White House, moved this country toward more equality and justice, but before most of the programs accomplished much, they were undermined by the escalating Vietnam War. In 1966 the federal government was spending more money monthly on that struggle than it put yearly into the war on poverty. Frustrated African-Americans and college-age youths turned to violence to hasten social change but produced instead a conservative backlash against further change.

VOCABULARY

The following terms are used in Chapter 30. To understand the chapter fully, it is important that you know what each of them means.

technocrat   an expert in technical fields and management

filibuster   to prevent a legislative vote by obstructive tactics, especially by making long speeches

monolithic   something made of or resembling a single piece of stone of massive size

immolating   offering a life in sacrifice

consensus   general agreement

cornucopia   an overflowing supply

anathema   a person or thing detested

intimate   hint; to make known indirectly

presaged   foreshadowed, forecasted, predicted

reactionary   someone or something on the far right politically; extremely conservative; favoring a return to conditions of an earlier time

due process   legal proceedings carried out in accordance with established rules and principles

bandolier   a broad belt worn over the shoulder, with small loops to hold cartridges; commonly worn by soldiers and paramilitary groups

ambivalent   having at one and the same time opposite and conflicting feelings about a person or thing

IDENTIFICATIONS

After reading Chapter 30, you should be able to identify and explain the historical significance of each of the following:

Greensboro and other sit-ins, 1960–1961

Michael Harrington, *The Other America*

Ralph Nader

Betty Friedan, *The Feminine Mystique*

Congress of Racial Equality (CORE) and freedom rides

Peace Corps and Alliance for Progress

Bay of Pigs invasion and Cuban missile crisis

Ngo Dinh Diem

National Liberation Front (Vietcong)

New Frontier

Great Society

Economic Opportunity Act (Job Corps, VISTA, Head Start) and war on poverty

Barry Goldwater

Medicare and Medicaid

Immigration Act, 1965

National Endowments for the Arts and the Humanities

Stewart Udall

Baker v. *Carr*

Miranda v. *Arizona*

Civil Rights Act, 1964

Mississippi Freedom Summer Project, 1964

Voting Rights Act, 1965

Kerner Commission and its report

Malcolm X and the Black Muslims

Stokely Carmichael, H. Rap Brown, and Black Power

Huey Newton, Bobby Seale, and the Black Panthers

American Indian Movement (AIM)

César Chávez

Chicanos and Chicanas

National Organization for Women (NOW)

Gulf of Tonkin Resolution

hawks versus doves

SKILL BUILDING: MAPS

On the map of Indochina, locate and explain the importance in U.S. foreign policy of each of the following:

Laos
North Vietnam
South Vietnam
Saigon
Gulf of Tonkin
Hanoi
Danang

SKILL BUILDING: CHARTS

Look at the figures in the chart on the election of 1964 in your textbook. How do the election results compare with the outcome in 1960? Can you explain the reasons for the great differences between the two elections?

HISTORICAL SOURCES

Chapter 30 takes advantage of a source that is available to the historian studying the recent past—interviews with eyewitnesses to and participants in the events discussed. Such observations are sprinkled throughout this chapter. What does the author use these quotes to illustrate? In addition, the historian studying the recent past can draw on television coverage and recordings as well as written accounts of significant demonstrations and speeches. Look at "A Place in Time: Washington, D.C., in 1963." In that description of the massive march on Washington at which Martin Luther King, Jr., made his famous "I Have a Dream" speech, what elements could the historian have learned from watching films and listening to recordings of the event? What parts of this capsule history could not be gathered simply by watching and listening? Where do you suppose the author got the information about the event and what came before and after that would not be evident from films and recordings?

MULTIPLE-CHOICE QUESTIONS

Circle the letter of the item that best completes each statement or answers the question.

1. The U.S. Supreme Court during the tenure of Chief Justice Earl Warren made all of the following rulings *except*
   a. requiring states to provide a lawyer at public expense for indigent defendants charged with a felony.
   b. outlawing racial segregation in public schools even if the separate facilities were equal.
   c. overturning the World War II legislation that allowed the government to intern Japanese-Americans.
   d. requiring police to tell a suspect of his or her constitutional rights to remain silent and have a lawyer present during questioning.

2. The Bay of Pigs invasion was
   a. a U.S.-backed attempt by anti-Castro forces to land in Cuba and overthrow the regime there.
   b. the first landing of U.S. marines in South Vietnam and the start of Americanization of that conflict.
   c. the name that southerners applied to the invasion of their region by northern college students and civil-rights activists in the summer of 1964.
   d. an attempt made by the West to supply East Berlin with food after the communists erected the Berlin Wall.

3. The purpose of the 1964 Freedom Summer Project in Mississippi was
    a. to protest the escalation of the Vietnam War.
    b. to help and encourage blacks to become registered voters.
    c. to force the Interstate Commerce Commission to declare segregated transportation facilities unconstitutional.
    d. to persuade the state legislature to ratify the Equal Rights Amendment.

4. Which of these leaders most closely followed the example of Martin Luther King, Jr., in using religion and nonviolent resistance to battle for social justice?
    a. H. Rap Brown
    b. César Chávez
    c. Malcolm X
    d. George Wallace

5. War was avoided in the Cuban missile crisis when
    a. the United States agreed to remove its missiles from Turkey in exchange for the Soviet Union's taking its missiles out of Cuba.
    b. Kennedy agreed to remove Western troops from East Berlin in exchange for Khrushchev's order to dismantle Soviet missiles in Cuba.
    c. the United States agreed to stop its bombing of North Vietnam in exchange for the Soviet Union's removal of missiles with nuclear warheads from Cuba.
    d. Khrushchev agreed to remove Soviet missiles from Cuba in exchange for Kennedy's pledge not to invade that country.

6. "Hawks" and "doves" divided over the issue of whether
    a. the U.S. government should overthrow the Castro regime in Cuba.
    b. the civil-rights movement should use violent acts to protect black rights or rely on nonviolent means.
    c. the United States should seek total victory in Vietnam or a negotiated settlement.
    d. the Warren Court had gone too far in protecting criminals at the expense of their innocent victims.

7. Belief in the domino theory would most likely lead a person to support
    a. federal intervention in the South to protect freedom riders and other civil-rights activists.
    b. a test-ban treaty with the Soviet Union to prevent further atmospheric and ocean firing of nuclear weapons.
    c. American intervention in the Vietnam War to prevent a Vietcong victory.
    d. appointment of more conservative justices to the Supreme Court to prevent it from falling completely under the influence of Warren liberals.

8. Before his assassination in 1963, John F. Kennedy had succeeded in
    a. stimulating the U.S. economy by increased military spending.
    b. getting through Congress a new immigration law that did away with the discriminatory national-origins quota system.
    c. getting through Congress the most far-reaching voting-rights bill since Reconstruction.
    d. all of the above.

9. The feminist revival in the 1960s was brought about by
    a. continuing employment discrimination.
    b. the publication of Betty Friedan's *The Feminine Mystique*.
    c. the sexism that women activists encountered in the peace and civil-rights movements.
    d. all of the above.

10. During the last two years of Lyndon Johnson's presidency, the majority of public funds went into
    a. Medicare and Medicaid.
    b. the Vietnam War.
    c. Head Start and other federally assisted educational programs.
    d. public housing, the Job Corps, and other public-works and employment programs.

SHORT-ANSWER QUESTIONS

1. Briefly explain the roles played by television in the election of 1960 and in John F. Kennedy's thousand-day presidency.

2. President Kennedy remarked in 1963, "The civil-rights movement should thank God for Bull Connor. He's helped it as much as Abraham Lincoln." Explain the meaning of this statement.

3. How and why did President Kennedy deepen U.S. involvement in Vietnam?

4. Describe four major pieces of legislation or programs that made up President Lyndon B. Johnson's Great Society and war on poverty initiatives.

5. Why in his second term did President Johnson go from electoral triumph to widespread rejection by the American people?

6. According to the Kerner Commission report, what caused the wave of race riots in the late sixties?

7. How did President Johnson convince Congress to pass the Gulf of Tonkin resolution? What did LBJ mean when he compared the resolution to "grandma's nightshirt—it covered everything"?

ESSAY QUESTIONS

1. Discuss the accomplishments and failures of John F. Kennedy's thousand-day presidency.

2. Martin Luther King, Jr., observed that President Johnson's desire to end poverty and provide economic opportunity for all Americans was "shot down on the battlefields of Vietnam." Do you agree with King's statement? Why or why not?

3. Discuss the development of the 1960s civil-rights movement. What were its successes and its frustrations? How and why did the Black Power movement emerge from it?

4. Discuss the 1960s movements to gain opportunity, equality, and power for women, Mexican-Americans, and Native Americans. Who participated in them? Why? What tactics did they use? What did each movement owe to the civil-rights and Black Power movements?

5. Compare and contrast the United States in the 1950s and in the 1960s. How do you account for the great differences between the two decades?

31

A Troubled Journey: From Port Huron to Watergate

OUTLINE AND SUMMARY

I. The Rise and Fall of the Youth Movement

A. Toward a New Left

The founding of Students for a Democratic Society (SDS) in 1962 signaled the end of the campus apathy of the 1950s. Its Port Huron Statement, written by Tom Hayden, criticized American society and called on youth to build a true "participatory democracy." The perceived impersonality and bureaucracy of university administrations, the failings of New Frontier and Great Society liberalism, and above all the Vietnam War brought many followers to the movement. At no time, however, did the SDS speak for the majority of college students, who continued to care more about acquiring a good job, a home, a family, and a new car than about remaking America.

B. From Protest to Resistance

SDS adherents staged sit-ins, rallies, campus takeovers, and other demonstrations to protest racism, the military-industrial complex, and the war. Chanting "Hell, no, we won't go!" they encouraged young men to burn their draft cards and flee to Canada rather than serve in the armed forces. Their March Against Death in Washington, D.C., in 1969 drew some 300,000 participants.

C. The Waning of Student Radicalism

In 1970, when President Richard M. Nixon widened the fighting with an invasion of Cambodia, a new wave of campus unrest spread across the country. At Kent State University in Ohio, National Guardsmen opened fire on demonstrators, killing four, and at Mississippi's Jackson State College, highway patrolmen shot two students to death. Students condemned Nixon and the repressive violence, but many older citizens turned against the protestors, saying they got what they deserved for undercutting the president's foreign policy. Frustrated by its inability to end the war much less remake American society, the SDS began to disintegrate. A handful of former members went underground and engaged in terrorism, giving the government a handy excuse for more crackdowns. Other New Left activists drifted into the environmentalist, consumer, antinuclear, and women's movements. Many middle- and working-class people, alarmed by radicalism, began voting for political conservatives by the late 1960s. Still, the New Left did spur broad antiwar sentiment that eventually forced the Nixon administration to extricate itself from Indochina.

D. The Youth Culture

Besides the minority who engaged in radical politics, many young people in the sixties rebelled against accepted middle-class life-styles. Their "counterculture" rejected competitiveness, the work and success ethic, and responsibility in favor of love, cooperation, freedom, and experimentation with drugs and sex. Hippie men grew long hair and beards; they and young women wore tie-dyed T-shirts, torn jeans, and love beads. Probably half of all college students smoked marijuana, and a minority tried hallucinogens. The decade opened with folk-music concerts, proceeded to acid rock and Beatlemania, and in 1969 climaxed with a rock-music festival at Woodstock, New York. But by the late 1960s, the counterculture dream of an age of peace and harmony was already turning sour as the haunts of the flower children in San Francisco's Haight-Ashbury and New York's East Village attracted muggers, rapists, and dope peddlers.

E. The Sexual Revolution

One part of the counterculture, greater sexual openness and permissiveness, spread well beyond the hippies. The sexual revolution was made possible to a considerable extent by waning fear of unwanted pregnancy. In 1960 the Pill became available, and in 1973 the Supreme Court in *Roe* v. *Wade* declared unconstitutional state laws limiting women's right to an abortion during the first three months after conception. Films and plays became sexually explicit. Adult bookstores and moviehouses and topless bars proliferated. Live-in arrangements, divorces, and premarital and extramarital sex were common. Homosexuals organized the Gay Power movement and demanded acceptance and equal rights for gays. All of this erotic liberation, however, offended possibly a majority of citizens, who saw these developments as undermining moral decency. By the 1970s they responded by voting for politicians who promised to clean up the smut and protect the family. In the 1980s worry about AIDS also revived restraint.

II. 1968: The Politics of Strife

A. The Tet Offensive in Vietnam

On January 31, 1968, the start of Tet, the Vietnamese New Year, the Vietcong and North Vietnamese launched a major offensive, capturing much territory from the South and even staging attacks on the capital, Saigon. U.S. forces eventually repulsed the communists, but the heavy death toll on both sides made growing numbers skeptical about whether we could ever win the conflict at an acceptable cost. By March 1968, 42 percent of Americans described themselves as doves, and many of them looked approvingly upon Minnesota's antiwar senator Eugene McCarthy, who had announced that he would enter the upcoming Democratic primaries to challenge Johnson for the presidential nomination.

B. A Shaken President

After McCarthy did surprisingly well in the New Hampshire primary, a second antiwar candidate entered the race—Robert Kennedy. On March 31, Johnson, finally heeding key Democratic foreign-policy advisers, announced that he was deescalating in Vietnam by halting the bombing in the North. Embittered by the hatred that had developed toward him and doubting his chances against the Kennedy charisma, the president added that he would not seek or accept another term in the White House.

C. Assassinations and Turmoil

On April 4, 1968, James Earl Ray assassinated Martin Luther King, Jr. Infuriated blacks rioted in Chicago, Washington, D.C., and other cities. In the midst of the national turmoil, Vice President Hubert Humphrey entered the Democratic race. Humphrey, with a liberal record on civil-rights and domestic reform, received backing from union leaders, Johnson loyalists, and most party officials, who supported the president's Vietnam policies. McCarthy appealed mainly to affluent, educated liberal doves; Kennedy, to the less privileged and various ethnic and racial minorities, as well as peace advocates. On June 5, just hours after he won the California primary, Robert Kennedy was assassinated by a Palestinian refugee, thus removing the best hope for success of the peace forces. In August the Democrats nominated Humphrey, while in the Chicago streets surrounding the convention hall, Mayor Richard Daley's police clubbed antiwar demonstrators.

D. Conservative Resurgence

Richard Nixon, the Republican candidate, made the most of the unrest by promising he could end civil strife; achieve an honorable peace in Vietnam; crack down on radicals; and uphold law and order for the silent majority of hardworking, tax-paying, patriotic Americans. George Wallace, running as a third-party candidate, also appealed to resentful and fearful blue-collar workers, white racists, and people fed up with the counterculture and radicalism.

Wallace captured nearly 14 percent of the vote; Nixon nosed out Humphrey with just over 43 percent. These results indicated that a new conservative coalition had emerged. Fifty-seven percent of the electorate, including much of the old New Deal constituency, had voted for Nixon and Wallace, politicians who repudiated liberal ideals.

III. Nixon and World Politics

A. Introduction

Nixon and his national security adviser and later secretary of state, Henry Kissinger, believed in realpolitik—that is, making foreign-policy moves pragmatically on the basis of power politics and what would advance the national interest, without reference to morality or ideology. They also shared a liking for diplomatic intrigue, hidden from the public.

B. Vietnamization

Nixon and Kissinger decided that the United States must somehow extricate itself from Vietnam. The 1969 Nixon Doctrine pointed to a new course in Asia: henceforth the United

States would supply economic and military assistance to countries threatened by communist subversion or invasion, but it would expect them to do the fighting. The need to recall American ground forces from Vietnam was overwhelmingly apparent. Their morale and discipline had snapped, desertions mounted, and frustration led some American soldiers to commit atrocities against Vietnamese civilians, as in My Lai. Nixon began removing American troops from Vietnam, but at the same time he sought "peace with honor" by sending Kissinger to hold secret peace talks with the North Vietnamese. In hope of wringing concessions from the North Vietnamese, Nixon also authorized bombing raids over the North and over their supply lines in neutral Cambodia and Laos.

C. LBJ's War Becomes Nixon's War

The raids did not accomplish their purpose. Hanoi stood its ground, and the bombing touched off a civil war in Cambodia between the communist Khmer Rouge and pro-American factions. In 1970 the North Vietnamese increased their infiltration of Cambodia, and Nixon, in turn, ordered a joint U.S.–South Vietnamese invasion of that beleaguered country. Nixon also pushed the South Vietnamese into an attack on Laos to destroy communist bases there. The soldiers of the South were routed, and in April 1972 the North mounted a major offensive against Cambodia and the South. Nixon ordered the military to mine North Vietnam's harbors and step up bombing of its supply bases and cities.

D. America's Longest War Ends

The massive bombing finally broke the deadlock in the negotiations that had begun in 1968. In January 1973 the United States and North Vietnam signed the Paris Accords, ending the fighting between them but leaving South Vietnam's future to be settled by the final battles between North and South. America's longest war had cost us 58,000 dead, 300,000 wounded, and $150 billion. The Vietnamese suffered 2 million casualties, the war had ravaged much of Indochina, and the communist regime that gained control of the once peaceful Cambodia killed 40 percent of its people.

E. Détente

Our withdrawal from the war opened the way for détente with China and the U.S.S.R. The falling-out between the two communist giants also made them receptive to easing tensions with the United States. After two decades in which successive American administrations had refused to recognize the People's Republic of China and had blocked its admission to the United Nations, Kissinger paid a secret visit to Beijing in June 1971, followed by a Nixon trip in February 1972, at which Sino-American relations were normalized. In May the president flew to Moscow and signed agreements with the Soviets on trade, technological cooperation, and arms control, including the SALT I pact limiting antiballistic missiles. These moves not only improved the world outlook for peace but also enhanced Nixon's image in an election year.

F. A Multipolar World

In October 1973 the Middle East was again embroiled in war, as Syria and Egypt attacked Israel. U.S. equipment helped the Israelis to repel the assault and counterattack. In retaliation, the oil-producing Arab states imposed an embargo on shipments of petroleum to the United States and its allies. This led to acute shortages, skyrocketing prices, and rampant inflation in the United States. To ease the fuel crisis and reduce Soviet influence in the Middle East, the Nixon administration tried to cultivate better relations with the Arabs and to mediate between them and Israel. In October 1973 Kissinger began his "shuttle diplomacy," flying from one Mideastern capital to another to negotiate peace settlements. He managed to engineer an Israeli-Egyptian cease-fire, a withdrawal of Israeli forces from Egyptian and Syrian territories captured in 1973, and an end to the oil embargo. His efforts improved U.S. relations with Egypt, which began receiving American aid, but Syria and Palestine Liberation Organization (PLO) hard-liners became even more antagonistic toward Israel and increased terrorist attacks on Israeli and U.S. citizens.

In line with realpolitik, Nixon and Kissinger gave economic and military assistance to any country that they thought important to American financial and strategic interests, especially to countries willing to oppose Soviet influence. This policy often included nations ruled by brutal dictatorships, such as Iran under the shah and the Philippines under Ferdinand Marcos. Nixon also secretly handed the CIA $10 million to help a military junta overthrow Chile's democratically elected Marxist president, Salvador Allende.

IV. Domestic Problems and Divisions

A. Richard Nixon: Man and Politician

Nixon possessed traits that made him a successful political leader—intelligence, energy, and concentration. But his personality contained darker elements, too, that ultimately brought about his downfall. Nixon was almost paranoid in his belief that his enemies, especially the "eastern liberal establishment," were out to get him. Therefore, he must destroy them first.

B. The Nixon Presidency

At first Nixon followed a moderate course, signing into law bills passed by the Democratic Congress that increased social-security benefits, subsidized housing for low- and middle-income families, and created the Environmental Protection Agency and the Occupational Safety and Health Administration. Meanwhile many Americans demonstrated increased ecological concern. Former antiwar and civil-rights activists organized the first Earth Day in April 1970, denounced the "obsession with industrial growth and consumerism" that was despoiling the planet, and called for alternative life-styles and government policies to protect the environment. Conservatives decried the cost to business of additional regulations, as well as the increased expenditures that the administration's proposed welfare reform would entail. Thus, Nixon's Family Assistance Plan, guaranteeing a minimal annual income for all Americans, died in the Senate. Subsequent cuts in federal spending on social services left cities more overwhelmed than ever with the burden of providing for their poor.

C. A Troubled Economy

Nixon inherited a budget deficit and inflation from the Johnson administration. To combat these Nixon cut government expenditures and urged the Federal Reserve Board to drive up interest rates. Rising unemployment and a recession resulted, and inflation persisted. Worried about the political impact of hard times, the president tried Keynesian economics. In

1971 he deliberately proposed an unbalanced federal budget, and subsequently he levied surcharges on imports, allowed the value of the dollar to decline, and imposed wage and price ceilings. These policies stimulated the economy and reduced the trade deficit and inflation sufficiently to help get Nixon reelected in 1972. Afterward he ended price and wage controls, and in 1973 inflation and sluggish economic growth (stagflation) resumed.

D. Law and Order

Nixon signed legislation to strengthen the powers of the police. He also used law-enforcement agencies in legal and illegal ways to harass peace advocates, radicals, and his enemies. The Internal Revenue Service paid special attention to tax returns from people in these categories; the FBI and CIA wiretapped their phones and infiltrated their organizations to foment discord and provoke violence. Nixon established the White House "plumbers" to spy on and discredit his opponents. Daniel Ellsberg, who had turned over to the press the secret Pentagon Papers disclosing government lies about U.S. actions in Vietnam, became the plumbers' first target. They broke into his psychiatrist's office to look for medical records that might put Ellsberg in a poor light, and the Justice Department indicted him for theft and espionage.

E. The Southern Strategy

Nixon wooed whites tired of civil-rights activism, especially southerners. His administration opposed extension of the 1965 Voting Rights Act and school busing as a means to further integration. The president pushed the Supreme Court toward the right by his appointments of Chief Justice Warren Burger and three other conservatives.

F. The Silent Majority Speaks

To build a new Republican majority, Nixon also played the role of defender of the family and traditional values against the Democrats, whom the administration identified as the party of the New Left, hippies, the drug culture, abortion, and disorder.

G. The Election of 1972

When the Democrats nominated liberal senator George McGovern for president, they had little chance of winning. Nonetheless, Nixon and his Committee to Reelect the President (CREEP) decided to use every means possible to destroy the opposition, including having the White House plumbers break into Democratic National Committee headquarters in the Watergate complex to install secret wiretaps on the phones. After the burglars were caught, the administration began its attempt to hide the trail to higher-ups. It succeeded long enough to get Nixon overwhelmingly reelected, although the Democrats retained control of Congress.

V. The Crisis of the Presidency

A. *The Watergate Cover-Up*

In 1973 the cover-up began to unravel. One of the convicted Watergate burglars confessed that White House aides were involved. Then *Washington Post* reporters Carl Bernstein and Bob Woodward wrote a series of articles exposing CREEP's use of illegal campaign contributions to finance "dirty tricks" against the Democrats. In February 1973 the Senate established a special committee to probe alleged election misdeeds. It heard damaging testimony and, learning that Nixon had secretly taped all conversations held in the Oval Office, demanded that the president turn the recordings over to the committee. Meanwhile Nixon, pretending to cooperate in the investigation, appointed a new attorney general, Elliot Richardson, who chose a special Watergate prosecutor, Archibald Cox. When Cox also requested the tapes, Nixon fired Cox and accepted Richardson's resignation. This "Saturday Night Massacre" prompted the House Judiciary Committee to start impeachment proceedings against the president.

B. *A President Disgraced*

The administration was further discredited when Vice President Spiro Agnew resigned after pleading no contest to charges of bribe taking and tax evading. Nixon nominated Gerald Ford to replace Agnew. The president continued to stall on releasing the full, unedited recordings. In July 1974 the Supreme Court ruled that he must do so. The following month he surrendered the subpoenaed tapes, and they revealed that Nixon had personally ordered the Watergate cover-up and had lied about his role for two years. Warned that he would almost certainly be impeached and convicted, Nixon, on August 9, became the first chief executive in American history to resign, bringing Ford into office as the first nonelected president.

VI. Conclusion

Nixon's departure marked the end of a period of rancor and polarization. Troubled by the Vietnam experience, rebellious youths, energy shortages, a declining economy, and failure of the Democrats to deliver on the promises of the Kennedy and Johnson administrations, Americans had lost faith in Washington. Nixon had capitalized on the disillusionment to put together a new majority coalition for the Republicans. Although he promised to unite Americans and defend law and order, Nixon engaged in numerous illegal acts. Nearly fifty administration members would eventually be indicted for fraud, extortion, perjury, and other crimes. The Watergate affair would leave many citizens even more distrustful of government, making it difficult for Nixon's successors to lead the nation effectively.

VOCABULARY

The following terms are used in Chapter 31. To understand the chapter fully, it is important that you know what each of them means.

iconoclast   attacker of cherished beliefs or institutions

alienation   feelings of withdrawal or estrangement from a person, thing, or society

maverick   a dissenter

participatory democracy   a society in which most citizens directly share in governmental decisions by holding office or making policy

napalm and Agent Orange   chemicals used by the United States in Vietnam to burn villages and defoliate forests

ecology   the scientific study of the relations between organisms and their environment; the political and social movement to protect those relations

chauvinism   zealous and belligerent patriotism or devotion to any cause

taboo   a prohibition; something set apart or forbidden

monogamy   marriage of one woman with one man

pubescent   arriving or arrived at puberty

realpolitik   a pragmatic politics (especially as applied to foreign policy) based on advancement of the national interest without concern for ideology or morality

paranoid   displaying the traits of a mental disorder in which one mistakenly believes that others have hostile intentions toward him or her

innuendo   an indirect intimation (or hint) about a person or thing, especially of an unfavorable nature

dossier   a file of documents relating to the same matter, subject, or person

vendetta   a blood feud or private war of revenge

prior restraint   a type of government censorship that stops publication beforehand of materials deemed objectionable on moral, political, military, or other grounds, rather than punishing the publisher or writer after the material is printed

impeachment   the charging of a public official, such as the president, with misconduct in office

---

IDENTIFICATIONS

After reading Chapter 31, you should be able to identify and explain the historical significance of each of the following:

Mario Savio and the Berkeley Free Speech Movement

the New Left and red-diaper babies

Students for a Democratic Society, the Port Huron Statement, and Tom Hayden

Kent State and Jackson State killings

hippies and the counterculture

Woodstock

flower children and Haight-Ashbury

sexual revolution, the Pill, *Roe* v. *Wade*, and the Gay Power movement

Tet offensive

Eugene McCarthy

Robert Kennedy

Hubert Humphrey

George Wallace

Mayor Richard Daley versus the Yippies

Henry Kissinger

Nixon Doctrine

My Lai massacre

SALT I

Palestine Liberation Organization (PLO)

Salvador Allende

Neil Armstrong and Apollo II

Daniel Ellsberg and the Pentagon Papers

Warren Burger

Spiro Agnew

George McGovern

Carl Bernstein and Bob Woodward

the White House "plumbers" and the Watergate break-in and cover-up

Saturday Night Massacre

Senator Sam Ervin

SKILL BUILDING: MAPS

1. On the map of China and Indochina on p. 216, locate and explain the importance in U.S. foreign policy of each of the following:

   South Vietnam

   Saigon

   Danang

   Cambodia (Kampuchea)

   Laos

   North Vietnam

   Hanoi

   Haiphong

   People's Republic of China

   Beijing

   Sino-Soviet border

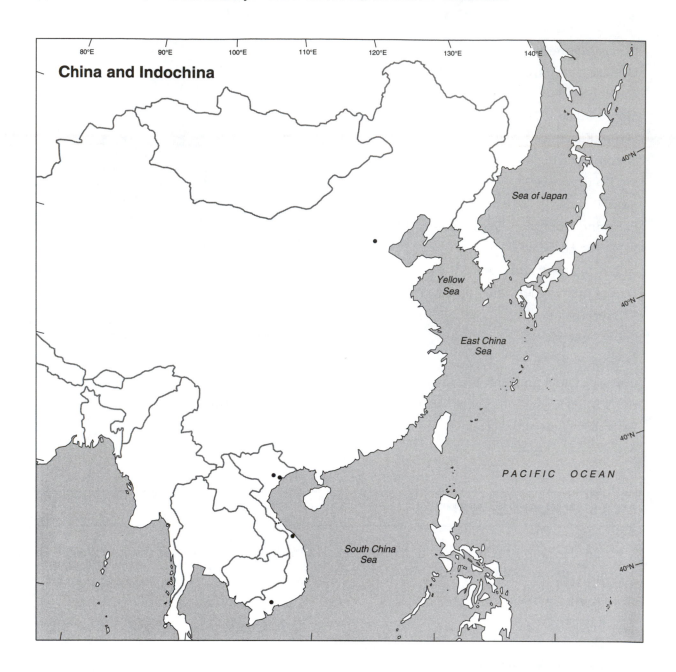

2. On the map of the Middle East on the following page, locate and explain the importance in U.S. foreign policy of each of the places below:

Syria

Israel

Golan Heights

Egypt

Sinai Peninsula

West Bank

Jerusalem

Jordan

Saudi Arabia

Iran

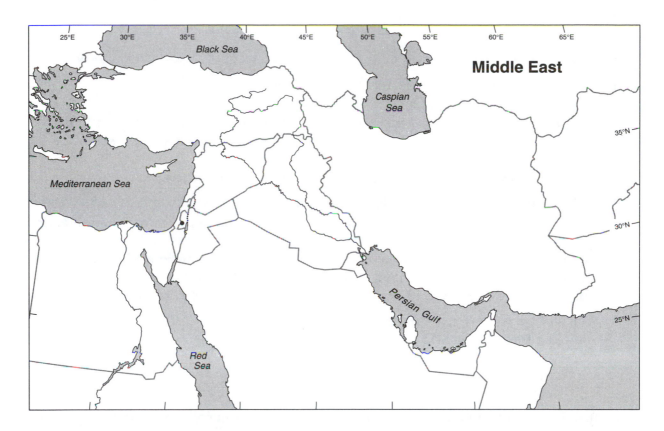

HISTORICAL SOURCES

Authors writing social history often use a variety of cultural artifacts as sources. In Chapter 31 these include the messages on the signs carried by demonstrators, slogans and chants (remembered or learned from films and tapes), songs and music popular during the period, clothing of the time, hairstyles (remembered or seen in photographs), and bumper stickers. Find places in the chapter where each of these artifacts is referred to or quoted. In each case why is the historian using that source?

Now look at "A Place in Time: Haight-Ashbury in the Mid-1960s." What cultural artifacts are mentioned in that capsule history to paint a picture of the life-style that briefly prevailed there in the 1960s?

The author of Chapter 31 also uses more formal, traditional historical sources, such as the published reports of congressional investigating committees. For example, on pages 1017–1019 the author discusses the testimony about wrongdoing in the Nixon White House given before Sam Ervin's committee. That information can be found in U.S. Senate, Select Committee on Presidential Campaign Activities, *Final Report,* 93rd Cong., 2d Sess., 1974. On page 1019 the writer summarizes the articles of impeachment against Nixon drawn up by the House Judiciary Committee. The full text of those articles can be read in U.S. Congress, House of Representatives, *Report of the Committee on the Judiciary,* 93rd Cong., 2d Sess., 1974.

MULTIPLE-CHOICE QUESTIONS

Circle the letter of the item that best completes each statement or answers the question.

1. Most of the early SDS and New Left members were
   a. from working-class families.
   b. children of parents who had been radicals and activists in the 1930s and 1940s.
   c. from upper-class families who were unhappy with the declining status of the "eastern liberal establishment."
   d. students who were already active in sororities and fraternities.

2. With regard to China, President Richard Nixon
   a. ordered its harbors mined and its southern cities bombed to stop it from aiding the Vietcong.
   b. traveled to Beijing to normalize relations with its communist government.
   c. cut off all trade with it until it improved its human rights record.
   d. authorized the CIA to finance secret plots to overthrow Mao Zedong.

3. Which of the following are *incorrectly* paired?
   a. Tom Hayden and SDS
   b. Mario Savio and the Free Speech Movement
   c. Carl Bernstein and the Yippies
   d. Timothy Leary and LSD

4. It is estimated that in the 1960s at least half of all American college students
   a. tried marijuana.
   b. burned their draft cards.
   c. became hippies or Yippies.
   d. had to leave their studies for two years to serve in Vietnam.

5. Which of the following facts about the election of 1968 indicates that a new conservative majority had supplanted the long-standing New Deal coalition?
   a. Between them, Nixon and Wallace received a majority of the votes of unskilled and semiskilled workers.
   b. Nixon won 43.4 percent of the popular vote.
   c. The great majority of blacks voted for Hubert Humphrey.
   d. Almost all union leaders supported Hubert Humphrey.

6. Which of the following did U.S. involvement in Vietnam accomplish?
   a. It prevented the communists from taking power in Cambodia.
   b. It saved South Vietnam from falling under the control of communist North Vietnam.
   c. It stimulated the U.S. economy sufficiently to ensure full employment, business growth, and balanced federal budgets.
   d. none of the above

7. "That's one small step for man, one giant leap for mankind." This quote refers to
    a. Nixon's decision to resign from the presidency.
    b. the signing of the Paris Accords ending the U.S. presence in Vietnam.
    c. the peaceful inauguration of Gerald Ford after the long nightmare of Watergate.
    d. astronaut Neil Armstrong's walk on the moon.

8. Nixon established the White House "plumbers" to
    a. persuade Congress to confirm his conservative nominees to the Supreme Court.
    b. guard administration security and discredit the president's enemies.
    c. repair the executive mansion after Congress refused to appropriate funds for the work.
    d. drain support away from school busing as a means of reducing segregation.

9. Which of the following statements about Nixon's relations with the Democratic-controlled Congress is correct?
    a. Nixon vetoed bills creating the Environmental Protection Agency and the Occupational Safety and Health Administration.
    b. Nixon never released to Congress the subpoenaed, unedited tapes of conversations in the Oval Office.
    c. The Senate rejected two of Nixon's Supreme Court nominees.
    d. Congress passed an equal rights amendment, but Nixon vetoed it.

10. Why did John Mitchell, E. Howard Hunt, and G. Gordon Liddy arrange the break-in at the Watergate complex?
    a. to find information about Daniel Ellsberg that would discredit him in the eyes of the peace movement
    b. to destroy the Democratic National Committee's files of potential campaign contributors
    c. to wiretap the telephones of the Democratic National Committee
    d. all of the above

SHORT-ANSWER QUESTIONS

1. What were the students at Kent State University protesting in 1970? What happened there? How did students and liberals react? How did the majority of Americans react?

2. Describe the youth counterculture of the 1960s. What caused it to wane by the 1970s?

3. What was the sexual revolution of the 1960s and 1970s? What caused it? What brought about a backlash against it by the 1980s?

4. Discuss what happened inside and outside the Democratic National Convention in Chicago in August 1968. What effect did these events have on the Democrats' chances for victory in November?

5. Explain what President Nixon meant by the policy of Vietnamization.

6. What were the terms of the 1973 Paris Accords between the United States and North Vietnam?

7. Discuss Henry Kissinger's "shuttle diplomacy" in the Middle East. What did it accomplish?

8. How did the Nixon administration bring about the overthrow of the Allende government in Chile?

ESSAY QUESTIONS

1. Discuss the rise and decline of college-student radicalism in the period 1960–1970. What caused the radicalism? Who became radicalized? What forms did radical protest take? Why did radical protest wane?

2. In 1964 Lyndon Johnson was elected president by a landslide. In 1972 Richard Nixon won an equally decisive victory. Yet each man was driven from office in disgrace. Explain the reasons for each one's electoral triumph and subsequent downfall.

3. Nixon, "who had built his reputation as a hard-line Cold Warrior, initiated a new era of détente with the communist powers." Discuss how and why the president accomplished this.

4. "While claiming to be the defender of law and order, the Nixon administration committed numerous illegal acts." Write an essay agreeing or disagreeing with this statement, and back what you say with as many facts as possible.

5. Some political commentators claimed that "the outcome of Watergate proved that the constitutional system had worked." Others believed that it further eroded trust in government and the ability of presidents to lead effectively. What is your interpretation of the outcome and its impact on the United States?

32

Turning Inward: Society and Politics from Ford to Reagan

OUTLINE AND SUMMARY

I. After the Sixties: Changing Social and Cultural Contours

A. America Turns Inward

The social activism of the sixties diminished or turned to other causes. The environmental movement intensified, with fear about nuclear hazards peaking in 1979 after the near-catastrophe at Three Mile Island. The 1960s student radical gave way to the 1970s and 1980s yuppie (young urban professional), preoccupied with personal health, fulfillment, and "a consumption lifestyle." Americans of all ages watched more hours of television and increasingly tuned in to the proliferating cable channels. They also enjoyed the new electronic gadgets: videocassette recorders, compact discs, and personal computers.

B. The Women's Movement: Gains and Uncertainties

The women's movement continued into the 1970s and 1980s. The National Organization for Women (NOW) had almost fifty thousand members by the mid-1970s, but the Equal Rights Amendment it worked for was not ratified. *Roe* v. *Wade* (1973), establishing women's constitutional right to an abortion, was attacked by the right-to-life movement. The controversy between the right-to-lifers and pro-choicers became one of the most politically divisive issues of the 1980s.

Women continued to enter the labor force in record numbers. Fifty-eight percent were working outside the home in 1992. Women made significant gains in business and the professions, but most of them still worked in gender-segregated, low-paying, low-prestige occupations, and their average earnings lagged behind those of men. The conservative presidential administrations of the 1970s and 1980s often instituted policies harmful to women. In 1972 Nixon vetoed a bill creating a national day-care system for the children of working mothers. In 1976 Congress cut off Medicaid funding for most abortions, and the welfare cuts under Reagan especially hurt the large proportion of single mothers and their children who depended on welfare payments.

The 1970s and 1980s saw later marriages, fewer children per family, and more unwed couples living together. By 1991, the divorce rate was over 50 percent.

C. The Two Worlds of Black America

In the 1970s and 1980s the black middle class grew in size and made significant advances: 46 percent of blacks held white-collar jobs by 1990, and 12 percent of the nation's college students were black. However, the plight of the black underclass worsened if anything. About one-third of blacks were trapped in inner-city slums. There half of all youths dropped out of high school, and 60 percent were unemployed. Cocaine addiction, violence, illegitimacy, and welfare dependency were prevalent.

D. New Patterns of Immigration

Since 1965 immigration to the United States has been heavy. Most of the newcomers have arrived from the Western Hemisphere (45 percent) and Asia (30 percent). Today the fastest-growing ethnic group is Hispanics. As in the past, the majority of the immigrants are fleeing poverty, but many have encountered rough conditions in the United States as well. To stem the tide of illegal immigrants, Congress passed the 1986 Immigration Reform and Control Act.

E. Brightening Prospects for Native Americans

In the late 1960s and 1970s Indian militance brought changes in destructive federal policies. The 1974 Indian Self-Determination Act granted tribes the right to administer government-aid programs and schools on their reservations. Native Americans also have won important court cases, including a 1980 award to the Sioux of $107 million for lands in South Dakota wrongfully taken in the nineteenth century. Although Indian pride and rights are on the rise, Native Americans still struggle with high unemployment, alcoholism, and disease.

F. Sexuality in the Era of AIDS

The trend toward greater sexual permissiveness and acceptance of homosexuals was partially reversed by the outbreak of the AIDS epidemic. By 1994 more than 220,000 Americans had died of the disease, and public-health officials exhorted those who would not abstain from sex to practice safer sex by using condoms.

G. The Evangelical Renaissance

In the religious revival of the 1970s and 1980s, some people joined cults such as the "Moonies." Others attended evangelical Protestant churches and watched and contributed to television preachers. The born-again Christians exerted a conservative political influence, condemning the communist world, abortion, and pornography and demanding prayer in public schools.

II. Years of Malaise: Post-Watergate Politics and Diplomacy

A. The Caretaker Presidency of Gerald Ford

After he became president on August 9, 1974, Gerald R. Ford pardoned Richard Nixon for "any and all crimes" he might have committed. On domestic issues Ford proved more conservative than his predecessor. He vetoed environmental, social-welfare, and federal regulatory bills, but a heavily Democratic Congress overrode him on quite a few. Already troublesome, inflation soared, as prices rose by 12 percent in 1974. Ford responded by cutting government spending and backing the Federal Reserve Board's decision to tighten credit, which it did by raising the discount rate. These anti-inflation moves resulted in a severe recession, with an unemployment rate hovering around 11 percent by 1975. Then Ford proposed tax cuts to stimulate consumer spending. This did not end the economic trouble, however. Particularly hard hit was the U.S. auto industry, as high gasoline prices persuaded millions of consumers to buy smaller, fuel-efficient imports rather than American-made gas-guzzlers.

In foreign policy there was considerable continuity between the Nixon and Ford administrations. Ford kept Nixon's secretary of state, Henry Kissinger, and carried on his predecessor's efforts to improve relations with China and the U.S.S.R. In 1975, Ford, Soviet leader Leonid Brezhnev, and the heads of thirty-one other nations signed the Helsinki Accords, which formalized Europe's post-1945 borders and promised respect for human rights and freedom of travel. The accords also encouraged Soviet dissidents, who were starting to demand democratization in the communist countries. Additionally, Ford's presidency witnessed the final collapse of the South Vietnamese government as the North Vietnamese captured Saigon and soon renamed it Ho Chi Minh City.

B. The Outsider as Insider: President Jimmy Carter

The Republicans nominated Ford for president in 1976. The Democrats ran a former governor of Georgia, Jimmy Carter. In the aftermath of Watergate, Carter appealed to the nation with his promise never to lie to the people and the fact that he was a Washington outsider. Carter, who won in a close race, entered office with no clear political philosophy. In his first year he managed to bring unemployment down by implementing a tax cut and increased public works, but thereafter he showed little inclination to launch social-welfare programs that involved federal spending. Having poor relations with Congress, he failed to get it to enact national health insurance and welfare and tax reforms. He did appoint a significant number of women and minority-group members as federal judges.

In foreign policy, Carter was somewhat more successful than in domestic affairs. He and his secretary of state, Cyrus Vance, tried to combat human rights abuses in foreign countries, including Chile, Ethiopia, and South Africa, and moved to forge friendlier ties with the black peoples of Africa. They successfully completed negotiations on and got ratification of treaties transferring control of the Panama Canal and Canal Zone to the Panamanians by 1999 and completed normalization of relations with the People's Republic of China. Carter's initial conciliatory stance toward the Soviets turned tough when the U.S.S.R. invaded Afghanistan in 1980. The president then adopted a series of anti-Soviet measures inspired by his hard-line national security adviser, Zbigniew Brzezinski.

C. The Middle East: Peace Accords and Hostages

Carter's foremost foreign-policy achievement was to invite Egypt's Anwar el-Sadat and Israel's Menachem Begin to Camp David, Maryland, in September 1978. There, with the president's encouragement, the two hammered out an Israeli-Egyptian understanding which was formalized in a treaty in 1979. The Camp David Accords did not end the Arab-Israeli conflict, as Israel continued to build Jewish settlements in occupied Arab territories, the other Arab states refused to talk to Israel, and an Islamic fundamentalist assassinated Sadat.

Carter's worst foreign-policy nightmare also came from the Middle East in 1980, an election year. After Islamic fundamentals overthrew the United States' ally, the shah of Iran, Carter admitted the cancer-stricken monarch to the United States for treatment. Infuriated Iranians stormed the U.S. embassy in Tehran and took some fifty American hostages. A military rescue attempt failed, and Carter was unable to negotiate their release. Not until Reagan's inauguration did the Iranians let the Americans go.

D. A Sea of Troubles as Carter's Term Ends

Inflation grew steadily worse—13 percent annually in 1979 and 1980—largely because of OPEC's repeated price hikes. The Federal Reserve Board countered with an ever-higher discount rate, making borrowing so expensive that home building and other industry stagnated. Carter, believing the answer to our woes lay in fuel conservation, created the Department of Energy and proposed to Congress legislation that would penalize waste and reward restraint. Capitol Hill passed only a fraction of what he asked. Americans blamed the austerity-preaching president for the economic mess, and his popularity plunged farther when he was unable to free U.S. hostages held in Iran. When the Democrats renominated Carter in 1980, he had no hope of winning.

III. The Reagan Revolution

A. Background of the Revolution

Several things prepared the way for the Reagan revolution. Despite the New Deal and Great Society experiences, the old beliefs in rugged individualism and unregulated free enterprise never disappeared entirely. Decades of Cold War rhetoric left a deep suspicion of the Soviet Union and communism. A New Right cultural conservatism had emerged in reaction to the social turmoil and sexual revolution of the 1960s. Thus groups such as Jerry Falwell's Moral Majority threw their support to right-wing politicians. The shift of population to the traditionally more conservative Sun Belt also set the stage for Ronald Reagan.

B. The Man Behind the Movement

Ronald Reagan, ex-movie actor and General Electric spokesman, former governor of California, and the favorite of conservatives, took the 1980 Republican nomination. In November Reagan swept to victory over Carter and independent candidate John Anderson, and his party gained a majority in the Senate for the first time since 1955. Reagan carried the southern and western states and a majority of the blue-collar vote. Of the old Roosevelt coalition, only blacks remained solidly in the Democratic camp. On the day Reagan was inaugurated, Iran finally released the American captives.

C. Reaganomics

Reagan believed that the way to make the economy prosper was to lift government regulation and taxes off the back of business. In 1981 he persuaded Congress to cut income taxes by 25 percent and make up for the lost revenue with drastic reductions in domestic spending. He also appointed persons who shared his commitment to deregulation to head federal agencies. Secretary of the Interior James Watt opened national forest and wilderness areas to private developers. The secretary of transportation rescinded 1970s regulations for reducing air pollution and making cars safer and more efficient. By 1982 the economy was in a deep recession. The unemployment rate reached 10 percent. Minorities and the inner-city poor suffered severely as social-welfare programs dried up. The nation also experienced enormous foreign-trade deficits. Obsolete plants in the industrial heartland could not meet foreign competition and from 1979 to 1983 laid off 11.5 million workers as they shut down. Farm exports dropped, causing thousands of family-run farms to go under. Because military spending increased rapidly and the sluggish economy resulted in less tax revenue collected, the federal deficit soared. By 1983, with inflation at last licked, the economy began to rebound.

D. The Great Bull Market

The period 1982–1987 witnessed numerous corporate mergers, many insider-trading and other get-rich-quick schemes, and a great bull market that tripled the average price of stocks. Then, on October 19, 1987, the market crashed, with the biggest single-day drop in its history. Unlike 1929, however, a depression did not follow.

E. Reagan Confronts the "Evil Empire"

During his first term Reagan was hostile toward the U.S.S.R., calling it an "evil empire." Claiming that the Soviet and Cuban communists were trying to gain footholds in Central America, the administration supported a military junta in El Salvador in its brutal attempts to suppress left-wing rebellion. It also funded and trained the contras in Nicaragua in their efforts to overthrow the pro-Marxist Sandinista government. When Congress banned further military aid for the contras, the White House secretly raised money from private right-wing groups and foreign governments to continue the arming. The president also dispatched marines to Grenada to topple a radical government.

F. Tragedy and Frustration in the Middle East

Reagan had no success in bringing peace to the Middle East. In 1982 Israel invaded Lebanon to force the Palestine Liberation Organization (PLO) out of its stronghold there. As a result of the raid, the PLO withdrew, but civil war between rival Lebanese Christian and Muslim factions heated up. The president sent two thousand U.S. marines into Lebanon as part of an international peacekeeping force to oversee the orderly exit of the PLO, but in October 1983 a Muslim terrorist attack killed 239 of the Americans. In 1984 Reagan recalled the remaining men.

G. Military Buildup and Antinuclear Protest

Reagan launched the biggest peacetime military buildup in U.S. history. By 1985 the Pentagon's annual budget exceeded $300 billion, almost double what it had been in 1981. Much of the spending went into developing and deploying more nuclear-warhead missiles and other atomic weapons. Alarmed by this buildup, hundreds of thousands of Americans joined the nuclear-freeze movement, seeking a verifiable halt by the superpowers in the manufacture and deployment of nuclear weapons. The 1982 rally of freeze activists and sympathizers in New York City's Central Park drew 800,000, the largest demonstration in U.S. history, and in the fall of that year freeze resolutions passed in nine states. Reagan responded by starting talks with the Soviets on strategic-arms reduction and proposing to build a vast space-based antimissile defense system known as the Strategic Defense Initiative (SDI), nicknamed Star Wars. Opponents of SDI pointed out its prohibitive cost, its technical implausibility, and the great likelihood of its further escalating the arms race.

H. Reagan Reelected

By 1984 Reagan had nearly doubled military spending, aggravated Cold War tensions, produced huge federal-budget and foreign-trade deficits, drastically curtailed social welfare, and weakened government regulatory agencies. The economy had rebounded, however; inflation was almost beaten, and the president was as popular as ever. The Republicans again nominated Reagan and Vice President George Bush in 1984. Walter Mondale, the Democratic candidate for president, ran with Representative Geraldine Ferraro, the first woman to run on the national ticket of a major political party. Reagan won decisively.

IV. Conclusion

In the 1970s and 1980s the United States more than ever had become two societies: millions of young, middle-class Americans concentrated on their psychic well-being and upward socioeconomic mobility, while the poor, minorities, and recent immigrants lived in decaying inner cities plagued by crime, drugs, violence, and inadequate public services. In contrast to the socially conscious New Deal era or the 1960s, the affluent middle class of the 1970s and 1980s ignored the plight of the less fortunate and in 1980 and 1984 voted into the presidency a man who promised to reduce the role of government at home and escalate the nation's anticommunist stance abroad.

VOCABULARY

The following terms are used in Chapter 32. To understand the chapter fully, it is important that you know what each of them means.

yuppie   young urban professional

gentrification   the process whereby middle-class people buy run-down housing in poor inner-city neighborhoods and expensively restore it, resulting in the revival of the area but usually pushing out former residents who can no longer afford to live there

enervated   unnerved, weakened (especially psychologically)

discount rate   the interest rate that the Federal Reserve Board charges banks in the Federal Reserve system for giving them Federal Reserve notes in exchange for promissory notes; when the discount rate is raised, banks have to charge borrowers higher interest

stagflation   a combination of business stagnation and high inflation; the condition that beset the U.S. economy in the late 1970s and early 1980s

euphemistic   substituting a pleasant expression for an unpleasant, harsh, or offensive one; for example, *He passed away* instead of *He died*

insider trading   profiting on the stock market through private knowledge of planned corporate actions

---

IDENTIFICATIONS

After reading Chapter 32, you should be able to identify and explain the historical significance of each of the following:

Sam Walton and discount stores

Three Mile Island

Me Generation

Silicon Valley

Roe v. *Wade*, right-to-life movement, and pro-choice supporters

National Organization for Women (NOW)

Equal Rights Amendment

"feminization of poverty"

Immigration Reform and Control Act, 1986

American Indian Movement (AIM)

Indian Self-Determination Act, 1974

Moonies

Jerry Falwell and the Moral Majority; Pat Robertson and the Christian Coalition

Helsinki Accords

Zbigniew Brzezinski

Camp David Israeli-Egyptian Accords

Iranian hostage crisis

political action committees (PACs)

Reaganomics

Secretary of the Interior James Watt and the Sagebrush Rebellion

Donald Trump and Ivan Boesky

Sandinistas versus contras

Palestine Liberation Organization (PLO)

nuclear-freeze movement

Strategic Defense Initiative (Star Wars)

Sandra Day O'Connor

Walter Mondale and Geraldine Ferraro

SKILL BUILDING: MAPS

1. On the map of North Africa and the Middle East which follows, locate and explain the importance to U.S. foreign policy of each of the following:

    Afghanistan

    Israel

    West Bank

    Egypt

    Port Said

    Syria

    Jordan

    Iran

    Tehran

    Lebanon

    Iraq

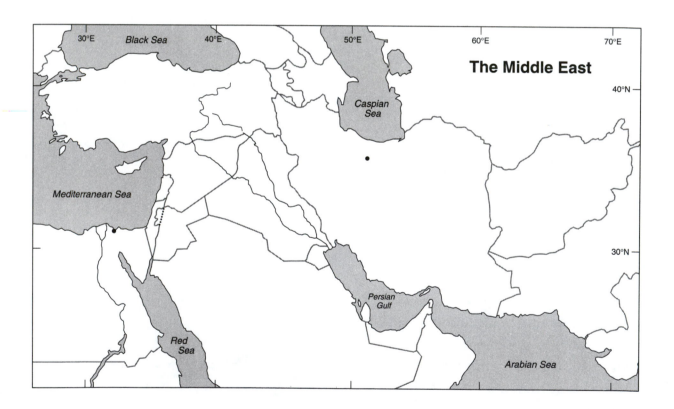

2. On the map of the Caribbean and Central America below, locate and explain the importance to U.S. foreign policy of each of the following:

Panama

Panama Canal Zone

El Salvador

Nicaragua

Honduras

Costa Rica

Cuba

Grenada

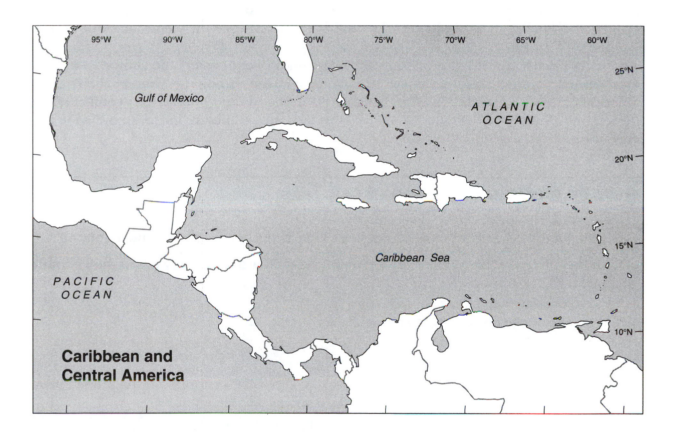

SKILL BUILDING: GRAPHS

Look at the graphs in Chapter 32. From glancing at the one titled "Changing Demographics," you should be able to answer the following questions:

1. About how many Hispanics lived in the United States in 1992?

2. About how many Asians and Pacific Islanders are there likely to be by 2050?

Now look at the graph "The Election of 1980" and answer the following questions:

1. Was this a close election or a landslide?
2. The losing candidate, Jimmy Carter, won the electoral votes of which states?
3. Did the third-party candidate, John Anderson, carry any state?

HISTORICAL SOURCES

In Chapter 32 the author has used many of the historical sources we have noted earlier, including data from the U.S. Bureau of the Census. For example, many of the chapter's observations about family patterns, women in the work force, conditions of the black underclass, and ethnic make-up of America's population come from census studies. Look at page 1030, where the author makes statements about Hispanics based on Census Bureau estimates. What are these findings? Why can't the historian rely on the accuracy of census figures?

In "A Place in Time: Houston Rides the Economic Roller Coaster" the author again uses local history to illuminate the impact of national and international events on the lives of American citizens. How did OPEC's changing price policies and Middle East conflict affect life in Houston in the 1970s and 1980s? Why was the impact different in Houston than in the cities of the Northeast and Midwest?

MULTIPLE-CHOICE QUESTIONS

Circle the letter of the item that best completes each statement or answers the question.

1. In the 1970s and early 1980s the Federal Reserve Board repeatedly raised the discount rate to
   a. stimulate new-home construction.
   b. encourage borrowing for new-plant construction.
   c. combat inflation.
   d. combat unemployment.

2. The only sector of the Roosevelt New Deal coalition that continued through the 1980s to vote consistently for the Democratic presidential candidate was
   a. blue-collar workers.
   b. farmers.
   c. Irish, Polish, and other ethnic Americans.
   d. blacks.

3. Which of the following happened during Jimmy Carter's presidency?
   a. Treaties transferring control of the Panama Canal and Canal Zone to Panama by 1999 were ratified.
   b. The inflation rate was finally slowed to 6 percent annually.
   c. The United States invaded Grenada to topple an anti-American left-wing regime.
   d. The INF Treaty was negotiated and ratified.

4. Jerry Falwell's Moral Majority and other evangelical Protestant groups
    a. tended to be politically conservative and therefore strongly pro-Reagan.
    b. were concentrated in the South and therefore almost always supported Democratic candidates.
    c. were the strongest supporters of peaceful coexistence with the U.S.S.R. and China.
    d. opposed prayer in public schools and other attempts to disregard the separation of church and state.

5. All of the following happened during Ronald Reagan's first term as president *except*
    a. the most massive military spending in U.S. peacetime history.
    b. runaway inflation.
    c. a drop in U.S. exports of both agricultural and industrial products.
    d. deregulation of many industries.

6. Three Mile Island is associated with
    a. the Star Wars defense system.
    b. a near-disastrous accident at a nuclear-power plant.
    c. gentrification of a run-down area.
    d. the "feminization of poverty."

7. Which of the following statements about women in the 1980s is correct?
    a. The majority held paying jobs outside the home.
    b. They were close to achieving equality of pay with men.
    c. Almost half of the lawyers, doctors, and engineers in this country were women.
    d. They were likely to marry at a younger age and have more children than women in the 1950s.

8. The Reagan administration extended military aid and training to the contras in hope that the contras would overthrow a leftist government in
    a. Afghanistan.
    b. Grenada.
    c. Cuba.
    d. Nicaragua.

9. Which of the following statements about the Camp David Accords is correct?
    a. The signers promised to respect human rights, which gave courage to Soviet dissidents.
    b. They were negotiated by Israel and Lebanon with the help and encouragement of President Reagan.
    c. They were agreed to by Israel's Menachem Begin and Egypt's Anwar el-Sadat and ended the long Arab-Israeli conflict.
    d. Getting Egypt's Sadat and Israel's Begin to negotiate an understanding between their countries was President Carter's greatest foreign-policy achievement.

10. Which of the following statements about the election of 1984 is correct?
    a. The Republicans won control of both the White House and Congress for the first time since the Eisenhower years.
    b. A major political party nominated a woman for vice president for the first time in U.S. history.
    c. An incumbent president was defeated by a candidate claiming to be an honest Washington "outsider."
    d. It was one of the three closest contests in the twentieth century.

SHORT-ANSWER QUESTIONS

1. Describe the new patterns of immigration into the United States that set in after 1965.

2. Which social activist movements of the 1960s continued strongly in the 1970s and 1980s? Why?

3. What was the *Roe* v. *Wade* decision? Why did it prove to be politically divisive throughout the 1980s?

4. In what ways did prospects for Native Americans improve in the late 1960s and 1970s? What significant problems continued to plague American Indians?

5. "Religious faith has always loomed large in American history, but after 1970 it played a more decisive cultural and political role than it had for years." Explain why the author of Chapter 32 makes this statement. Do you agree?

6. What were the troubles that overwhelmed the Carter administration and prevented Carter's reelection?

7. Explain the meaning of the term "Reaganomics."

ESSAY QUESTIONS

1. "The story of black America in the 1970s and 1980s was really two very different stories." Explain what this quotation means using as many facts as possible.

2. Discuss the waxing and waning of détente between the United States and the Soviet Union from the 1970s to 1984. What caused each of the periods of strain and relaxation of tensions?

3. Compare and contrast American society and culture in the 1960s and the 1980s.

4. Discuss the foreign policies of the United States in Africa, Latin America and the Caribbean, and the Middle East under the Ford, Carter, and first Reagan administrations.

5. What is meant by the term "the Reagan Revolution"? According to Chapter 32, what accounted for the appeal of Ronald Reagan and his policies to the American electorate in the 1980s?

33

Beyond the Cold War

OUTLINE AND SUMMARY

I. Problems and Opportunities in Reagan's Second Term

A. *Tax Reform, Budget Deficits, and Trade Gaps*

During Reagan's second term, immigration and tax-reform measures passed, but the legacy of Reaganomics—huge budget and foreign-trade deficits—continued.

B. *Middle East Encore: Talks and Terrorism*

The Middle East remained a thorny problem. In December 1987 the Intifada, a Palestinian uprising against Israel, began, and U.S. efforts to convince Jordan, the Palestinians, and Israel to negotiate failed. The Palestinians and their backers, especially Libya's Colonel Muammar el-Qaddafi, resorted to terrorist attacks against U.S. citizens, including bombing a Pan Am jet in 1988.

C. *The Iran-Contra Scandal*

The Iran-contra affair, the worst scandal of the Reagan administration, also originated in Middle Eastern problems. Robert McFarlane, Oliver North, and other members and staff of the National Security Council in 1985–1986 secretly arranged shipments of U.S. weapons to Iran. Then they diverted money from the sales to the Nicaraguan contras at a time when Congress had forbidden further aid to them. To hide their activities, North shredded incriminating documents requested by investigators. A congressional committee chaired by Senator Daniel Inouye found no evidence that Reagan had known of the scheme but criticized him for his casual style of supervision and disregard for the law, which invited such behavior from subordinates. North and others involved were subsequently tried and convicted. North's conviction was overturned in 1991 on technical grounds.

D. *More Scandals and Embarrassments*

Lesser scandals also marred Reagan's second term. Evidence of bribes and conspiracy in the granting of military contracts surfaced. Reagan's secretary of the interior, James Watt, and attorney general Edwin Meese were accused of influence peddling, which led to the latter's resignation. Despite these and other revelations, the president remained popular.

E. Reagan's Mission to Moscow

The U.S.S.R., bedeviled by domestic crises, sought an easing of tensions abroad, which was reflected in its willingness to make concessions in its arms-control talks with the United States. In 1987 the two superpowers negotiated the Intermediate Nuclear Forces (INF) Treaty. It removed twenty-five hundred U.S. and Soviet missiles from Europe and provided for on-site verification inspections. The agreement opened a new era of détente, capped by Reagan's visit to Moscow in May 1988 and the U.S.S.R.'s decision to withdraw its forces from Afghanistan. Ironically, Reagan, the Cold Warrior, denouncer of arms control, and architect of massive military buildup, "seemed destined to be remembered for . . . bettering relations with the Soviets and reducing the risk of global war."

F. The Election of 1988

Vice President George Bush captured the Republican nomination, and Massachusetts governor Michael Dukakis beat Jesse Jackson for the top spot on the Democratic ticket. Bush campaigned on Reagan's achievements, tried to distance himself from the Iran-contra scandal, and painted Dukakis as soft on crime and deficient in patriotism. The governor was unable to refute Bush's claims and articulate a strong vision of the United States' future. Both candidates avoided important issues, resorting instead to photo opportunities and televised spot commercials. Bush won 54 percent of the vote, while the Democrats widened their majorities in Congress.

II. The Bush Years: Resolve Abroad, Drift at Home

A. The Cold War Ends

Soon after Bush's inauguration, Soviet power collapsed. First the Eastern European countries discarded their U.S.S.R.-backed communist regimes. Then East and West Germany reunited, and the Baltic republics declared their independence from Moscow. With our former Cold War adversary clearly no longer a threat, in 1991 President Bush signed another treaty with Gorbachev reducing each country's strategic nuclear arsenal by 25 percent.

Meanwhile Gorbachev's attempts to revive the Soviet economy by introducing some free enterprise alarmed hard-line Communists, who in August 1991 tried to overthrow him. Boris Yeltsin, president of the Russian Republic, and his followers squelched the coup, outlawed the Communist party, and proclaimed the end of the U.S.S.R. Overwhelmed by the rush of anticommunism and resurgent nationalism, Gorbachev resigned.

President Bush and his secretary of state, James Baker III, reacted cautiously to the events in Eastern Europe. In 1992 Bush proposed economic aid for Russia, and Baker tried to see to it that the nuclear arsenal and know-how of the former Soviet republics did not fall into the wrong hands. The United States further cut back its nuclear stockpiles.

Bush abandoned Reagan's interventions in Nicaragua and El Salvador, and the long civil wars there subsided. However, the United States invaded Panama; toppled its leader, Manuel Noriega; and brought him to Florida to stand trial for drug selling. The United States withdrew support of corrupt Filipino president Ferdinand Marcos and recognized his democratically elected successor, Corazon Aquino.

When the economic sanctions of the United States and other countries against the racist white government of South Africa induced it to release Nelson Mandela and drop most apartheid laws, Bush resumed normal trade. The administration refused to impose trade sanctions on China in retaliation for its brutal suppression of prodemocracy demonstrators. The president traveled to Japan in hopes of persuading that prosperous nation to ease the U.S. trade deficit by buying more U.S. products. Little came of his attempt.

B. Operation Desert Storm

After years of weapons stockpiling, including nuclear and chemical, Saddam Hussein, dictator of Iraq, invaded Kuwait on August 2, 1990. Although the United States had favored Iraq in its earlier war against Iran, President Bush, as well as other world leaders, now saw Hussein as a serious menace. The president, enlisting the support of Congress, the American people, and the United Nations, demanded Iraqi withdrawal from Kuwait. When Hussein did not comply, on January 16, 1991, the United States and other U.N. members began daily bombing raids on Iraqi troops, supply depots, communication centers, and cities. Saddam Hussein retaliated by firing Scud missiles at Israel and Saudi Arabia. The United States tried to intercept these missiles with its Patriot missiles. On February 23, 1991, the U.N. and U.S. ground assault began, and within one hundred hours Kuwait was liberated and Bush declared a cease-fire. U.N. inspectors entered Iraq and began dismantling Hussein's nuclear-weapons plants, but the dictator remained in power, crushing Shiite Muslim and Kurdish uprisings against him.

In the wake of the Persian Gulf War, Bush attempted to reopen Arab-Israeli peace negotiations. In November 1991, Israel, the Palestinians, and various Arab states met for talks, first in Madrid and then Washington. Reaching agreements, however, proved extremely slow and difficult.

C. Domestic Discontents

Bush inherited economic ills stemming from his predecessor's policies. Savings-and-loan associations collapsed. Deregulation of the Reagan years that permitted savings-and-loan associations to extend risky loans and speculate in real-estate and other questionable ventures largely caused these disasters. Because deposits in these institutions were federally insured, making good on the losses cost the American taxpayers billions of dollars.

The huge federal deficit produced by Reagan's tax cuts and enormous military spending grew still larger due to the S&L bailout, Gulf War costs, welfare, and Medicare/Medicaid payments. The 1990 package of new taxes and reduced spending failed to stanch the fiscal bleeding. Then, in 1990, recession hit. Sales, housing starts, and tax revenues fell; unemployment climbed. States dropped social-welfare programs, and more than 2 million additional Americans sank below the poverty line. Those in the middle class, once enthusiastic about Reaganomics, became skeptical, but they still displayed little compassion for the poor.

The economic downturn highlighted deep-seated social maladies. Poverty and anger in inner cities worsened and in April 1992 erupted into rioting in Los Angeles and other places. Public schools languished. In 1989, the *Exxon Valdez* oil spill ruined six hundred acres of pristine Alaskan coastline, and the Environmental Protection Agency (EPA) pronounced the air in more than 100 U.S. cities hazardous to breathe. The Bush administration largely ignored these problems. It continued to favor more oil exploration and drilling in Alaska and undermined international treaties on global warming and mining in Antarctica. Bush did, however, sign the 1990 Federal Clean Air Act, passed by the Democratic-controlled Congress.

D. *The Supreme Court Moves Right*

To swing the Supreme Court farther to the right, Reagan appointed conservatives Sandra Day O'Connor, the first woman justice; Antonin Scalia; and Anthony Kennedy, as well as elevating William Rehnquist to chief justice to replace the retiring Warren Burger. Bush followed suit, naming two more conservatives, David Souter and Clarence Thomas. The Senate almost rejected the latter because of his questionable judicial qualifications and law professor Anita Hill's charges that he sexually harassed her. As early as 1989, court decisions reflected the new conservative majority. The justices hedged women's abortion rights, narrowed the interpretation of civil-rights laws, and removed some protections for arrested persons. However, in a five-to-four decision, the Court reaffirmed its earlier *Roe* v. *Wade* stand.

E. *The Politics of Frustration*

Bush's popularity, at a peak after Operation Desert Storm, plunged with the recession. In his 1992 State of the Union message, the president suggested such classic Republican formulas for recovery as middle- and upper-class tax cuts and incentives for business. Democrats denounced his proposals as "politically motivated and inadequate."

In 1992 the Democrats nominated Arkansas Governor Bill Clinton and Senator Al Gore of Tennessee for president and vice-president, respectively. They promised to create jobs, protect the environment, safeguard a woman's right to an abortion, reform welfare, and create a national health-care system. A Republican convention dominated by the right wing renominated Bush and Quayle and denounced abortion, sexual permissiveness, feminism, and other "threats" to family values. Clinton won with 43 percent of the popular vote to Bush's 38 percent. The strong showing of a third-party candidate, billionaire H. Ross Perot, indicated widespread dissatisfaction with both of the major parties. Perot garnered 19 percent of the vote, the most for any independent since Theodore Roosevelt in 1912. The Democrats retained control of Congress, and the number of women and minority members serving on Capitol Hill grew.

III. The Clinton Years: Democratic Disarray, Republican Resurgence

A. *Struggling to Shape a Domestic Agenda*

In his domestic program, Clinton aimed particularly to please the middle class and blue-collar workers, as well as to advance some of the causes of the 1960s and 1970s, such as feminism. Clinton named many women to cabinet and other top government positions, including Ruth Bader Ginsberg to the Supreme Court and his wife, Hillary Rodham Clinton, to head his Task Force on National Health-Care Reform. The president had only modest success in getting key proposals through Congress. The lawmakers passed the federal spending cuts, tax increases, and the North American Free Trade Agreement with Mexico that Clinton requested but rejected his economic-stimulus package (especially when unemployment fell and new jobs increased in 1993–1994 without any spurt of inflation). The health-care plan eventually unveiled by Clinton's task force fell under such a barrage of lobbying and partisan attacks that by mid-1994 it had lost most of its support. Nor did Congress accept Clinton's ideas for revamping welfare, which both liberals and conservatives disliked, though for different reasons.

By 1994 allegations of sexual and other misconduct and complaints that he was too eager to please and compromise were seriously eroding Clinton's popularity and effectiveness. More ominous to any liberal or even moderate agenda was the expanding influence of the religious right. Pat Robertson's Christian Coalition, through voter registration drives and organizing workshops, had by 1994 gained control of many state Republican parties and local and state governments.

B. The Quest for a Coherent Foreign Policy

Clinton preferred to concentrate on domestic issues, but with the United States left as the only superpower, he had to respond to international crises. The collapse of communism in Eastern and Central Europe unleashed age-old ethnic hatreds. The former Yugoslavia erupted into civil war among Croats, Serbs, and Muslims, and various attempts at settlement by NATO, the United Nations, and the United States got nowhere. The former U.S.S.R. also seemed overwhelmed by economic chaos and national rivalries. Other than offering Russia and Ukraine economic assistance, there was little that Washington could do. Because Bush's humanitarian intervention in Somalia turned sour, Clinton refrained from similar military commitments in Rwanda. He found it more difficult, however, to ignore the brutal junta in Haiti and the Haitian refugees streaming to U.S. shores.

The Arab-Israeli-Palestinian talks begun in the aftermath of the Gulf War finally bore fruit when PLO head Yasir Arafat and Israeli prime minister Yitzhak Rabin signed an agreement at the White House for limited Palestinian self-rule in the Gaza Strip and Jericho. However, Muslim fundamentalist terrorism did not cease. In February 1993, Middle Eastern terrorists bombed the World Trade Center in New York.

In Asia, the Clinton administration followed Bush's lead in pressing Japan to ease the U.S. trade deficit by buying more U.S. goods and in refusing to impose trade sanctions on China for its human-rights abuses.

IV. The 1994 Elections and After: A Sharp Right Turn

In the 1994 mid-term elections, the voters made a sharp rightward turn, electing Republican majorities to both houses of Congress for the first time since 1954. Why did this happen? What did it mean? Some commentators mentioned widespread feelings of frustration among working- and middle-class Americans (perhaps fueled by the stagnation of real income). Others pointed to the organizing and spending of right-wing and special-interest groups, such as the Christian Coalition and the National Rifle Association. Republican politicians, especially Newt Gingrich as Speaker of the House, quickly proposed a "Contract with America," a series of conservative legislative goals. Although the election results seemed to demonstrate a significant ideological shift, it was hard to know if that was so since only 38 percent of eligible voters went to the polls in 1994. The leaders of the Republican-controlled Congress announced their intention to balance the federal budget, cut taxes for middle- and upper-income Americans, increase defense spending, and cut back on various federal welfare programs.

V. A Broader Perspective

A. Economic and Social Trends: Coping with Change

Regardless of who was president and which political party controlled the White House and/or Capitol Hill, certain economic and social trends persisted for several decades. Ever greater numbers of women entered the paid labor force: in 1992, 58 percent of women worked for wages. By the 1990s Americans had a troubling sense that economic opportunities were narrowing and that they were not likely to be better off than their parents. These perceptions rested on various developments. The nation's share of total world output of goods and services dropped from one-third in 1950 to one-fifth by 1990, and more foreigners held ownership in U.S. businesses, banks, and real estate than formerly. The proportion of Americans engaged in relatively high-paying unionized industrial jobs relentlessly shrank, while those having to settle for low-paid, non-union, no-security, no-benefits, service-sector positions grew. Between 1970 and 1990, average family real income barely rose, and that of factory workers declined. Unemployment, even during periods of national prosperity, was alarmingly high for unskilled, poorly educated young people. In the inner cities and among minorities, the problems were magnified. In 1994, Detroit's youths suffered almost a 50 percent jobless rate. Indeed, some commentators claimed that the United States had developed a permanent "outer class" that was "lacking work, uneducated, politically apathetic, [and] socially adrift."

The gap between the black middle and lower classes widened. More African-Americans than ever before graduated from college and held elective office by 1993, but for the one-third of blacks living below the poverty line, conditions worsened. A similar gap separated Hispanics as more of them moved into the middle class and political office, but over a quarter remained impoverished.

The 1990s also saw a pronounced rise in the hate rhetoric and organizing activity of the radical right (religious, cultural, and political).

B. An Imperiled Environment

The past decades witnessed American government's making halting and uncertain efforts to address long-term, worldwide environmental hazards. These included the disposal of radioactive nuclear waste, wildlife- and forest-destroying acid rain, depletion of the protective ozone layer, and global warming.

C. A New World Order?

In recent years we have seen the end of the Cold War and the disintegration of the Soviet Union, events that eased the threats of totalitarianism and nuclear war. However, new trouble spots have erupted around the globe. Complex issues, such as how to handle the disparity in living standards between the industrialized Northern Hemisphere and the impoverished, underdeveloped Southern Hemisphere, face the world. Defining what role the United States should play on the international scene and how it should relate to the United Nations are challenges with which the American people and government must wrestle.

VI. Conclusion

By the 1990s, the United States was increasingly divided into two Americas: the educated, prosperous, professional, and middle classes "thriving in the new service-based economy dominated by computers and . . . interactive communication" and "an outer class stuck in poverty and despair." Rapid social and demographic changes had spawned outbursts of fear and hate. In the years ahead, can America's multicultural society "find the resources to sustain a sense of common national identity or will fragmentation and mistrust prevail"?

VOCABULARY

The following terms are used in Chapter 33. To understand the chapter fully, it is important that you know what each of them means.

patrician   person of high birth; person born into the upper class

market economy   one in which decisions about production, pricing, and distribution are made by private entrepreneurs seeking profits and responding to economic forces such as supply and demand rather than by centralized government planning

commonwealth   a group of sovereign states associated by their own choice and linked by common objectives and interests; for example, the association that exists among Great Britain, Canada, India, and other countries known as the British Commonwealth

apartheid   South Africa's policy of racial separation

trade deficit   a condition that exists when a nation earns less from its exports than it spends on imports

colossus   something or someone of great size, scope, or importance

dichotomy   division into two contrasting groups

Newt Gingrich   Republican leader who proposed a "Contract with America" after the 1994 elections

IDENTIFICATIONS

After reading Chapter 33, you should be able to identify and explain the historical significance of each of the following:

Intifada and Middle East terrorist attacks

the Iran-contra scandal, Robert McFarlane, John Poindexter, and Oliver North

Donald Regan, Edwin Meese, and James Watt

INF Treaty and the Moscow summit

Jesse Jackson and Michael Dukakis

Mikhail Gorbachev and Boris Yeltsin

James Baker III

General Manuel Noriega

Nelson Mandela and the African National Congress

Saddam Hussein

Operation Desert Storm and General Norman Schwarzkopf

S&L bailout

Exxon Valdez

ozone shield

William Rehnquist

Clarence Thomas versus Anita Hill

H. Ross Perot

Ruth Bader Ginsberg

Hillary Rodham Clinton and the Task Force on National Health-Care Reform

gays, the military, and "Don't ask, don't tell"

North American Free Trade Agreement (NAFTA)

"ethnic cleansing": Serbs, Croats, and Muslims

Colin Powell

SKILL BUILDING: MAPS

1. On the map of Europe on the next page, locate and explain the historic changes that took place in the late 1980s and 1990s in each of the following:

   Germany

   Berlin

   Estonia

   Latvia

   Lithuania

   Belarus

   the Ukraine

   Poland

   Russian Federation

   states created from the former Yugoslavia

2. On the map of the Middle East and North Africa, which follows, locate and explain the historic events that occurred in each of the following in the late 1980s and 1990s:

Libya
Egypt
Afghanistan
Israel
West Bank
Jericho
Gaza Strip
Jordan
Syria
Kuwait
Kuwait City
Iraq
Baghdad
Saudi Arabia
Riyadh
Persian Gulf

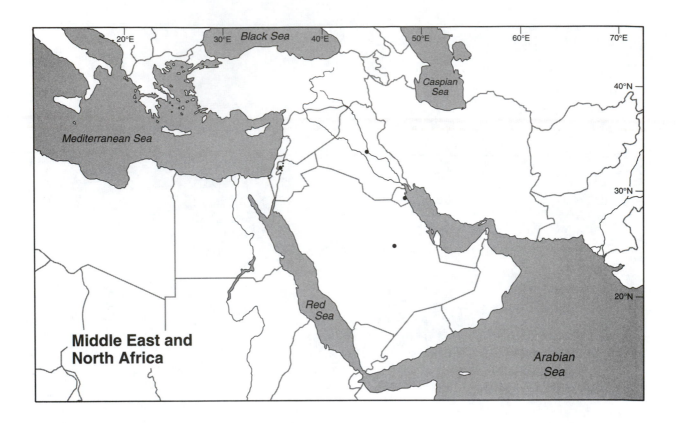

Middle East and North Africa

MULTIPLE-CHOICE QUESTIONS

Circle the letter of the item that best completes each statement or answers the question.

1. Which of the following statements about the election of 1992 is correct?
   a. The right wing of the Republican party dominated its national convention and wrote its platform.
   b. An independent candidate for the presidency won a larger portion of the vote than any other third-party candidate had since the election of 1912.
   c. Bill Clinton's victory owed much to his success in reviving the New Deal Democratic coalition.
   d. all of the above

2. The only arms-control treaty to provide for destruction of a class of existing weapons and for on-site inspection for compliance is
   a. SALT I.
   b. SALT II.
   c. the Non-Proliferation Treaty.
   d. the INF Treaty.

3. During President Bush's administration, the United States dispatched military forces to
    a. Afghanistan and Iran.
    b. Syria and Egypt.
    c. Panama and the Middle East.
    d. all of the above

4. All of the following events occurred internationally in the late 1980s and early 1990s *except*
    a. Ferdinand Marcos was driven from power in the Philippines.
    b. the Kurds of Iraq successfully defied Saddam Hussein and established an independent state.
    c. Mikhail Gorbachev resigned from office, and the Soviet Union ceased to exist.
    d. East and West Germany reunited, and the Baltic states declared their independence.

5. The collapse of the savings-and-loan industry
    a. was caused by the excessive federal regulation that kept savings-and-loan associations from making profitable investments.
    b. led to the ruin of depositors in those institutions, who lost all they had in their accounts.
    c. triggered a serious depression, much as the 1929 stock market crash did.
    d. worsened the budget deficit because Washington had to spend billions of dollars to repay federally insured depositors.

6. By 1990 what portion of African-Americans lived below the poverty line?
    a. one-half
    b. one-fourth
    c. one-third
    d. one-fifth

7. The *Exxon Valdez* incident involved
    a. an oil spill that fouled the waters off Alaska.
    b. a terrorist attack on an American oil tanker.
    c. an OPEC conspiracy to jack up the price of oil.
    d. Exxon's offering illegal payments to members of Reagan's cabinet to obtain leases to drill for oil in the Alaska wilderness.

8. Which of the following statements about Presidents Reagan and Bush and the Supreme Court is correct?
    a. There were too few resignations from the Supreme Court to give Reagan and Bush a chance to appoint a new majority reflecting their political philosophies.
    b. Because of Reagan's and Bush's political conservatism, they appointed only white males as justices.
    c. Through their appointments to the Supreme Court, Reagan and Bush created a conservative majority that is likely to continue into the twenty-first century.
    d. Despite the fact that their appointees had to be confirmed by the Democratic-controlled Senate, Reagan and Bush won approval for all the justices they nominated.

9. During his first year in office, President Bill Clinton successfully pushed through Congress
    a. a plan for national health-care reform.
    b. the North American Free Trade Agreement (NAFTA) with Mexico.
    c. a budget that provided for a much expanded federal-jobs program and other pump-priming measures to stimulate the economy.
    d. a measure opening opportunities for military service to declared homosexuals.

10. Between 1970 and 1990 the average annual income, adjusted for inflation, of American industrial workers
    a. declined.
    b. nearly doubled.
    c. rose slightly.
    d. increased by 25 percent.

SHORT-ANSWER QUESTIONS

1. Explain the Iran-contra affair.

2. Discuss briefly the record of the Reagan and Bush administrations on environmental issues.

3. What actions did the Bush administration take in Central America (Nicaragua, El Salvador, Panama)? Why did it take those actions in each case?

4. What were the main foreign-policy initiatives of the United States toward Japan and China during the Bush and Clinton administrations?

5. What were President Clinton's suggestions for revamping America's welfare system? Why were they controversial? What happened to them?

6. What has been the political impact of Pat Robertson's Christian Coalition?

7. Discuss the reasons for the decline in union membership and union influence in national politics.

ESSAY QUESTIONS

1. The author of Chapter 33 says of President Reagan, "The vigorous Cold Warrior, denouncer of earlier arms-control treaties, and champion of massive military spending seemed destined to be remembered for his part in bettering relations with the Soviets and reducing the risk of global war." Discuss this statement, using as many specific facts as possible, and offer some possible explanations of this paradox.

2. In 1991 a *New York Times* editorial commented, "George Bush remains mystifyingly incomplete: shrewd and energetic in foreign policy and just the reverse—clumsy and irresolute—at home." Write an essay agreeing or disagreeing with this assessment and explain your reasons with as many specific facts as possible.

3. "Clinton began his presidency in January 1993 with confidence and high energy. But grueling difficulties on both the domestic and foreign-policy fronts quickly propelled his administration into rough waters." Discuss the domestic and foreign policies of the Clinton administration, and explain in what respects it floundered in "rough waters."

4. Discuss the Persian Gulf War. What caused it? Why and how did the United States intervene? How was it fought? What effects did it have on developments in the Middle East and on the U.S. domestic scene?

5. In "A Place in Time: Miami in the 1990s," the author writes, "In this vibrant, garish . . . city, many of the most urgent social issues facing contemporary America emerge in particularly stark fashion." Write an essay identifying those social issues and discussing how they were illustrated in both Miami and the rest of the nation.

EPILOGUE

Looking Ahead—Looking Back

OUTLINE AND SUMMARY

I. Changes and Challenges Ahead

Experts predict that the population of the United States will grow to 310 million by 2080 and that the portion of the population over sixty-five years of age will continue to climb. These demographic trends will challenge American society to find ways to provide for and employ about a third of a billion citizens, and they put great pressure on America's social security and medical-care systems. In the twenty-first century, U.S. society will become increasingly multicultural and nonwhite. It is projected that by 2050 today's minorities (Hispanics, blacks, Asians, and Native Americans) will comprise almost half the nation. The U.S. economy is likely to remain the world's largest for a long while, but it will face escalating competition from the European Common Market and the Pacific Rim countries. The economic and social maladies of America's inner cities will probably persist into the next century despite overall prosperity. In the post–Cold War period, the United States is just starting to feel its way toward a suitable international role for itself.

II. Facing Up to Change

Rather than viewing change as offering positive challenges, some Americans are reacting with fear and hostility toward the country's democratic traditions, government, and cultural and ethnic diversity. These people fail to see the many positive aspects of contemporary national life. Despite its faults, the U.S. educational system is one of the most open and equal in the world. American political thinkers and social scientists are calling attention to thorny economic and social problems and offering creative solutions in a spate of books, such as Robert Reich's *The World of Nations* and Albert Gore's *Earth in the Balance*.

III. Drawing Strength from the Past

Our national past should encourage us in facing today's problems. The U.S. Constitution, written in 1787 for an agrarian population of 4 million, has proved through time to be a wise and flexible instrument that still works in the 1990s for a modern industrial society of 255 million. The federal system allows creative experiments in solving social ills to emanate not just from Washington but also from state and local governments. Since 1787, slowly and sometimes painfully, the American political system has moved from including only propertied white males to embracing all adult citizens. When economic troubles, such as those accompanying the industrial revolution, threatened the welfare of large numbers of people, muckraking journalists exposed the dangers, and government acted to protect society. Although we have sometimes violated our own best traditions, for most of our history and to the present day, our respect for human rights has been a beacon for the rest of the world. With all of these strengths in our heritage, our great challenge is "to pass on to future generations the enduring vision of freedom and common purpose that others have transmitted to us from the past."

VOCABULARY

The following terms are used in the Epilogue. To understand it fully, it is important that you know what each of them means.

quincentennial   five hundredth anniversary

cacophony   harsh noise

cursory   hastily done

franchise   the right to vote

IDENTIFICATIONS

Woodstock festival

D-Day ceremonies

Robert Reich, *The World of Nations*

Albert Gore, *Earth in the Balance*

Vaclav Havel

MULTIPLE-CHOICE QUESTIONS

Circle the letter of the item that best completes each statement or answers the question.

1. Demographers predict that in the twenty-first century, the U.S. population will
    a. grow by some 60 million people.
    b. contain a larger percentage of children than it does in the 1990s.
    c. contain a smaller percentage of elderly people than in 1990.
    d. become more ethnically and racially homogeneous.

2. By the year 2000, America's largest ethnic minority will probably be
    a. blacks.
    b. Asians.
    c. Hispanics.
    d. Indians.

3. By what date did all adult Americans first have the constitutional right to vote regardless of race, gender, or economic standing?

   a. 1877
   b. 1950
   c. 1990
   d. 1920

4. In 1989 Chinese students demonstrating for more freedom in their country used which of the following symbols?

   a. the hammer and sickle
   b. the Statue of Liberty
   c. the swastika
   d. all of the above

SHORT-ANSWER QUESTIONS

1. What are some of the challenges that the United States will face in the twenty-first century because of the demographic trends noted in the Epilogue?

2. What predictions about the U.S. economy does the Epilogue make?

3. The Epilogue states that one source of the U.S. tradition of respect for human rights comes from landmark judicial decisions. From your study of American history, discuss three specific cases.

ESSAY QUESTIONS

1. The British philosopher John Stuart Mill claimed that there is great value in "placing human beings in contact with persons dissimilar to themselves." Such contacts have "always been . . . one of the primary sources of progress." Write an essay either agreeing or disagreeing with Mill, and back up your position with what you have learned from your study of American history.

2. The Epilogue states, "In contemplating the present tangle of problems, Americans . . . feel apprehensive, . . . however, our national experience furnishes reason for encouragement." What in our national experience gives us reason to believe that we will be able to confront and conquer our contemporary problems?

Preparing for the Final Examination

As you approach the end of your American history course, you may well wonder how you are supposed to remember all those facts for the final. Here are some hints for preparing yourself to take that semester exam. (1) Do not wait until the night before the test (or even the last couple of days prior to it) to start your studying. (2) Review the notes that you have taken on class lectures and assigned readings other than your textbook. (3) Review the chapters of this study guide, rereading carefully the Outline and Summary portion of each. (4) As you follow steps 2 and 3, look for issues and themes that seem to come up again and again. History, after all, is about change and continuity over time. Therefore, ask yourself as you review, "What things about American society have changed between the Reconstruction era and the 1990s and why?" On the other hand, which things have remained essentially constant or recurred periodically throughout all those years?

The sample multiple-choice and essay questions that follow are designed to assist you in pulling together all those facts and seeing more clearly the patterns of change and continuity over the last century or so of American history.

MULTIPLE-CHOICE QUESTIONS

Circle the letter of the item that best completes each statement or answers the question.

1. In which two periods did the federal government make its greatest efforts to protect black Americans by passing civil-rights laws and constitutional amendments?
   a. in the 1920s and 1930s
   b. during the administrations of Ronald Reagan and George Bush
   c. during Reconstruction and the 1960s
   d. during World Wars I and II

2. Which of these was primarily a rural-based reform movement concerned particularly with farmers' economic problems?
   a. the New Frontier
   b. progressivism
   c. populism
   d. the Fair Deal

3. The social worker who established Hull House in Chicago was
    a. Harry Hopkins.
    b. Frances Perkins.
    c. Jane Addams.
    d. Jeannette Rankin.

4. Each of these was a muckraking writer whose book helped to secure passage of federal legislation *except*
    a. John Hay.
    b. Upton Sinclair.
    c. Michael Harrington.
    d. Rachel Carson.

5. Oliver H. Kelly, James B. Weaver, William Jennings Bryan, and Henry Wallace were all associated with promoting the interests of which group?
    a. blacks
    b. Native Americans
    c. organized labor
    d. farmers

6. Which of the following happened to the majority of southern blacks in the years between Reconstruction and 1900?
    a. They were driven out of the South by poverty and discrimination.
    b. They became tenants and sharecroppers on land owned by whites.
    c. They got jobs in factories opening in the Midwest and Far West.
    d. They became independent, landowning small farmers.

7. The administration that ran up the biggest federal budget deficits in U.S. history was that of
    a. Franklin Roosevelt.
    b. Lyndon Johnson.
    c. Ulysses Grant.
    d. Ronald Reagan.

8. All of the following administrations are particularly associated with corruption and wrongdoing in government *except* that of
    a. Ulysses Grant.
    b. Herbert Hoover.
    c. Warren Harding.
    d. Richard Nixon.

9. Which of the wars that the United States fought had the least popular support at home?
    a. Spanish-American War
    b. World War I
    c. World War II
    d. Vietnam War

10. By what year did the majority of the American people live in cities?
    a. 1890
    b. 1920
    c. 1940
    d. 1960

11. In which of these elections was foreign policy *not* an important issue?
    a. 1900
    b. 1916
    c. 1936
    d. 1968

12. After which of these events did women secure the right to vote in national elections?
    a. the Great Depression of the 1930s
    b. passage of the Equal Rights Amendment in the 1970s
    c. passage of the Fourteenth Amendment
    d. World War I

13. In which decade did the United States finally get rid of the discriminatory national-origins quota system in our immigration law?
    a. 1970s
    b. 1960s
    c. 1980s
    d. 1920s

14. The elections of 1912, 1924, and 1948 were similar in what way?
    a. In each one there was a third party calling itself progressive.
    b. In each one the winner received more than 60 percent of the votes.
    c. In each one there was no incumbent running.
    d. Each election was followed immediately by war.

15. Membership in the organized labor movement in the United States increased most rapidly during which decade?
    a. 1890s
    b. 1920s
    c. 1930s
    d. 1970s

16. American armed forces fought against Soviet armies in which of these conflicts?
    a. World War II
    b. Korean War
    c. Vietnam War
    d. none of the above

17. Which of these statements about Native Americans is correct?
    a. Indian tribes lost hundreds of thousands of acres of land to whites under the Dawes Act.
    b. Native Americans resented the Indian Reorganization Act of 1934 because it attempted to suppress Native American culture and force rapid assimilation.
    c. As a result of the termination policy, the great majority of Native Americans live in cities and all reservations have been closed.
    d. none of the above.

18. In which of these periods was the U.S. economy plagued by the highest rates of inflation?
    a. 1875 to 1897
    b. 1900 to World War I
    c. 1920s and 1930s
    d. 1970s and early 1980s

19. All of the following have been used to justify U.S. intervention in Asia *except*
    a. the need to uplift, educate, and teach democracy to backward peoples.
    b. the Good Neighbor policy.
    c. the Open Door policy.
    d. the domino theory.

20. American literature tended to concern itself more with great social and economic questions and less with the emotional state of the individual during which period?
    a. 1930s
    b. 1950s
    c. 1880s
    d. 1970s and 1980s

21. Which of the following happened after both World War I and World War II?
    a. The Senate rejected treaties permitting the United States to join international organizations created to keep the peace.
    b. There was a heightened fear of internal communism and radicalism and greater attempts to suppress them.
    c. There was a postwar depression.
    d. The party in power during the war was defeated in the next presidential election.

22. All of these people were leaders who opposed the United States' participation in a war being fought in their day *except*
    a. Eugene McCarthy.
    b. Jane Addams.
    c. Eugene Debs.
    d. Theodore Roosevelt.

23. Some critics have blamed Franklin D. Roosevelt for giving in to Soviet domination of Eastern Europe at which conference?
    a. Versailles
    b. Potsdam
    c. Yalta
    d. Geneva

24. The treaty granting the United States control over the Panama Canal and Canal Zone was signed and ratified under which president, and the treaty returning control by 1999 to Panama was signed and ratified under which president, respectively?

    a. Theodore Roosevelt and Jimmy Carter
    b. William H. Taft and Richard Nixon
    c. Woodrow Wilson and Lyndon Johnson
    d. William McKinley and Bill Clinton

25. Which of these leaders was the first to gain a mass following among black Americans?

    a. Booker T. Washington
    b. W. E. B. Du Bois
    c. Marcus Garvey
    d. Malcolm X

ESSAY QUESTIONS

1. Compare and contrast the old immigrants (pre-1880s), the new immigrants (1880–1920), and the post–1960 immigrants. Who composed each group? Why did each group come? What characteristics did each display? How did each fare in the United States and why?

2. One history of African-Americans is titled *From Plantation to Ghetto*. Considering the experiences of blacks from Reconstruction to the 1990s, do you think this is an appropriate title? Why or why not? Back up what you say with as many historical and demographic facts as possible.

3. Pretend that you are a filmmaker working on a forty-five-minute documentary about the changing role of women in American society from Reconstruction to 1990. Which persons, events, trends, and laws would you depict in your movie? Why did you make these particular choices?

4. Discuss the impact of World War I, World War II, and the Vietnam War on American society at home. In your answer consider effects on the economy, women, families, minorities, domestic reform, and civil or constitutional liberties.

5. Compare and contrast the Populist, progressive, New Deal, and Great Society reform programs. What do you see as the major achievements of each? What do you think were the most serious failures?

6. Discuss the Latin American policy of the United States from Theodore Roosevelt's corollary to the early 1990s.

7. Trace federal-government policies toward labor and unions from the late nineteenth century to the 1990s. During which periods has the government been most prolabor? During which periods has government been most hostile to unions? How have the changes in government policy affected the labor movement?

8. Initially the majority of the American people did not wish to enter either World War I or World War II. Yet the United States entered both conflicts. Why?

9. From the late nineteenth century to the present progressives-liberals and conservatives have argued over the proper role of the federal government in the economic and social life of the nation. Explain the positions of each side and the rationales for their positions. Discuss concrete examples of legislation, federal programs, and Supreme Court decisions, from the 1890s to the 1990s, that have followed the philosophy of each political camp.

10. Discuss the origins of the Cold War and its impact on U.S. domestic and foreign policy since 1945. When and why did the Cold War end?

11. How do you define the American dream? Based on your definition, during which period between the 1870s and the 1990s has American society come closest to fulfilling your vision? Explain your choice by discussing as many facts about that period as possible.

12. Discuss the preservation, conservation, and environmental movements in the United States from the late nineteenth to the late twentieth centuries. What environmental issues have these movements addressed at various periods? What obstacles and opposition have the movements faced? What do you consider the greatest achievements, if any, of these movements? (In your answer consider the roles played by such individuals as John Muir, Gifford Pinchot, Theodore Roosevelt, Franklin Roosevelt, Rachel Carson, and Albert Gore.)

Answers to Multiple-Choice Questions

Prologue

1. c
2. a
3. d
4. a
5. c

Chapter 16

1. c
2. b
3. d
4. a
5. c
6. b
7. b
8. c
9. a
10. a

Chapter 17

1. c
2. b
3. d
4. b
5. d
6. c
7. a
8. d
9. c
10. d

Chapter 18

1. b
2. a
3. d
4. c
5. a
6. a
7. c
8. d
9. b
10. a

Chapter 19

1. b
2. a
3. c
4. d
5. c
6. c
7. b
8. b
9. a
10. a

Chapter 20

1. c
2. b
3. c
4. d
5. a
6. d
7. d
8. c
9. a
10. d

Chapter 21

1. a
2. c
3. b
4. a
5. a
6. d
7. a
8. d
9. c
10. b

Chapter 22

1. a
2. d
3. c
4. b
5. c
6. b
7. c
8. a
9. a
10. d

Chapter 23	**Chapter 26**	**Chapter 29**	**Chapter 32**
1. a	1. a	1. a	1. c
2. c	2. b	2. c	2. d
3. b	3. c	3. d	3. a
4. b	4. b	4. b	4. a
5. b	5. c	5. b	5. b
6. a	6. b	6. a	6. b
7. b	7. c	7. d	7. a
8. c	8. d	8. c	8. d
9. c	9. a	9. b	9. d
10. d	10. c	10. c	10. b

Chapter 24	**Chapter 27**	**Chapter 30**	**Chapter 33**
1. c	1. a	1. c	1. d
2. b	2. c	2. a	2. d
3. c	3. a	3. b	3. c
4. d	4. d	4. b	4. b
5. c	5. c	5. d	5. d
6. a	6. a	6. c	6. c
7. b	7. d	7. c	7. a
8. c	8. b	8. a	8. c
9. b	9. a	9. d	9. b
10. d	10. b	10. b	10. a

Chapter 25	**Chapter 28**	**Chapter 31**	**Epilogue**
1. c	1. c	1. b	1. a
2. d	2. a	2. b	2. c
3. b	3. d	3. c	3. d
4. c	4. a	4. a	4. b
5. a	5. b	5. a	
6. c	6. c	6. d	
7. a	7. d	7. d	
8. d	8. d	8. b	
9. a	9. a	9. c	
10. b	10. c	10. c	

Preparing for the Final Examination

1. c
2. c
3. c
4. a
5. d
6. b
7. d
8. b
9. d
10. b
11. c
12. d
13. b
14. a
15. c
16. d
17. a
18. d
19. b
20. a
21. b
22. d
23. c
24. a
25. c